Oracle SOA Suite 11*g*
Administrator's Handbook

Create a reliable, secure, and flexible environment for your Oracle SOA Suite 11*g* Service Infrastructure and SOA composite applications

Ahmed Aboulnaga

Arun Pareek

BIRMINGHAM - MUMBAI

Oracle SOA Suite 11*g* Administrator's Handbook

First published: August 2012

Production Reference: 1170812

Published by Packt Publishing Ltd.
Livery Place
35 Livery Street
Birmingham B3 2PB, UK.

ISBN 978-1-84968-608-2

www.packtpub.com

Cover Image by Sandeep Babu (sandyjb@gmail.com)

Credits

Authors
Ahmed Aboulnaga
Arun Pareek

Reviewers
Mehmet Demir
Hans Forbrich
Tobias Luetticke
Shanthi Viswanathan

Acquisition Editor
Rashmi Phadnis

Lead Technical Editor
Dayan Hyames

Technical Editors
Prasad Dalvi
Prashant Salvi

Project Coordinator
Yashodhan Dere

Proofreader
Bernadette Watkins

Indexer
Monica Ajmera Mehta

Graphics
Valentina D'silva
Manu Joseph

Production Coordinator
Shantanu Zagade

Cover Work
Shantanu Zagade

About the Authors

Ahmed Aboulnaga is a Technical Director at IPN Web Inc., a full life cycle systems integrator headquartered in Maryland, USA. Ahmed's professional focus is on technical management, architecture, and consulting within the Oracle Fusion Middleware stack, having implemented enterprise solutions for commercial, government, and global customers over the years.

Ahmed is an Oracle SOA Architect Certified Expert and Oracle Application Server Certified Associate and has presented at OpenWorld, Collaborate, OAUG, IOUG, and various Oracle users groups in the past. He actively contributes to the online community in areas of WebLogic Server, SOA Suite, Application Integration Architecture, Oracle Service Bus, Grid Control, and other Oracle middleware technologies. Ahmed is currently the President of the Western Michigan Oracle Users Group.

I would like to thank my father for instilling in me a strong work ethic, encouraging my passion in technology, and supporting my efforts on this book. You are greatly missed.

Arun Pareek is an IASA certified Software Architect and has been actively working as an SOA and BPM practitioner. Over the past six years, he has worked in the capacity of Consultant and Architect in the implementation of a variety of SOA-based projects for customers across the globe. He has a knack for designing systems that are scalable, manageable, performant, and fault-tolerant, and is a keen enthusiast of automation techniques.

He is currently employed with Rubicon Red, Australia; an innovative IT professional services firm focused on enabling enterprise agility and operational excellence through the adoption of emerging technologies such as SOA, BPM, and Cloud Computing. Rubicon Red was founded in 2009 to focus on the emergent needs of Oracle Fusion Middleware customers, and offers a robust SOA adoption methodology incorporating agile development, reference architecture(s), automation, and governance.

Prior to working with Rubicon Red, Arun has worked for companies such as Dell and Accenture where he has successfully executed many SOA-based projects in the communications and utilities domain.

Arun Pareek has also been engaged with Packt Publishing as a Technical Reviewer for quite some time now; reviewing books such as *Oracle BAM 11gR1 Handbook* and *Oracle BPM Suite 11g Developer's cookbook*. He is also an active blogger on these technologies, and runs a widely popular blog at `http://beatechnologies.wordpress.com`. He can also be contacted at his personal e-mail address at `arrun.pareek@gmail.com`.

Acknowledgement

A large part of the knowledge in this book has come from the numerous great people I have worked with. Not all of them are listed here but they have certainly influenced me in my life and that has resulted in this work. First of all I am extremely grateful to Ahmed Aboulnaga for being humble enough and allowing me to co-author this book. Based on my interactions with him in the course of writing this book, I have found him to be a great technologist, and a wonderful man. He was always an e-mail away whenever I had any questions and has acted both as my educator and a guide.

I cannot thank my employers, Matt Wright and John Deeb, enough for being very appreciative and supportive about me completing this book. Both Matt and John are passionate exponents of SOA and BPM, exceptional leaders, and have allowed me to focus my energy on writing, and I greatly thank them for that. Matt is also an acclaimed author of the popular *Oracle SOA Suite Developer's Guide, Antony Reynolds, Matt Wright, Packt Publishing*.

The content of this book has significantly improved based on the feedback received from many reviewers. A book is never a single person's creation. I am grateful to all the reviewers of the book, the ones who have done it officially with Packt and also the ones who have gracefully accepted my request personally. Full credit goes to Hans Forbich, Tobias Luetticke, Shanthi Vishwanathan, Mehmet Demir and my colleagues from Rubicon Red, Craig Barr and Judy Nie, who have all provided invaluable feedback and suggestions to make the final version of the book much better than the original draft.

Rashmi Phadnis, Sayama Waghu, Yashodhan Dere, Dayan Haymes, and the entire team from Packt Publishing have shown exceptional professionalism and provided great support when we needed it and helped the book see light. Thank you all for believing in us and taking the initiative to publish so many great books on technology, including this one.

I would also like to thank all the clients, colleagues, peers, and superiors that I have worked with over the years. I learned something new from each one of you, and for that I am grateful.

Most importantly, I would like to appreciate the encouragement I have from my parents for helping me achieve many things in my life. My brother Amit, my sister Anita, and my friends Ravi, Amit, and Ankit have supported and encouraged me in every way possible, right from the time I began working on this book.

A special note of thanks to my wonderful wife Karuna for her constant support, cooperation, and patience without which it would have been impossible for me to manage my work and life together. Thank you for believing that I could write this book when I did not believe it myself and for supporting me even when my already busy schedule only got busier.

I have learned a lot from all of you and I have so much more to learn.

About the Reviewers

Mehmet Demir is a TOGAF certified Enterprise Architect with more than 15 years of experience designing systems for large companies. He has hands-on experience in developing and implementing SOA-based solutions using Oracle Fusion Middleware, WebCenter Portal, WebCenter Content, BEA WebLogic/AquaLogic product technologies and Oracle Identity Access Management Suite. As an Oracle certified SOA Architect, IBM certified SOA Designer, BEA certified Architect and Oracle WebCenter 11g Certified Implementation Specialist, Mehmet focuses on developing high quality solutions using best practices.

He is currently working for Thoughtcorp as an Enterprise Architect delivering high value IT solutions to many of Canada's most prominent companies such as CIBC, Home Hardware, and Bell TV. Prior to this Mehmet worked for BEA Systems where he was a principal member of the Canadian consulting team.

In addition to his technical capabilities, Mehmet has an MBA from the Schulich School of Business and is a certified Project Manager with a PMI PMP designation.

Mehmet can be contacted at: `http://ca.linkedin.com/in/demirmehmet`.

I would like to thank my beautiful wife Emily and my sweet daughter Lara for their support.

Hans Forbrich, an Oracle ACE Director, has been involved with Oracle products since 1984. As for the later 1990s, Hans has been heavily involved in Oracle's middleware products, whether Oracle Application Server or WebLogic Server, and the operations administration of application infrastructure, such as SOA, deployed into the middle tier.

Hans is the owner of Forbrich Computing, specializing in Oracle training. He is also an Oracle University partner and founding member of SHEN Group—a consortium of consultants in the Oracle technology field, ranging from Database to Oracle Business Intelligence and SOA Suite.

I'd like to thank my wife for her patience and support with my book projects and also my partners Edelweiss Kammermann and Nelson Calero for their encouragement and technical expertise as well frequent tech discussions.

Tobias Luetticke has more than 12 years of experience in the software field. As a Consultant and Software Architect he shaped various mission-critical applications for German blue chip companies and his current employer. His background also includes project management and teaching software development best practices. Early in his career, Tobias developed a passion for open source and agile development methodologies that still drives his work. His main focus is on finding the best means to deliver business value. When not working, he and his family explore the beautiful country of New Zealand.

Tobias is a certified Scrum Master, Project Management Professional (PMP), and holds a Computer Science degree from Karlsruhe Institute of Technology, Excellence University, Germany.

Currently, he works as a Senior Application Solution Architect for a New Zealand government entity, where he architects enterprise applications and leads development teams to see his solutions through to fruition.

Tobias enjoys writing and shares his experience in the software development space through articles he publishes in various magazines as well as through his book on OpenSSH.

Shanthi Viswanathan is an Oracle technologies evangelist and predominantly provides consulting services in Oracle products. She has worked on several Oracle Fusion projects in various different roles spanning the entire life cycle. Shanthi has also helped clients with high availability, performance tuning, and capacity planning of Oracle Fusion Middleware products. She has trained and mentored clients and assisted in jump starting projects. She is currently a Principal Solution Architect at Canon Europe. In addition, Shanthi is an avid yoga practitioner and teacher.

www.PacktPub.com

Support files, eBooks, discount offers and more

You might want to visit www.PacktPub.com for support files and downloads related to your book.

Did you know that Packt offers eBook versions of every book published, with PDF and ePub files available? You can upgrade to the eBook version at www.PacktPub.com and as a print book customer, you are entitled to a discount on the eBook copy. Get in touch with us at service@packtpub.com for more details.

At www.PacktPub.com, you can also read a collection of free technical articles, sign up for a range of free newsletters and receive exclusive discounts and offers on Packt books and eBooks.

http://PacktLib.PacktPub.com

Do you need instant solutions to your IT questions? PacktLib is Packt's online digital book library. Here, you can access, read and search across Packt's entire library of books.

Why Subscribe?

- Fully searchable across every book published by Packt
- Copy and paste, print and bookmark content
- On demand and accessible via web browser

Free Access for Packt account holders

If you have an account with Packt at www.PacktPub.com, you can use this to access PacktLib today and view nine entirely free books. Simply use your login credentials for immediate access.

Instant Updates on New Packt Books

Get notified! Find out when new books are published by following @PacktEnterprise on Twitter, or the *Packt Enterprise* Facebook page.

Table of Contents

Preface

Oracle SOA Suite 11*g* is the backbone of messaging and application integration in a service oriented architecture. An Application Administrator is responsible for end-to-end administration and management of this infrastructure. The role extends to other areas such as architecting an SOA infrastructure, troubleshooting, monitoring, performance tuning, and securing transactions that flow over loosely coupled components. Understanding the underlying components, services, and configuration and their relation to each other is necessary to effectively administer the Oracle SOA Suite 11*g* environment. Due to its sheer size, administering Oracle SOA Suite 11*g* is a daunting task, but this book provides detailed explanations and walkthroughs of all of the core administrative areas.

We begin with an introduction to SOA and quickly move on to management of SOA composite applications. You will learn how to manage composite applications, their deployments, and lifecycles, followed by detailed explanations surrounding monitoring and performance tuning the Oracle SOA Suite 11*g* infrastructure. In-depth explanations of numerous configuration and administration areas are also covered. You will be taken through troubleshooting approaches on how to identify faults and exceptions through extended logging and thread dumps, finding solutions to common startup problems, and deployment issues. We also explain how to secure the deployed services by leveraging Oracle Web Services Manager. Later chapters deal with managing the metadata services repository, backup, and recovery, and will conclude with advanced topics such as silent installs, cloning, and high availability installations.

What this book covers

Chapter 1, SOA Infrastructure Management: What You Need to Know, introduces Oracle SOA Suite 11g, a complete, best-of-breed, and hot-pluggable product set that helps to deliver robust, agile, and reliable SOA solutions. This chapter introduces the capabilities of Oracle SOA Suite 11g and provides a snapshot of several important aspects surrounding its administration and how it can be leveraged to effectively manage and monitor the SOA infrastructure.

Chapter 2, Management of SOA Composite Applications, focuses on the management of composites, describing composite lifecycles, revisions and states, leveraging ant for automated build and deployments, using configuration plans for code promotion, and defining partitions to logically separate composites. It also describes ways to optimally save instance data, explaining the relation between database usages with respect to various audit levels that can be set.

Chapter 3, Monitoring Oracle SOA Suite 11g, emphasizes monitoring of the service engines and instances, understanding their states as well as obtaining performance metrics of composite instances running on the Oracle SOA Suite 11g infrastructure. This chapter also describes other areas that include a detailed explanation of sensors, ECID, Oracle WebLogic Server infrastructure monitoring, and the break down of the log files in an easy to understand format.

Chapter 4, Tuning Oracle SOA Suite 11g for Optimum Performance, is one of the more important chapters, as it provides guidelines and recommendations on how to drastically improve the performance of your Oracle SOA Suite 11g infrastructure, covering areas of Oracle WebLogic Server, service engines, code considerations, Oracle Database, and operating system tuning recommendations.

Chapter 5, Configuring and Administering Oracle SOA Suite 11g, is quite a long chapter, as it details the numerous administrative areas around BPEL, Mediator, UMS, BAM, and Human Workflow components in varying detail. Other topics such as startup and shutdown of the infrastructure, administration of DVMs and XREFs, configuration of log rotation, setting up UMS, and the creation of read-only MDS accounts for developers are also described.

Chapter 6, Troubleshooting the Oracle SOA Suite 11g Infrastructure, unlike other troubleshooting guides which simply list out solutions to common errors, presents a comprehensive troubleshooting methodology, which, when coupled with the foundational knowledge of the previous chapters, provides you with a better ability to solve most issues related to the infrastructure.

Chapter 7, Configuring Security Policies, introduces Oracle Web Services Manager, a central policy framework for service oriented applications used by Oracle SOA Suite 11*g* to implement service-level security. This chapter explains the OWSM security semantics such as policy assertions, templates, keystores, and credential stores. It also covers how they can be used to apply security to components within a composite along with the configurations required at the infrastructure. The chapter also covers administration topics that range from logging, exporting, importing, and versioning the various policies by using a combination of WLST and console approaches.

Chapter 8, Managing the Metadata Services Repository and Dehydration Store, discusses operational aspects of the metadata services layer including deploying applications to use an MDS repository, exporting and importing metadata across environments, and database growth management activities, such as tuning and purging. It also discusses partitioning surrounding the Dehydration Store.

Chapter 9, Backup and Recovery, identifies exactly what components need to be backed up (such as the Middleware Home, JDK, Windows registry keys, and runtime artifacts), what would need to be restored in the event of a failure, and to what point in time a recovery would be needed. The chapter provides the necessary approach to recover your environment from the backup point and also explains ways to leverage cloning to backup and restore a middleware installation and domain from one environment to another.

Chapter 10, Advanced Administration Topics, covers several advanced, disjoined topics that most Oracle SOA Suite 11*g* administrators will be engaged in, namely, patching Oracle SOA Suite components, upgrading from Oracle SOA Suite 10*g*, installing a highly available clustered setup of the infrastructure, and performing silent installations. You can download this chapter from `http://www.packtpub.com/sites/default/files/downloads/6082EN_Chapter10_ Advanced Administration Topics.pdf`.

What you need for this book

This book expects the readers to have a basic knowledge of WebLogic Server, scripting using WLST, and a conceptual understanding of Oracle SOA Suite 11*g*.

Who this book is for

This book is intended for Oracle SOA Suite 11*g* administrators who have some familiarity with the tool but need detailed explanations and walkthroughs covering all facets of administration. WebLogic Server Administrators, Database Administrators, and even developers looking into entering the world of SOA Suite administration will find this book valuable, as the definitive guide to real world administration of Oracle SOA Suite 11*g*.

Conventions

In this book, you will find a number of styles of text that distinguish between different kinds of information. Here are some examples of these styles, and an explanation of their meaning.

Code words in text are shown as follows: "Click on the Browse button and locate your SAR file (for example, `C:\svn\SOA11g\HelloWorld\deploy\sca_HelloWorld_rev1.0.jar`)."

A block of code is set as follows:

```
export USERNAME=weblogic
export PASSWORD=welcome1
export SOAHOST=soahost1
export SOAPORT=8001
```

When we wish to draw your attention to a particular part of a code block, the relevant lines or items are set in bold:

```
export USERNAME=weblogic
export PASSWORD=welcome1
export SOAHOST=soahost1
export SOAPORT=8001
```

Any command-line input or output is written as follows:

```
ant -f ant-sca-mgmt.xml startComposite -Duser=$USERNAME
-Dpassword=$PASSWORD -Dhost=$SOAHOST -Dport=$SOAPORT
-DcompositeName=HelloWorld -Dpartition=default -Drevision=1.0
```

New terms and **important words** are shown in bold. Words that you see on the screen, in menus or dialog boxes for example, appear in the text like this: "clicking the **Next** button moves you to the next screen".

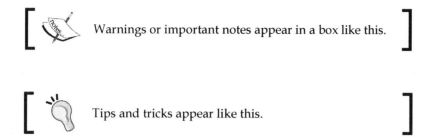

Warnings or important notes appear in a box like this.

Tips and tricks appear like this.

Reader feedback

Feedback from our readers is always welcome. Let us know what you think about this book—what you liked or may have disliked. Reader feedback is important for us to develop titles that you really get the most out of.

To send us general feedback, simply send an e-mail to feedback@packtpub.com, and mention the book title through the subject of your message.

If there is a topic that you have expertise in and you are interested in either writing or contributing to a book, see our author guide on www.packtpub.com/authors.

Customer support

Now that you are the proud owner of a Packt book, we have a number of things to help you to get the most from your purchase.

Downloading the example code

You can download the example code files for all Packt books you have purchased from your account at http://www.packtpub.com. If you purchased this book elsewhere, you can visit http://www.packtpub.com/support and register to have the files e-mailed directly to you.

Errata

Although we have taken every care to ensure the accuracy of our content, mistakes do happen. If you find a mistake in one of our books—maybe a mistake in the text or the code—we would be grateful if you would report this to us. By doing so, you can save other readers from frustration and help us improve subsequent versions of this book. If you find any errata, please report them by visiting http://www.packtpub.com/support, selecting your book, clicking on the **errata submission form** link, and entering the details of your errata. Once your errata are verified, your submission will be accepted and the errata will be uploaded to our website, or added to any list of existing errata, under the Errata section of that title.

Piracy

Piracy of copyright material on the Internet is an ongoing problem across all media. At Packt, we take the protection of our copyright and licenses very seriously. If you come across any illegal copies of our works, in any form, on the Internet, please provide us with the location address or website name immediately so that we can pursue a remedy.

Please contact us at copyright@packtpub.com with a link to the suspected pirated material.

We appreciate your help in protecting our authors, and our ability to bring you valuable content.

Questions

You can contact us at questions@packtpub.com if you are having a problem with any aspect of the book, and we will do our best to address it.

1
SOA Infrastructure Management: What you Need to Know

Today every organization is facing the need to predict changes in the global business environment, to rapidly respond to competitors, and to best exploit organizational assets to prepare for growth. Your enterprise application infrastructure can either help you meet these business imperatives or it can impede your ability to adapt to change.

To proactively respond to these challenges and dynamics of change, major companies worldwide are adopting **Service-Oriented Architecture (SOA)** as a means of delivering on these requirements. The adoption of SOA and **Business Process Management (BPM)** methodologies is helping them overcome the complexity of their application and IT environments, and also aligning IT and business together. SOA represents a fundamental shift in the way new applications are designed, developed, and integrated with legacy business applications, and facilitates the development of enterprise applications as modular business services that can be easily integrated and reused.

Oracle SOA Suite 11*g* is a comprehensive suite of products that includes BPEL Process Modeler, Business Rules Editor, Mediator, Web Services Manager, and Business Process Manager, all designed to help build, deploy, and manage SOA and BPM-based implementations. For the full list of Oracle SOA Suite 11*g* components, have a look at `http://docs.oracle.com/cd/E12839_01/integration.1111/ e10223/01_components.htm`. The deployment of the Oracle SOA Suite 11*g* platform within the enterprise is accelerated by the continued alignment of business and IT as a result of the rapid adoption of Service Oriented and Event Driven Architectures and Business Process Management.

While businesses strive to be more agile and dynamic, the need for administration, management, and monitoring of the underlying SOA infrastructure is essential. These are particularly important for the following reasons:

- An essential aspect of any successful SOA deployment is the ability to continuously monitor mission-critical services, business processes, events, and service levels in real time to immediately identify problems and take corrective action.

- SOA infrastructure monitoring provides visibility into the performance of each individual service transaction across distributed and heterogeneous systems. With this end-to-end visibility, problems could be spotted quickly and corrected to ensure reliable operations.

- The SOA infrastructure is also expected to enforce policies for runtime governance.

- The ability to easily and efficiently automate deployments is equally important as it enables the administrator to rapidly respond to continuous code changes.

- Proper management of **Service Level Agreements (SLAs)** is required by defining, tracking, and controlling appropriate service levels. It also provides a necessary alert mechanism in the event of an SLA violation.

In this chapter, we will provide an overview of Oracle SOA Suite 11*g* monitoring and management, which ultimately serves as a prelude for the remainder of this book. Here, we will introduce various topics ranging from centralized monitoring and code deployment to performance tuning and scaling the infrastructure. This book describes each of these areas and more, in varying degrees of detail, to arm you with the necessary background and understanding, as well as detailed instructions on how to perform key administrative tasks within the Oracle SOA Suite 11*g* product stack. In this chapter, we will introduce the following:

- Overcoming monitoring and management challenges in SOA
- Monitoring the SOA platform — centralized management and monitoring
- Oracle SOA Suite 11*g* Infrastructure Stack
- Performance monitoring and management
- Managing composite application lifecycles
- Cloning domains from test to production
- Introducing Oracle Enterprise Manager Fusion Middleware Control

Identifying and overcoming monitoring and management challenges in SOA

The very nature of SOA involves implementation of services that are distributed and loosely coupled, and thus monitoring these services is complex due to the involvement of disparate systems that may include external systems and external resources (for example, messaging queues, databases, and so on). Tracing transactions across a loosely coupled implementation, particularly if it involves invocations to external systems, is extremely complicated. The reusable nature of SOA increases the importance of managing availability and performance of these services and greatly increases the need for closed loop governance. In order to achieve the desired **Quality of Service (QoS)**, each service endpoint must literally be managed like a resource. Managed services should have near zero downtime, performance metrics, and a defined service level agreement. In a composite service's infrastructure, it's necessary to monitor and manage the end-to-end view of the systems, as well as provide detailed information about the performance and availability metrics of individual services. Each part of the overall SOA system can appear healthy while individual service transactions can be suffering.

Another important aspect of SOA monitoring is logging. The distributed nature of SOA makes a standardized logging approach difficult to implement. In addition to monitoring services in real time, the administrator is also required to perform standard administrative duties such as backups, code deployments, performance tuning, purging of old data, and more. In general, SOA infrastructure administrators are swamped with the following tasks and activities:

- Managing multi-tier transaction flows
    - Spanning shared components/services
    - Deployed across several tiers in different containers
    - Across the enterprise

- Obtaining performance metrics and visibility into SOA services
    - Beyond generic Java classes and methods
    - Framework and metadata visibility
    - Specific knowledge of the Oracle platform

- Maintaining control over configuration changes
- Performance tuning the service infrastructure
- Performing time consuming administrative tasks
- Code deployments

- Cloning and scale up
- Backups and restores
- Purging and cleanup
- Troubleshooting faults and exceptions
- Policy and security administration

This book is intended to provide you, the Oracle SOA Suite 11*g* administrator, with a thorough understanding of how to perform each of these tasks and activities.

Monitoring the SOA platform—centralized management and monitoring

Monitoring in Oracle SOA Suite 11*g* enables closed loop governance by connecting design-time with runtime. Once services, their metadata, and associated policies are deployed, they begin to be automatically monitored and managed by the service infrastructure by regularly updating the console with a scorecard of runtime metrics collected.

Oracle SOA Suite 11*g* runs on top of numerous infrastructure components that include database management systems, J2EE compliant application servers and centralized identity management solutions. All Oracle SOA Suite 11*g* components have specific functions for administering and managing parts of an SOA infrastructure, each from a different perspective or for a different audience. In order to address the monitoring and management challenges described earlier, several areas need to be considered:

- Monitoring solutions need to be provided at an enterprise level that encompass all related applications. This can begin with monitoring composite endpoints as well as the overall operational health of the infrastructure.
- Real-time monitoring and proactive alerting based on runtime statistics of configured KPIs, availability, performance metrics, and service level agreements should be implemented.
- Reporting of important information in the message (that is, payload), captured as a part of reporting functionality, can aid system administrators in better analysis and troubleshooting.

Oracle Enterprise Manager Fusion Middleware Control

Oracle Enterprise Manager Fusion Middleware Control, the web-based console into all Oracle SOA Suite 11*g* administrative functions, enables a bird's-eye view of your processes and their instances through a centralized management and monitoring console. It organizes a wide variety of performance data and administrative functions into distinct, web-based home pages. These home pages make it easy to locate the most important monitoring and performance data, and the most commonly used administrative functions for any Fusion Middleware component—all from your web browser!

Via Oracle Enterprise Manager Fusion Middleware Control, you can browse running servers, applications, and service engines to easily recognize and troubleshoot runtime problems in the SOA platform. As depicted in the following screenshot, the dashboard provides a comprehensive snapshot of the environment, including recent composite instances, state of currently deployed composites, and recently faulted transactions and their errors. From here, we typically drill down as necessary.

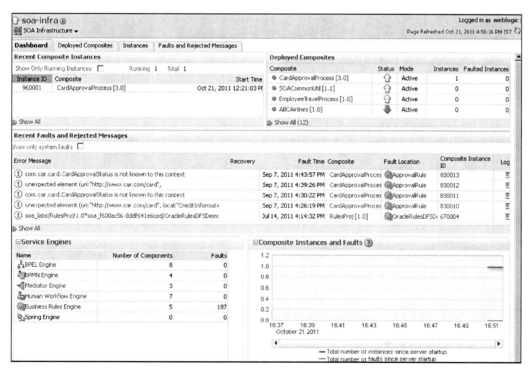

With out-of-the-box functionality provided by Oracle Enterprise Manager Fusion Middleware Control, you can obtain a real-time end-to-end view of the business transaction for SLA management, fault tracing, and problem determination, including the following:

- Web services message processing totals and processing times
- Transaction discovery/availability/state/status
- Transaction performance
- SOA registry and security
- Service discovery and relationship/dependency mapping
- Transaction audit trail and flow, faults, and rejected messages
- JMX-based monitoring of all components of the SOA infrastructure

In addition, Oracle Enterprise Manager Fusion Middleware Control provides a comprehensive infrastructure management console that includes the following capabilities:

- Code deployment and undeployment
- Startup and shut down
- Performance, metrics, and transaction monitoring
- Security and policy management
- Log management
- Instance monitoring and management
- Runtime exceptions and fault management
- Diagnostics and tuning
- Browsing, viewing, and modifying runtime MBeans
- Web service testing

The following diagram shows the runtime architecture of Oracle Enterprise Manager Fusion Middleware Control. It describes how Oracle Enterprise Manager Fusion Middleware Control aggregates runtime metrics from different components.

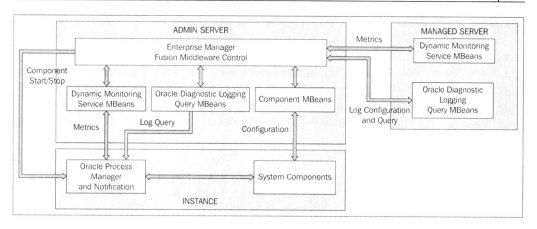

Several internal services are leveraged to automatically collect these metrics behind the scenes:

- **Oracle Process Manager and Notification (OPMN)**: OPMN is responsible for aggregation of component status, runtime metrics, and component logs, and provides a central access point for this information. It can also act as an agent that can start/stop registered components.

- **Dynamic Monitoring Service (DMS)**: DMS hooks up with the runtime MBeans of all participating managed servers controlled by Oracle Enterprise Manager Fusion Middleware Control. This MBean periodically collects performance and monitoring statistics for all available components, and makes it available for the DMS collection MBeans on the Admin Server.

- **Oracle Diagnostics Logging (ODL)**: ODL is a standard Java API utility framework that is leveraged in Oracle Enterprise Manager Fusion Middleware Control to log diagnostic messages in a standard format across each domain.

Apart from Oracle Enterprise Manager Fusion Middleware Control, there are a host of other management and monitoring frameworks available to administer various facets of your SOA infrastructure to help pinpoint issues. This includes JRockit Mission Control, **WebLogic Diagnostics Framework (WLDF)**, **Weblogic Scripting Tool (WLST)**, Oracle Enterprise Manager Grid Control, and more. Although these frameworks and tools are beyond the scope of this book, the following diagram provides a holistic view of each of these frameworks:

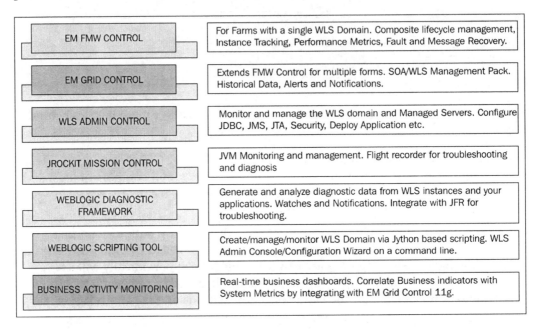

Oracle SOA Suite 11*g* infrastructure stack

Oracle SOA Suite 11*g* is a member of the Oracle Fusion Middleware family of products. Oracle has put in the effort to make this stack robust, extensible, and agile, in part by including some of the best technologies available on the market. Instead of cobbling together enterprise solutions from disparate vendors and products, Oracle SOA Suite 11*g* provides you with a unified product suite to meet all of your SOA needs. This results in a single design-time experience, single runtime infrastructure, and end-to-end monitoring that greatly simplifies the building, maintenance, and monitoring of distributed SOA implementations.

The following diagram shows how Oracle SOA Suite 11*g* brings out a seamless integration capability for an enterprise wide SOA adoption and implementation by using an array of standard components suited to achieve a specific business objective:

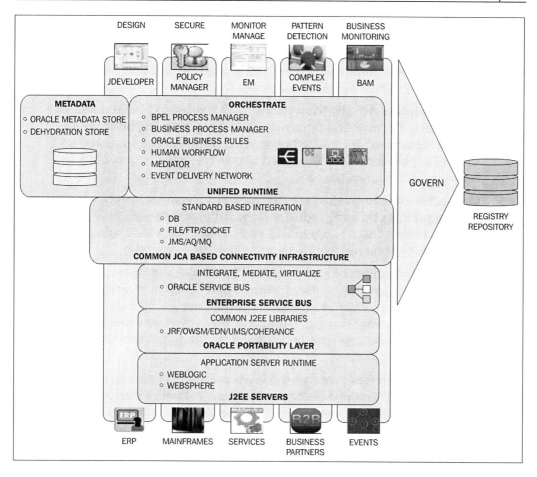

Here are some points about the Oracle SOA Suite 11*g* infrastructure stack:

- JDeveloper provides a design and development environment for software developers and architects, using the Oracle SOA Suite 11*g* to create standards based reusable enterprise software assets.

- Service components can be built as BPEL and/or BPMN processes, business rules and decision components, human task, events and mediator, or a combination thereof. They are the building blocks used to construct SOA composite applications. The service infrastructure, comprising a unified platform for services, processes, and events, provides the internal message transport infrastructure capabilities for connecting service components and enabling data flow. Service engines, such as the BPEL Process Manager Engine, Mediator Engine, and BPM Engine, process messages received | from the service infrastructure.

- Oracle Service Bus provides a framework for lightweight, scalable, and reliable service orchestration designed to connect, mediate, and manage interaction between heterogeneous systems and services. It is widely adopted in all major SOA implementations, and is used to transform protocols and messages between different components.

- Oracle **Business Activity Monitoring (BAM)** is used to build interactive real-time dashboards and proactive alerts for monitoring business processes and services, giving business executives and operation managers the information they need to take corrective action, if the business environment changes.

- Oracle **Business-to-Business (B2B) Integration** enables integration with trading partners by using industry standard protocols such as RossettaNet, **Electronic Data Interchange (EDI)**, and so on, to provide a solution for establishing online collaborations and automated processes.

- Oracle **Complex Event Processing (CEP)** provides a mechanism to process multiple event streams to detect patterns and trends in real time, and provide enterprises the necessary visibility via BAM. Oracle CEP is designed to look across discrete event streams to find only the important events/trends within a given time frame, and to detect missing events and events that should have occurred but did not.

- **Oracle Web Services Manager (OWSM)** is used to govern interactions with shared services through security and operational policy management and enforcement to ensure service reuse remains under control. Starting with the Oracle SOA Suite 11*g* release, OWSM is a component that is built into the suite. Every Oracle SOA Suite 11*g* domain has this component built-in by default to facilitate the management of web services.

Oracle SOA Suite 11*g* relies on 100 percent standard integration approaches using BPEL, BPMN, JCA, J2EE, and web services, and hence extending its reach to other service-based and process-centric applications. This makes it highly pluggable with your existing enterprise IT infrastructure. Oracle SOA Suite 11*g* can be installed to run on any number of standards compliant application servers including Oracle WebLogic Server, IBM WebSphere, and Red Hat JBoss, and can run on any number of certified database management systems such as the Oracle Database, IBM DB2, and Microsoft SQL Server.

What differentiates Oracle SOA Suite 11*g* from other comparable products on the market is the consolidation of the stack into a unified service platform that translates into major user benefits. **Service Component Architecture (SCA)**, an emerging standard, is the key enabler here. SCA enables you to manage, version, and deploy components and metadata as a single unit. All artifacts are stored in a single repository, the **Metadata Store (MDS)**. But the story doesn't stop here, Oracle SOA Suite 11*g* also consolidates all the runtime into a modular architecture of engines plugging into a common service infrastructure. And the engine consolidation naturally leads to a rationalization of the monitoring infrastructure, still maintaining a vendor neutral J2EE platform! All of this translates into numerous design-time, runtime, and monitoring benefits, many of which we will explore throughout this book.

Performance monitoring and management

Performance means different things to different people. For some, it translates to transaction response time, while others view it as the volume of work that can be processed within a given time period. In order to maximize performance, you will need to monitor, analyze, and tune all of the components that make up your application and infrastructure.

Performance of your SOA composites can be directly impacted by the design and implementation of the SOA code itself, the setting and configuration of the service infrastructure, or performance of external resources such as services or queues. Where do you begin to identify the performance bottleneck?

Fortunately, Oracle Enterprise Manager Fusion Middleware Control provides a single tool that you require to capture key information such as WebLogic Server performance statistics and composite performance details. The following screenshot highlights the capturing of performance snapshots by using Oracle Enterprise Manager Fusion Middleware Control:

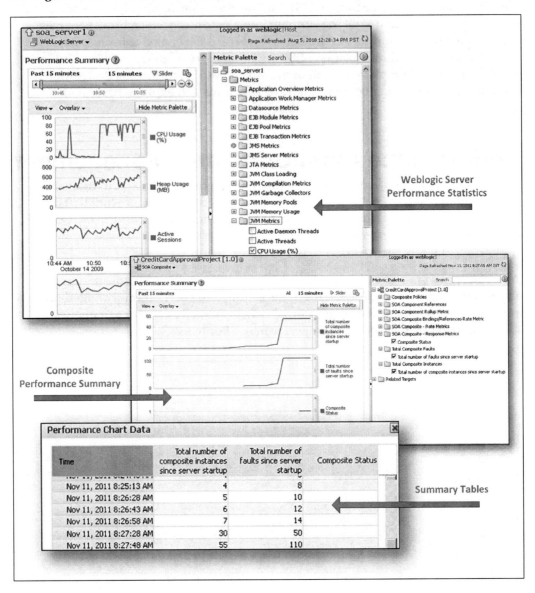

It is also important to understand that performance tuning is an iterative process. You need to make the adjustments, measure the impact, and then perform an analysis before possibly making further adjustments, and so on. Due to the varying expectations of a performant system, there is no one-size-fits-all solution that works well in every environment. Improving performance is a process of learning and testing.

Chapter 4, Tuning Oracle SOA Suite 11g for Optimum Performance provides detail on how to tune the performance of the Oracle SOA Suite 11g service infrastructure. It will describe the various knobs that you can adjust, and when and how you might want to adjust them. It is not unusual to obtain considerable performance gains by implementing certain settings or applying specific configurations. Though tuning the service infrastructure is not the only area that impacts performance, it is undoubtedly a key area.

 Did you know that by simply setting `CaptureCompositeInstanceState` to `Disabled` yields an additional 24 percent performance improvement on average across all instances?

Managing composite application lifecycles

The typical software development lifecycle is comprised of multiple phases such as requirements, analysis, design, development, testing, and promotion. Within the Oracle SOA development lifecycle, deployment and runtime management tend to introduce certain complexities. As an SOA composite is being developed, it may reference an endpoint (effectively a fully qualified URL) on a development server. This reference will need to change as the composite is promoted to higher up environments such as test and production. For example, your developers may have developed code that processes payments against PayPal. Naturally, they would be pointing to the PayPal sandbox server at `https://api.sandbox.paypal.com/2.0/` during development. What happens when this code is deployed to production? How are these references automatically updated to reference the PayPal production servers?

Oracle SOA Suite 11*g* offers comprehensive lifecycle management features starting from development, packaging, deployment, and post-deployment:

- It offers the ability to deploy multiple versions of a given composite application and specify a default version from either JDeveloper, Oracle Enterprise Manager Fusion Middleware Control, or ant/WLST-based scripts.

- Oracle SOA Suite tooling allows you to make/compile your composite applications and export a deployable **SOA archive (SAR)**.

 An **SOA archive (SAR)** is a deployment unit that describes the SOA composite application. The SAR packages service components such as BPEL/BPMN processes, business rules, human tasks, and mediator routing services into a single application.

- It has built-in capabilities to connect with versioning systems to version control your composite artifacts.

- It offers configuration plans that are composite-wide to customize environment specific values, such as a web service URL that is different in the dev/test environment than in the actual production environment. With configuration plans, here are a few things you can modify:
  - WSDL and schema includes/imports and endpoints
  - Endpoints and imports in `composite.xml`
  - Adapter properties
  - Web Service Policies can be attached/detached to either composite endpoints

The following screenshot illustrates how a developer IDE such as JDeveloper (top-left) is used to build and compile SOA composites that can eventually be packed and deployed as a JAR file to the Oracle SOA Suite 11*g* infrastructure for execution. The composites along with their instances can be instantaneously managed and monitored from the Oracle Enterprise Manager Fusion Middleware Control console (bottom-left).

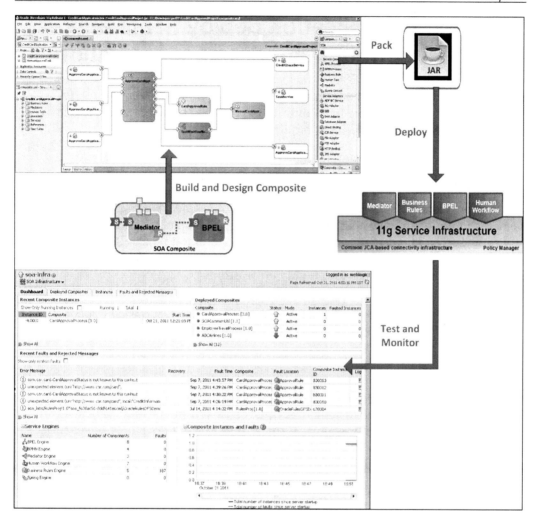

For managing your complete end-to-end lifecycle, you can also consider an enterprise repository solution such as the **Oracle Enterprise Repository (OER)**, which integrates with JDeveloper and related tools. It provides a system of record for all SOA asset information, automatically detects usage of these artifacts, tracks compliance, as well as many other governance capabilities and features. OER focuses on the SOA governance aspect of the lifecycle, but is not part of Oracle SOA Suite 11*g* or its infrastructure. Additional information on Oracle Enterprise Repository can be found at http://www.oracle.com/technology/products/soa/repository/index.html.

Automating application deployments and migrations through continuous integration

One of the key principles of SOA is that systems are no longer built to last, but rather built to change. As an administrator of the Oracle SOA Suite 11*g* platform, you should expect more rapid and continuous changes by development teams in response to ever changing business requirements.

Being able to adapt to the changing business requirements is not only important once a system has gone live, but it is also equally important during development. This would mean expecting a greater number of builds, packaging, and deployments. The process of deployment involves piecing together multiple relevant components, compiling them, deploying the final package into a target environment, and finally running a series of tests to validate the build. This would have to be repeated in each environment until promoted to production. This process is manual, resource intensive, and highly error prone.

 Automating application deployments is a practice that is widely adopted within the software industry to alleviate manual, resource intensive, and highly error prone processes.

Oracle SOA Suite 11*g* is unique in that it provides several ant scripts to assist in the compilation, build, and deployment of composites. These scripts can be executed manually, automated through custom scripts, or used from a continuous integration tool such as Hudson. As you read on, *Chapter 2, Management of SOA Composite Applications* of this book will cover details of how you can automate your composite build and deployment with ant scripts.

Think of a script which runs at regular time intervals or at the click of a button every time an administrator needs to deploy an application to the platform. By having automated build reports detailing the execution and/or issues of compilation and deployment, your time is freed up considerably to focus on other administrative activities. The following screenshot shows the continuous integration with the Oracle SOA Suite 11*g* platform:

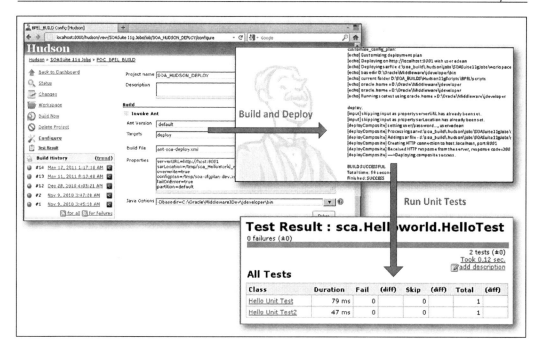

The preceding screenshot shows the Hudson console for a build job and the output of an automated build, which is followed by an automated unit test. By leveraging continuous integration tools such as Hudson, the deployment and validation efforts required by the Oracle SOA Suite administrator are greatly reduced.

Cloning domains from test to production

Oracle SOA Suite 11*g* enables administrators to further minimize manual steps involved when moving the domain infrastructure across physical machines. It allows what is referred to as green field movement, which entails leveraging existing out-of-the-box tools and capabilities to perform this activity without the reliance on external or third-party tools.

The following diagram depicts, at a high level, the process involved when moving Oracle Fusion Middleware components. This minimizes the amount of work that would otherwise be required to reapply all the customization and configuration changes made in one environment to another. You can install, configure, customize, and validate Oracle Fusion Middleware in a test environment. Once the system is stable and performs as desired, you can create the production environment by moving a copy of the components and their configurations from the test environment, instead of reimplementing all the changes that were incorporated into the test environment.

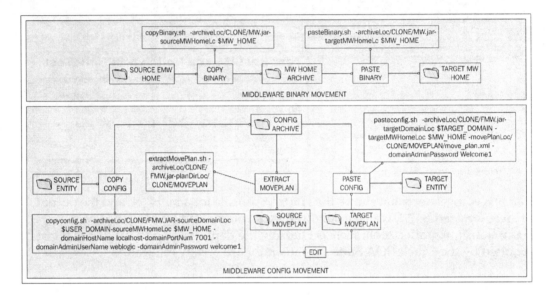

What is moved exactly?

- Installed binaries and patches
- Configuration and metadata
- Security configuration (for example, OPSS policies)
- Supports MDS metadata and JCA connection factories
- MovePlan—rewiring external references to match target
- Data sources and endpoint addresses

Introducing Oracle Enterprise Manager Fusion Middleware Control

Oracle Enterprise Manager Fusion Middleware Control is the Oracle SOA Suite 11*g* administrator's primary console to perform all necessary monitoring, management, and deployment activities. This includes administering areas such as the SOA infrastructure, composite applications, partitions, Java EE applications, and more. Through the console, you can perform the following functions:

- Create and delete partitions to provide a logical grouping of composites
- Manage composite state, including starting, stopping, activating, retiring, and setting the default revision of a deployed composite
- Manage composite instances, including deleting, terminating, and in some cases recovering instances
- Deploy and undeploy composites
- Export a composite or its metadata to a JAR file
- Automate unit testing
- Manual testing of composite applications
- Attach policies to composites, service components, and binding components
- Manage human workflows and notifications
- Publish or subscribe to business events
- Publish web services to a **Universal Description, Discovery and Integration (UDDI)** registry such as Oracle Service Registry

Subsequent chapters delve into each of these areas in varying levels of detail.

Accessing the Oracle Enterprise Manager Fusion Middleware Control Console

To log in to the Oracle Enterprise Manager Fusion Middleware Control, simply navigate to the following URL in your web browser:

- `http://<host>:<port>/em`

The default port for HTTP is 7001 and the default port for HTTPS is 7002, though this depends on the settings used during the installation. The default username is `weblogic` and the password is the one provided at installation or subsequently changed.

All information related to the ports that the servers run on, the deployments that are targeted to them along with their deployment orders and other resources configured on the servers are present in the `config.xml` file located under the `$DOMAIN_HOME/config` directory.

Navigating the console through the navigator

After logging in to the Oracle Enterprise Manager Fusion Middleware Control, the vertical navigation tree on the left, or the **navigator**, is your primary means to navigating to all other areas within the console. Here, you can right-click on many, but not all, menu items to pop up additional navigation menus. The navigator is the leftmost column as shown in the first screenshot under the *Presenting the dashboards* section.

Presenting the dashboards

Once you log in to Oracle Enterprise Manager Fusion Middleware Control, you are presented with the overall server state in a dashboard format. As shown in the following screenshot, deployment statuses are summarized in a pie chart, indicating a summary of the composites that are up, down, or in an unknown state. The state of deployed Java EE applications and infrastructure components are also shown. For example, out-of-the-box SOA Suite Java applications such as the BPM Composer (see **BPMComposer** in the following screenshot) are shown to have an up status. These Java applications, for example, are additional consoles and capabilities that are installed as part of Oracle SOA Suite 11*g*.

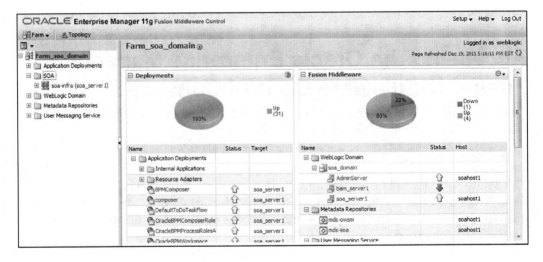

This dashboard is particularly useful to quickly and immediately get a snapshot of the overall health of the system.

On the navigation tree, when you expand **SOA** and click on **soa-infra**, you are presented with the SOA Infrastructure dashboard, which includes recent composite instances, deployed composites, and recent faults and rejected messages. By clicking on the various tabs, you are taken to a more detailed view.

For example, the **Instances** tab would show all instances, not just the recent ones. Clicking on the instance ID will pop up a new window, displaying the flow trace of that particular instance as shown in the following screenshot:

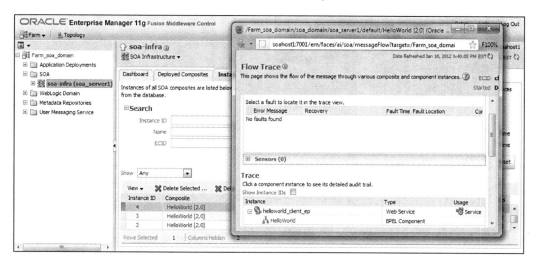

SOA suite configuration

Oracle Enterprise Manager Fusion Middleware Control allows you to configure areas of the SOA Infrastructure and service engines. This is done by expanding **SOA** in the navigator and right-clicking on **soa-infra**:

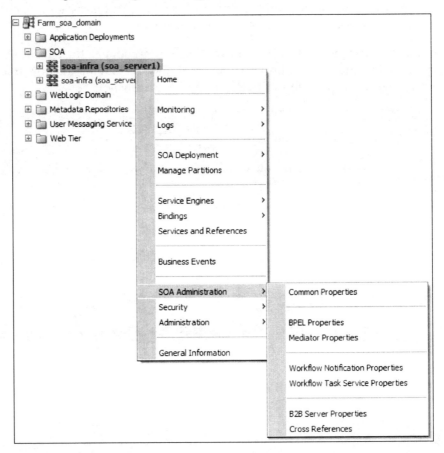

By expanding the **SOA Administration** menu as shown in the preceding screenshot, the various menu options will allow you to perform a number of configurations and setups on various SOA Infrastructure components and service engines that include the following.

- **Common Properties**: Here, you can modify server settings that impact the entire infrastructure. This includes global audit levels, capturing the state of composite instances, performing payload validation, configuring callback URLs, setting UDDI registry properties, setting retry counts, Enterprise Manager Fusion Middleware Control console optimization parameters, and more.

- **BPEL Properties**: This page provides the ability to set the maximum document size for a variable, enable or disable payload validation, disable sensors, configure BPEL Service Engine properties such as dispatcher system threads, invoke threads, engine threads, and more.

- **BPMN Properties**: This page provides the ability to set the audit trail size, set the maximum document size for a variable, enable or disable payload validation, configure dispatcher system threads, invoke threads, engine threads, and more.

- **Mediator Properties**: This page provides options for setting the audit level, DMS metrics level, number of parallel worker threads, number of maximum rows retrieved for parallel processing, parallel thread sleep values, error thread sleep values, and more.

- **Workflow Notification Properties**: Here, properties such as the workflow service notification mode and actionable e-mail address, and more, can be set for human workflow notifications.

- **Workflow Task Service Properties**: This page provides the ability to configure the actionable e-mail account, add the URL of the worklist application, select the pushback assignee, add portal realm mapping, and more.

- **B2B Server Properties**: Allows you to enable DMS metrics.

- **Cross References**: This page provides options for selecting cross-reference values.

Deployed Java EE applications

By expanding **Application Deployments** on the navigator, a list of deployed Java EE applications is shown. In parentheses, the managed server that this application is targeted to is shown. For example, the **composer** application is targeted to the AdminServer. The default applications installed with Oracle SOA Suite 11*g* include:

- soa-infra
- BPMComposer
- composer
- DefaultToDoTaskFlow
- OracleBPMComposerRolesApp
- OracleBPMProcessRolesApp
- OracleBPMWorkspace
- SimpleApprovalTaskFlow
- worklistapp

When expanding **Application Deployments | Internal Applications**, a further list of applications is shown. The default internal applications installed with Oracle SOA Suite 11*g* include:

- b2bui
- DMS Application
- em
- FMW Welcome Page Application
- wsil-wls

It is fairly common to deploy additional Java applications and target them to the SOA Server (for example, `soa_server1`) such as Java web services designed to supplement your SOA code, although it is probably recommended to dedicate a separate managed server for them. Java applications can be deployed either through Oracle WebLogic Server Administration Control or Oracle Enterprise Manager Fusion Middleware Control.

The other consoles

Oracle SOA Suite 11*g* includes many other application and server specific consoles. The two consoles we mainly focus on in this book are the Oracle Enterprise Manager Fusion Middleware Control and WebLogic Server Administration Console. The WebLogic Server Administration Console is used to administer all application server areas such as Java/JEE application deployments, managed server setup, configuration, and started, security, resource management, and much, much more. We will go over key areas of the WebLogic Server Administration Console in this as well as other chapters of the book. It can be accessed at (default port is 7001) `http://<host>:<port>/console`.

Other consoles include the SOA Composer, which is used to manage business rules, **domain value maps (DVMs)**, and tasks. The console can be accessed at (default port is 8001) `http://<host>:<port>/soa/composer`.

The BPM Worklist is where users (including business users) can view and manage all workflows and tasks delegated to them. The console can be accessed at (default port is 8001) `http://<host>:<port>/integration/worklistapp`.

The BPM console is used to manage users, partners, agreements, documents, and channels required for your B2B integrations. The console can be accessed at (default port is 8001) `http://<host>:<port>/b2b`.

The BAM console includes three separate functional areas—the BAM Architect, BAM ActiveStudio, and BAM ActiveViewer. These are used to create BAM users and data objects, create reports, and view reports. The console, which is only supported with Microsoft Internet Explorer, can be accessed at (default port is 9001) `http://<host>:<port>/OracleBAM`.

Summary

In this chapter, we provided a snapshot of some of the important aspects of Oracle SOA Suite 11*g* administration and the capabilities that can be leveraged to effectively manage and monitor the SOA infrastructure.

To summarize this chapter's key takeaways:

- One of the main challenges of monitoring an SOA infrastructure is the need to obtain an end-to-end view of loosely coupled services that may span multiple disparate systems.

- Oracle SOA Suite 11*g* is a complete, integrated, best-of-breed, and hot-pluggable product set that helps to deliver robust, agile, and reliable SOA solutions.

- Oracle SOA Suite 11*g* is 100 percent standards-based, and can run on any number of J2EE application servers (for example, WebLogic Server, WebSphere, and JBoss) and certified database management systems (for example, Oracle database, DB2, and SQL Server).

- Oracle Enterprise Manager Fusion Middleware Control allows you to both manage and monitor all components and services within the Oracle SOA Suite 11*g* stack, from a single web-based console.

- OPMN, DMS, and ODL are internal services used to automatically gather and aggregate metrics that are ultimately reported by Oracle Enterprise Manager Fusion Middleware Control.

- Deployment of SOA code is often one of the more challenging activities an administrator faces, but through the use of configuration plans and out-of-the-box ant scripts shipped with Oracle SOA Suite 11*g*, this task is finally made easier.

- Oracle SOA Suite 11*g* has been designed to allow easy integration with continuous integration tools and engines by provisioning out-of-the-box build, deploy, and management scripts.

- Oracle SOA Suite 11g provides the ability to move test to production environments easily, without the need to rely on external or third-party tools. Administrators no longer have to reapply configurations or customizations when building higher up environments.

Chapter 2, Management of SOA Composite Applications, dives deeper into the management aspects of Oracle SOA Suite 11g that were briefly touched upon here:

- Focusing on managing composites
- Leveraging ant for automated deployments
- Promoting code by using Oracle SOA Suite 11g's new configuration plan feature
- Delving into a comprehensive discussion on audit levels

2
Management of SOA Composite Applications

Developers typically create composite applications or simply composites that are packaged into single, deployable JAR files. These applications can contain any number of service components that include BPEL or BPMN processes, Mediator services, human tasks and workflows, and business rules. Composites include logic and code that form the foundation of SOA-based integrations. Though the design and development of composites are not the ultimate responsibility of the Oracle SOA Suite 11g administrator, the deployment, monitoring, and management of them are.

In this chapter, we will discuss the concepts that enable you to manage these composites, and cover the following areas in more detail:

- Managing composite lifecycles
- Structuring composite deployments with partitions
- Setting up ant for automated composite build management
- Promoting code, using configuration plans
- Understanding and configuring composite audit levels

Managing composite lifecycles

Every composite has a state, mode, and associated metadata. The state can be up (started) or down (shut down). The mode can either be active or retired. Metadata is stored in the **Metadata Store** (**MDS**), which is a database-based repository used by Oracle SOA Suite 11g, and consists of information that includes default revision number, last modification date, deployment and redeployment times, and instance statistics. Before walking through how to manage the state and mode of composites, we will begin by describing composite revisions.

Understanding revisions

When a `HelloWorld` composite is deployed to the server, a revision is required during the deployment. Thus, the service's **Web Services Description Language (WSDL)** can be accessed via a URL similar to the following, clearly indicating a revision of "1.0" after the composite name:

```
http://soahost1:8001/soa-infra/services/default/HelloWorld!1.0/
HelloWorld.wsdl
```

However, there may be a case where a new version of the service needs to be deployed and that this version has a different implementation from the existing one. Overwriting the existing version may not be the right option as it would break all client applications that are already utilizing the service. Thus, it makes sense to deploy the new service using a different revision, such as revision "2.0", and thus make both the versions available simultaneously. It would, therefore, be accessible at a different URL:

```
http://soahost1:8001/soa-infra/services/default/HelloWorld!2.0/
HelloWorld.wsdl
```

Now, the old and new services are both available and accessible. Clients accessing revision 1.0 of the composite may transition to revision 2.0 at their own pace. If multiple revisions of the same service are deployed, one of them must be specified as the default revision. This can be specified during deployment time or changed at runtime. The default revision would thus be accessed at a revision-independent URL:

```
http://soahost1:8001/soa-infra/services/default/HelloWorld/
HelloWorld.wsdl
```

Typically, client applications will access the default revision. Revisions are advantageous in environments where maintaining old and new versions of the same composite is required, particularly if it involves breaking changes.

As shown in the following screenshot, default revisions are indicated by a green dot in the list of composites for a given partition. Partitions will be explained in detail later in this chapter.

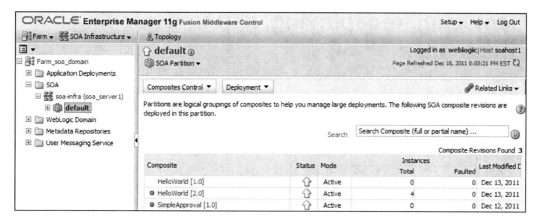

Changing the composite default revision at runtime

If a composite is not the default revision, the **Set As Default...** button will appear in the composite page, as shown in the following screenshot. By clicking on this button, it is possible at this point to set the revision of this composite as the default revision if you choose to.

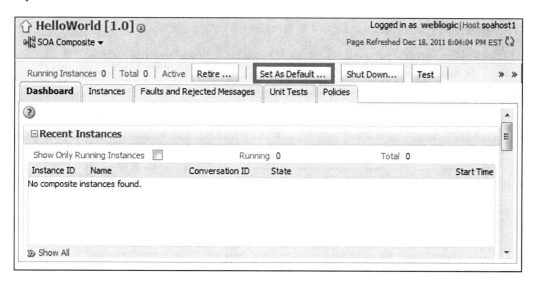

If a default composite application is undeployed, the default revision is automatically changed to the last deployed revision.

Deploying, redeploying, and undeploying composites

Composites are deployed and redeployed as SOA Archives or SARs, which are similar to traditional JAR files. Oracle Enterprise Manager Fusion Middleware Control provides the ability to deploy, redeploy, and undeploy a SAR from the convenience and simplicity of a web browser. Though deploying via the console is extremely easy, the following two important points should be considered:

- A SAR file is a special JAR file that requires a prefix of `sca_` and may include environment-specific information bundled within the JAR file. For example, the composite may reference a web service on some external development server. The URL of this web service is hardcoded in the JAR file. Deploying the same JAR to a production server would not be valid.
- Deployment of multiple composites via the console is cumbersome and time consuming. Using ant is the preferred method for deploying multiple SARs and this will be covered in a subsequent section in this chapter.

Deploying a composite

To deploy a single composite from the console:

1. On the navigator, expand **Farm_[Domain] | SOA** and right-click on **soa-infra**.
2. Navigate to **SOA Deployment | Deploy**.
3. In the field labeled **Archive is on the machine where the web browser is running**, click on the **Browse...** button and locate your SAR file (for example, `C:\svn\SOA11g\HelloWorld\deploy\sca_HelloWorld_rev1.0.jar`).

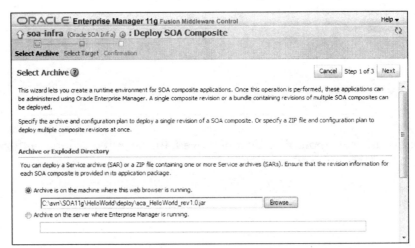

4. Click on **Next**.

5. From the drop-down list, select the partition to which you wish to deploy this composite.

6. Click on **Next**.

7. Choose the radio button **Deploy as default revision** or **Do not change the default revision**.

8. Click on the **Deploy** button.

When the `HelloWorld` composite is deployed as revision 1.0 and as the default version, an entry is logged in the `soa_server1.out` file (located under `$MW_HOME/user_projects/domains/soa_domain/servers/soa_server1/logs/soa_server1.out`) as follows:

```
INFO: DeploymentEventPublisher.invoke Publishing deploy
event for default/HelloWorld!1.0*soa_fe9ee226-4f29-4db7-b4be-
d7410bbc13ffdefault/HelloWorld!1.0*soa_fe9ee226-4f29-4db7-b4be-
d7410bbc13ff
```

Once it is deployed, the service becomes available immediately. If the composite uses inbound resources (such as the JMS Adapter, which consumes from a JMS queue), the consumption begins immediately once the composite is deployed.

The rest of the instructions in this chapter assume that the **HelloWorld** composite is deployed to the **default** partition.

Redeploying a composite

To redeploy a single composite from the console:

1. On the navigator, expand **Farm_[Domain]** | **SOA** | **soa-infra**.

2. Expand the partition (for example, **default**) and right-click on the composite name that you wish to redeploy (for example, **HelloWorld**).

3. Navigate to **SOA Deployment** | **Redeploy**.

4. In the field labeled **Archive is on the machine where the web browser is running**, click on the **Browse** button and locate your SAR file (for example, `C:\svn\SOA11g\HelloWorld\deploy\sca_HelloWorld_rev1.0.jar`).

5. Click on **Next**.

6. Choose the radio button **Deploy as default revision** or **Do not change the default revision**.

7. Click on the **Redeploy** button.

Redeploying a composite overwrites the existing revision. The state of the instances of the older revision are all changed to stale (instance states are described in detail in *Chapter 3, Monitoring Oracle SOA Suite 11g*).

Undeploying a composite

To undeploy a single composite from the console:

1. On the navigator, expand **Farm_[Domain]** | **SOA** | **soa-infra**.
2. Expand the partition (for example, **default**) and right-click on the composite name that you wish to undeploy (for example, **HelloWorld**).
3. Navigate to **SOA Deployment** | **Undeploy**.
4. Click on the **Undeploy** button.

In addition to the service no longer being available, undeploying a composite (or a composite revision) changes the state of all historical instances to stale, denoted by the icon ◎. If the default revision of the composite is undeployed, the last deployed revision of the composite becomes the default.

Starting up and shutting down composites

Composites are automatically started up when they are deployed. If a composite is shut down, all requests to the composite are rejected, including callbacks. New requests are not served and new instances are not created. However, all running instances are allowed to complete.

Though starting up and shutting down composites via the console is extremely easy, if you require to start up or shut down multiple composites, two approaches are available (discussed in detail later in this chapter):

- Composites deployed to the same partition can all be started up or all be shut down with a single operation.
- Ant can be used to automate the startup and shutdown of composites.

Starting a composite

To start up a single composite from the console:

1. On the navigator, expand **Farm_[Domain]** | **SOA** | **soa-infra**.
2. Expand the **default** partition, and click on the **HelloWorld** composite and the revision.

3. Click on the **Start Up** button, which will only appear if the composite is already shut down.

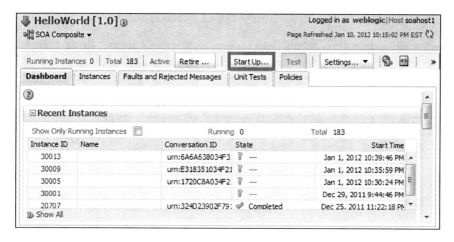

Shutting down a composite

To shut down a single composite from the console:

1. On the navigator, expand **Farm_[Domain]** | **SOA** | **soa-infra**.
2. Expand the partition (for example, **default**), choose from among the deployed composites, and click on the composite name and the revision (for example, **HelloWorld[1.0]**).
3. Click on the **Shut Down** button, which will only appear if the composite is already started up.

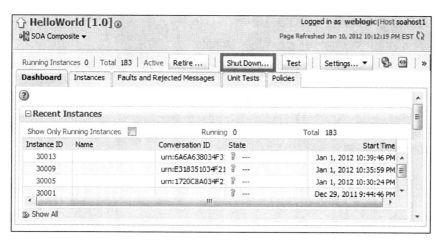

Retiring and activating composites

Composites have two modes — active and retired. These are often confused with composite states, which can be up (started) and down (shut down).

Composites are automatically activated when they are deployed (in fact, they are also started up as well, so active and started composites are really identical in nature). However, when a composite is retired, new instances cannot be created. Existing instances, however, continue to completion. This includes instances that receive callbacks. The ability to receive callbacks and time based waits is the primary difference between a retired composite and a composite that has been shut down.

> The only difference between activating a composite and starting up a composite is that activating the composite affects the retired mode, while starting up a composite affects the shutdown state.

Retiring a composite

To retire a single composite from the console:

1. On the navigator, expand **Farm_[Domain] | SOA | soa-infra**.
2. Expand the partition (for example, **default**) and click on the composite name (for example, **HelloWorld**).
3. Click on the **Retire** button, which will only appear if the composite is already active.

Activating a composite

To activate a single composite from the console:

1. On the navigator, expand **Farm_[Domain] | SOA | soa-infra**.
2. Expand the partition (for exampple, **default**) and click on the composite name (for example, **HelloWorld**).
3. Click on the **Activate** button, which will only appear if the composite is already retired.

Deleting instances

When an SOA composite application is invoked, a new composite instance is created. Every instance has a unique ID and its details can be retrieved from Oracle Enterprise Manager Fusion Middleware Control. Administrators are expected to delete completed instances and free up their data periodically to control growth. Too much instance-related data requires additional storage and it also impacts the performance of the console. We will discuss management of the instance data in *Chapter 8, Managing the Metadata Services Repository and Dehydration Store*, but it may be worthwhile briefly describing how to delete instances, thereby purging all data related to it, manually from Oracle Enterprise Manager Fusion Middleware Control as part of composite management activities. Deleting instances is quite easy as demonstrated in the following steps:

1. On the navigator, expand **Farm_[Domain]** | **SOA** | **soa-infra**.
2. Expand the partition (for example, **default**) and click on the composite name (for example, **HelloWorld**).
3. Click on the **Instances** tab.
4. At this point, you can delete instances in one of the following two ways:

    ○   Highlight the list of instances (press the *Ctrl* key and click on each composite one by one) and click on the **Delete Selected** button.
    ○   Click on the **Delete With Options** button. From here you can delete instances older than a specific time or delete all instances within a time frame that have a certain state.

We can also bulk delete/purge composite instances from the underlying database dehydration store through the use of SQL scripts. Again, this will be covered in more detail in *Chapter 8, Managing the Metadata Services Repository and Dehydration Store*.

Structuring composite deployments with partitions

Prior to Oracle SOA Suite 11*g* PS2 (11.1.1.3), as hundreds of composites were deployed to the SOA server, they were all listed in alphabetical order on the console, which made it a burden to manage and was not very structured. Oracle recognized the lack of structure and, therefore, introduced the concept of partitions to help better organize where to deploy your composites. However, partitions are just logical separations to group your composites together. Domain libraries, extension modules, server **Java Naming and Directory Interface (JNDI)**, and infrastructure properties are shared across all partitions.

Partitions do not have their own configuration or logging. They serve no purpose other than grouping composites into separate categories. Thus, for example, code for your Human Resources integrations can reside in a partition separate from your EBS integrations, offering better structuring and organization. There are a few bulk lifecycle management tasks that can be performed on all SOA composite applications in a partition, as we will describe in this section. For example, all composites within a partition can be shut down with a single operation.

The preceding screenshot shows a list of partitions in the navigator under **soa-infra**. Each partition may have one or more composite applications deployed to it. Partitions cannot be cascaded (that is, a partition cannot have a child partition).

The default partition

Oracle SOA Suite 11*g* should have, as a minimum, one partition. The default partition is created automatically when the product is installed, but it can be deleted afterwards if you choose to. You must always have at least one partition to allow you to deploy composites.

Managing partitions

You can perform several management tasks pertaining to partitions. These tasks include:

- Creating a partition
- Deleting a partition, including all composites within the partition
- Starting up and shutting down all composites in a partition
- Retiring and activating all composites in a partition
- Undeploying all composites in a partition

The simplest method to manage partitions is via the **Manage Partitions** page. Simply navigate to this page to create, delete, or perform bulk lifecycle management operations on the partitions:

1. Right-click on **soa-infra**, then click on **Manage Partitions** to access the **Manage Partitions** page.

2. At this point, you can do one of the following four things:

   a. Click on the **Create** button to create a partition.

   b. Highlight an existing partition and click on the **Delete** button to delete the partition.

   c. Highlight an existing partition and click on the **Composites Control** button to start up, shut down, activate, or retire all composites within that partition.

   d. Highlight an existing partition and click on the **Deployment** button to undeploy all composites within this partition, or to deploy a single composite to this partition.

The **Manage Partitions** page with each of its action buttons is shown in the following screenshot. The **Composites Control** and **Deployment** buttons are only activated when a partition is highlighted.

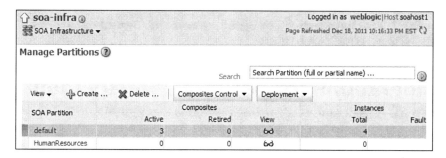

 Partitions do not have a state or a mode. Thus, for example, you are not shutting down the partition, you are actually shutting down all composites within the partition.

Creating a partition

When creating a partition, be mindful of the following naming conventions:

- Letters, numbers, underscores, and dashes are allowed (dashes are not allowed as the first character)

- Spaces are not allowed

Also, be aware that partitions cannot be renamed once they are created.

Deleting a partition

When considering deleting partitions, remember that there always needs to be one partition in existence. If you delete all partitions, it will not be possible to deploy any code to the server. If you delete a partition, all composites within that partition are automatically undeployed.

Grouping SOA composite applications into partitions

Typically developers choose a partition to which a particular composite should be deployed, but as an administrator, you must understand its implications.

When composites are deployed — whether through JDeveloper, the console, or ant — a partition name must be specified. Code deployed to the default partition will result in a different WSDL URL than that deployed to, for example, the `HumanResources` partition as shown here:

- `http://soahost1:8001/soa-infra/services/default/HelloWorld/HelloWorld.wsdl`
- `http://soahost1:8001/soa-infra/services/HumanResources/HelloWorld/HelloWorld.wsdl`

Considerations for partition management

There are some considerations regarding partitions that you should be aware of:

- Avoid creating partitions called Dev, Test, and Prod. Though possible, partitions are not designed to separate by environment.
- Domain libraries and SOA extensions (such as MQs and AQs) are shared by all partitions, so it is not possible to have different versions of these libraries or extensions for each partition.
- It is not possible to have the same JNDI address for outbound connection pools in Resource Adapters pointing to different queue manager or data sources for composites deployed in different partitions.
- Oracle SOA Suite 11g parameters such as timeouts, threads, and recovery configurations are defined by WebLogic Server domain, not by partition.

- If composites that use inbound adapters (such as the inbound AQ Adapter, in which messages are automatically dequeued from an Oracle AQ) are deployed to multiple partitions, it is not guaranteed which composite will dequeue the inbound message (that is, they will compete with each other).

Setting up ant for automated composite management

All component management tasks that can be performed manually through the web-based Oracle Enterprise Manager Fusion Middleware Control console can also be executed with a script through the command-line utility ant. In this section, we describe how to use ant to start up, shut down, activate, and retire composites, as well as package and deploy them. Oracle SOA Suite 11g ships all necessary ant scripts to perform these tasks, and they are quite easy to use.

Setting the environment

Here, we will describe how to set both Linux and Microsoft Windows based environments to allow you to run your ant commands through the command line. Your ant scripts do not have to be installed on the same machine running Oracle SOA Suite 11g. In fact, it is not unusual to dedicate a single machine or server, which would host your ant scripts, allowing you to centralize the startup, shutdown, and deployment of your SOA composites to multiple target environments. You will also see how ant enables automated build management for your environment in later sections of this chapter.

Setting the environment path for ant

In your environment, we assume that Oracle SOA Suite 11g is installed, which is recommended, as it will include all the required binaries to run ant. The Middleware Home, the Oracle SOA Suite 11g Home, the Java Home, WebLogic Server username and password, and SOA server host and port will need to be updated appropriately to reflect your environment. Directory locations and JDK versions may differ depending on the patchset of Oracle SOA Suite 11g installed. These commands must be executed to set your environment paths before running any ant command.

On Linux/Unix

In this chapter, we will assume that your code will reside under $CODE under the same Unix account where the Middleware Home and other binaries are installed. This is because the ant scripts require access to specific product libraries. The scripts assume a bash-based shell, so some changes may be required if other shells are used.

To set your environment, we recommend first creating a shell script setAntEnv.sh with the following content while keeping in mind to replace the highlighted values to suit your environment and installation:

```
export USERNAME=weblogic
export PASSWORD=welcome1
export SOAHOST=soahost1
export SOAPORT=8001
export SOAURL=http://${SOAHOST}:${SOAPORT}export CODE=/u01/svn/SOA11g
export MW_HOME=/u01/app/oracle/Middleware
export ORACLE_HOME=$MW_HOME/Oracle_SOA1
export JAVA_HOME=$MW_HOME/jdk160_24
export ANT_HOME=$MW_HOME/modules/org.apache.ant_1.7.1
export PATH=$JAVA_HOME/bin:$ANT_HOME/bin:$ANT_HOME/lib:$PATH:.
```

Don't forget to change the permissions of the script to executable:

```
chmod 750 setAntEnv.sh
```

Prior to running any ant command in the remainder of the chapter, simply source this shell script once to set your environment for your session as follows:

```
source setAntEnv.sh
```

Finally, make sure to change to the $ORACLE_HOME/bin directory before running any of the ant commands:

```
cd $ORACLE_HOME/bin
```

On Windows

We will assume that your code will reside under %CODE%. To set your environment, we recommend first creating a shell script setAntEnv.bat with the following content:

```
set USERNAME=weblogic
set PASSWORD=welcome1
set SOAHOST=soahost1
set SOAPORT=8001
set SOAURL=http://soaHost:soaPort
set CODE=c:\svn\SOA11g
set MW_HOME=C:\Oracle\Middleware
set ORACLE_HOME=%MW_HOME%\Oracle_SOA1
set JAVA_HOME=%ORACLE_HOME%\jdk160_24
set ANT_HOME=%ORACLE_HOME%\modules\org.apache.ant_1.7.1
set PATH=%JAVA_HOME%\bin;%ANT_HOME%\bin;%ANT_HOME%\lib;%PATH%
```

Make sure to update the highlighted text in the preceding script, to reflect your actual environment and installation.

In your Windows environment, if you do not have Oracle SOA Suite 11*g* and instead only have Oracle JDeveloper 11*g* installed, only a few modifications are required, and you should use the following commands instead:

```
set USERNAME=weblogic
set PASSWORD=welcome1
set SOAHOST=soahost1
set SOAPORT=8001
set SOAURL=http://%SOAHOST%:%SOAPORT%
set CODE=c:\svn\SOA11g
set ORACLE_HOME=C:\Oracle\jdev\jdeveloper
set JAVA_HOME=%ORACLE_HOME%\..\jdk160_24
set ANT_HOME=%ORACLE_HOME%\..\modules\org.apache.ant_1.7.1
set PATH=%JAVA_HOME%\bin;%ANT_HOME%\bin;%ANT_HOME%\lib;%PATH%
```

But only for installations of Oracle JDeveloper 11*g*, you must also perform a one-time copy of `ant-contrib-1.0b3.jar`. The file can be downloaded from `http://sourceforge.net/projects/ant-contrib/files/ant-contrib/`. Simply copy the file to `%ANT_HOME%\lib` as follows:

```
copy c:\temp\ant-contrib-1.0b3.jar %ANT_HOME%\lib
```

Now that your batch script is created, simply run it once in the command prompt to set your environment for your session:

```
setAntEnv.bat
```

Finally, make sure to change to the `%ORACLE_HOME%\bin` directory before running any of the ant commands:

```
cd %ORACLE_HOME%\bin
```

All ant commands in the remainder of this chapter will be Linux based. For Windows, simply replace the Linux specific environment variables such as `$USERNAME` and `$SOAHOST` with their Windows equivalent of `%USERNAME%` and `%SOAHOST%`. Also ensure that the slashes are reversed in the code paths. For example, `$CODE/HelloWorld/deploy/sca_HelloWorld_rev1.0.jar` in Linux would be `%CODE%\HelloWorld\deploy\sca_HelloWorld_rev1.0.jar` in Windows.

Starting and stopping composites with ant

Once you set the environment, you can start up a composite on Linux by running the following command:

```
ant -f ant-sca-mgmt.xml startComposite -Duser=$USERNAME
-Dpassword=$PASSWORD -Dhost=$SOAHOST -Dport=$SOAPORT
-DcompositeName=HelloWorld -Dpartition=default -Drevision=1.0
```

Likewise, you can stop a composite on Linux using the following:

```
ant -f ant-sca-mgmt.xml stopComposite -Duser=$USERNAME
-Dpassword=$PASSWORD -Dhost=$SOAHOST -Dport=$SOAPORT
-DcompositeName=HelloWorld -Dpartition=default -Drevision=1.0
```

You must also specify the composite name, the partition name it is deployed to, and the revision of the composite you wish to start up and shut down.

Packaging, deploying, and undeploying composites with ant

The commands in the following sections demonstrate how to package the HelloWorld composite project. This creates a deployable JAR file under the project's ~/deploy subdirectory. This JAR file can then either be manually deployed via Oracle Enterprise Manager Fusion Middleware Control as we have demonstrated earlier in this chapter, or through ant as shown in this section.

Packaging a composite via ant

The process of packaging a composite is equivalent to using the Make command in JDeveloper. The composite project is validated, compiled, and eventually built into a single deployable JAR file.

To package the HelloWorld composite application in Linux, simply run:

```
ant -f ant-sca-package.xml package -DcompositeDir=$CODE/HelloWorld
-DcompositeName=HelloWorld -Drevision=1.0
```

If no errors are encountered, you should expect to find the sca_HelloWorld_rev1.0.jar under the $CODE/HelloWorld/deploy directory.

Deploying a composite via ant

Now that the composite application is packaged, the SAR (or JAR file) can be deployed. The ant command references the path to the SAR directly (in Linux) as shown:

```
ant -f ant-sca-deploy.xml deploy -DserverURL=$SOAURL/soa-infra/deployer
-Duser=$USERNAME -Dpassword=$PASSWORD -DsarLocation=$CODE/HelloWorld/
deploy/sca_HelloWorld_rev1.0.jar -Dpartition=default -Doverwrite=true
-DforceDefault=true
```

As shown in these examples, the server URL, username, and password to the Oracle SOA Suite 11*g* runtime environment must be supplied. The fully qualified path to the SAR file must be provided in the sarLocation argument. Similar to deploying to the console, you must specify the partition to which you want to deploy. If a partition is not specified then the composite is deployed to the default partition. In this example, you can see that we do not provide a revision for the composite. This is because the revision was already specified during compilation (that is, packaging) time.

The overwrite argument specifies if you want to overwrite the composite already deployed to the server and the forceDefault argument specifies if you want this revision to be set as the default revision once it is deployed. The overwrite flag has to be specified if the composite is already deployed with the same revision number in the same partition. For first time deployments, specifying the overwrite flag is optional.

Undeploying a composite via ant

A composite can be undeployed via ant as well. On Linux, this is done by simply running the following command:

```
ant -f ant-sca-deploy.xml undeploy -DserverURL=$SOAURL/soa-infra/
deployer -Duser=$USERNAME -Dpassword=$PASSWORD -DcompositeName=HelloWorld
-Dpartition=default -revision=1.0
```

Exporting MDS artifacts with ant

The MDS, or Metadata Store, is a database-based repository, which stores various artifacts that can be referenced from within your SOA code. This can include shared schemas (that is, XSD files), WSDLs, fault policies and bindings, **domain value maps (DVMs)**, configuration files, and more.

Often, it is necessary to export the contents of the MDS either for backup, export, or management purposes. Fortunately, Oracle has provided an ant target that allows the easy export of MDS contents into a single JAR file. Once the JAR file is exported, it can be unzipped to your local filesystem and browsed through any file browser.

This command demonstrates how to execute ant to export the contents of your entire MDS to a single JAR file:

```
ant -f ant-sca-deploy.xml exportSharedData -DserverURL=$SOAURL/soa-infra/
deployer -Duser=$USERNAME -Dpassword=$PASSWORD -DjarFile=SOAMetaData.jar
-Dpattern=**
```

The JAR file SOAMetaData.jar can now be unzipped and browsed through the filesystem. When extracted to a temporary folder such as /tmp/svn, it may extract the following files:

```
/tmp/svn/SOAMetaData/faultPolicies/fault-bindings.xml
/tmp/svn/SOAMetaData/faultPolicies/fault-policies.xml
```

These files can now be navigated through the filesystem.

The pattern argument can be used to filter the contents you wish to export, allowing you to pick and choose what you want to export if you choose not to export the entire MDS content. For example, specifying a pattern of /apps/SOAMetaData/ dvm/**;/apps/SOAMetaData/faultPolicies/** will only export the artifacts under those two subfolders within the MDS.

Importing artifacts to the MDS with ant

Since MDS artifacts and contents are exported as a JAR file, it makes sense for it to be imported in the same manner.

For example, you may have the following files that you just updated on your local file system and wish to import them to the MDS. This may include fault policies, DVMs, and schemas located in the following local directory structure:

```
/tmp/svn/tmp/svn/SOAMetaData/faultPolicies/fault-bindings.xml
/tmp/svn/SOAMetaData/faultPolicies/fault-policies.xml
/tmp/svn/SOAMetaData/dvm/CurrencyCode.dvm
/tmp/svn/SOAMetaData/xsd/ErrorHandling/errorEvent.xsd
```

Firstly, you should zip up the contents of the ~/SOAMetaData subfolder generating a single SOAMetaData.jar file:

```
cd /tmp/svn
zip -r SOAMetaData.jar SOAMetaData
```

The JAR file is now ready to be imported to the MDS to maintain the same directory structure inside the MDS:

```
ant -f ant-sca-deploy.xml deploy -Dwl_home=/u01/app/middleware/
wlserver_10.3 -Doracle.home=$ORACLE_HOME -DserverURL=$SOAURL/soa-
infra/deployer -Duser=$USERNAME -Dpassword=$PASSWORD -Doverwrite=true
-DforceDefault=true -DsarLocation=SOAMetaData.jar
```

Promoting code using configuration plans

Promoting code refers to the activity of taking code from one environment, such as the development environment, and deploying it to the next one, such as the test environment. A typical software development promotion lifecycle sees code moving from development to test to QA (quality assurance) to production. As code is successfully tested in one environment, it is deployed to the next.

Why we need configuration plans

Unlike Java applications, SOA composite applications do not rely on property files to maintain environment specific configuration. Many SOA projects may include references to other external services, for example, `http://payment-processing-server-dev:7777/proc/servlet/createCustomer`. As you can see from this URL, the developer is referencing some external development server as identified by the hostname `payment-processing-server-dev`. This URL is hardcoded within the code and ultimately included within the deployable SAR. Prior to deploying this code to the test environment, the administrator must find a way to ensure that the test URL is referenced instead (which may have a different host, port, and protocol) as shown by `https://payment-processing-server-test:7778/proc/servlet/createCustomer`.

The SAR may potentially have other environment-specific settings such as URLs, JNDIs, and hostnames hardcoded in the SAR. One option is to manually extract the contents of the JAR file, manually edit all entries, and re-JAR it. This is a manual, cumbersome, and error prone process. Another approach is to attach a configuration plan to your composite at deployment.

The configuration plan is a single XML file that is attached to the SAR at deployment time. It is similar to a search-and-replace functionality, ensuring that references of one environment (such as development) are replaced with the next one (such as the test environment).

Understanding configuration plan contents

The following `cfgplan_test.xml` file is a configuration plan designed to be attached to the SAR at deployment time. It is used when deploying code written against a development environment to a test environment.

```xml
<?xml version="1.0" encoding="UTF-8"?>
<SOAConfigPlan xmlns:jca="http://platform.integration.oracle/blocks/
adapter/fw/metadata"
  xmlns:wsp="http://schemas.xmlsoap.org/ws/2004/09/policy"
  xmlns:orawsp="http://schemas.oracle.com/ws/2006/01/policy"
  xmlns:edl="http://schemas.oracle.com/events/edl"
  xmlns="http://schemas.oracle.com/soa/configplan">
<composite name="*">
  <import>
    <searchReplace>
      <search>http://soa11gdev:8001</search>
      <replace>http://soa11gtest:8001</replace>
    </searchReplace>
  </import>
  <service name="readFile">
    <binding type="*">
      <property name="inFileFolder">
        <replace>/u01/input/test</replace>
      </property>
    </binding>
  </service>
  <reference name="*">
    <binding type="ws">
      <attribute name="location">
        <searchReplace>
          <search> http://payment-processing-server-
          dev:7777/proc/servlet</search>
          <replace> https://payment-processing-server-
          test:7778/proc/servlet</replace>
        </searchReplace>
      </attribute>
    </binding>
  </reference>
</composite>
<wsdlAndSchema name="HelloWorld.wsdl|xsd/HelloWorld.xsd">
  <searchReplace>
    <search>sharedSchemaServerDev</search>
    <replace>sharedSchemaServerTest</replace>
  </searchReplace>
```

```
    <searchReplace>
      <search>7777</search>
      <replace>80</replace>
    </searchReplace>
  </wsdlAndSchema>
</SOAConfigPlan>
```

The file contains two main sections—`composite` and `wsdlAndSchema`. All entries within the `<composite>` tags apply to the `composite.xml` file in the SOA composite application. In this example, the `<wsdlAndSchema>` tag is specifically applied to the `HelloWorld.wsdl` and `xsd/HelloWorld.xsd` files within the project.

Let's walk through the preceding configuration plan in more detail.

<composite name="*">

This indicates that no matter what composite this configuration plan is attached to, the search-replace rules will apply to all, designated by *. Alternatively, it is possible to create different rules, which apply to different composites, such as:

```
<composite "HelloWorld1">
  <import>
    <searchReplace>
      <search>http://soa11gdev:8001</search>
      <replace>http://soa11gtest:8001</replace>
    </searchReplace>
  </import>
</composite "HelloWorld1">
<composite "HelloWorld2">
  <import>
    <searchReplace>
      <search>http://soa11gdev:8001</search>
      <replace>http://soa11gtest:8001</replace>
    </searchReplace>
  </import>
</composite "HelloWorld2">
```

The only reason to separate composite configuration as shown in the preceding configuration snippet is because the search-replace rules are different for each composite. If you do not envision any difference in the search-replace rules, we recommend sticking to `<composite "*">` instead in order to maintain simplicity.

<import>

The import tag is a subelement of the `<composite>` tag. Essentially, any search-replace within the `<import>` tag will apply to the `<import>` sections in `composite.xml`. You can have any number of search-replace elements here.

<service>

All composites will likely have a service. A service definition is synonymous to the input of the composite. A composite may have multiple services (for multiple interfaces), each of which can be invoked separately.

In the configuration plan, the `<service>` and `<reference>` tags use similar approaches. In the preceding example, there appears to be an inbound File Adapter that has an `inFileFolder` property. The code may be hardcoded with folder property `/u01/input/dev`. But here, the configuration plan will overwrite that property with the setting of `/u01/input/test` as the input folder.

<reference>

Composites may or may not have references, which refer to other resources such as another web service or an adapter.

Often, the reference could be the fully qualified URL to some other service either on the same server or a different one. Here, the configuration plan will replace all references to `http://payment-processing-server-dev:7777/proc/servlet` (development server) with `https://payment-processing-server-test:7778/proc/servlet` (test server).

Attaching a configuration plan

Attaching a configuration plan is quite simple. The ant command to deploy a composite application does not change and only an additional argument, which is the references to the fully qualified path to the configuration plan, is required:

```
ant -f ant-sca-deploy.xml deploy -DserverURL=$SOAURL/soa-infra/deployer
-Duser=$USERNAME -Dpassword=$PASSWORD -DsarLocation=$CODE/HelloWorld/
deploy/sca_HelloWorld_rev1.0.jar -Dpartition=default -Doverwrite=true
-DforceDefault=true -Dconfigplan=/tmp/cfgplan_test.xml
```

Best practices with configuration plans

The approach to managing code promotion effectively involves following a simple process to maintain consistency, and ensure proper substitution of environment-specific settings and deployment to other environments.

The summarized approach we recommend is as follows:

1. Developers should ensure that all URLs, JNDIs, hostnames, ports, and so on, reference development environments and they should try to remain as consistent as possible.

   For example, if multiple developers are working on multiple pieces of code that reference the same external service, they should try to be as consistent as possible. If this is the reference:

   ```
   http://payment-processing-server-dev:7777/proc/servlet
   ```

   They should avoid being inconsistent across their code:

   ```
   http://payment-processing-server-dev.somedomain.org:7777/proc/
   servlet
   http://PAYMENT-PROCESSING-SERVER-DEV:7777/proc/servlet
   https://payment-processing-server-dev:7778/proc/servlet
   ```

   The lack of consistency only means that additional search-replace statements will need to be added in the configuration plans.

2. The Oracle SOA Suite 11*g* administrator should create a configuration plan for every environment:
   - **Test**: `cfgplan_test.xml`
   - **QA**: `cfgplan_qa.xml`
   - **Prod**: `cfgplan_prod.xml`

   The `cfgplan_test.xml` configuration plan should replace all development environment settings with the test equivalent. The `cfgplan_qa.xml` should, similarly, replace all development environment settings with the QA equivalent. The `cfgplan_prod.xml` should do the same.

   Thus, the code will always maintain development environment specific settings, and it is the configuration plan that will ensure that these settings are replaced appropriately when the code is deployed to the target environment.

3. Every time a new environment-specific setting is used, the administrator should ensure that it is added to each of the configuration plans.

4. The administrator should always attach a configuration plan to every deployment.

Using configuration plans

In this example, we will exemplify the usage of configuration plans in a real world use case.

We have a simple `HelloWorld` BPEL project already deployed to both our development and test servers. On our development server, this is accessible at the URL `http://soa11gdev:8001/soa-infra/services/default/HelloWorldBPEL/helloworld_client_ep?WSDL`.

On our test server, it is accessible here, with only the hostname having changed. The URL is `http://soa11gtest:8001/soa-infra/services/default/HelloWorldBPEL/helloworld_client_ep?WSDL`.

When developing a Mediator composite that calls this BPEL service in our development environment, it will naturally invoke the development URL (accessible at `http://soa11gdev:8001`). When deploying this to the test server, this Mediator composite will continue to invoke the BPEL service on the development server! Our goal then, as the administrator, is to deploy this same Mediator project to the test server and change its references to the test environment accordingly.

Once the Mediator project is saved, the project will include two files with hardcoded URLs. The `composite.xml` file has the following code snippet:

```
<reference name="HelloWorldBPEL_BPEL"
  ui:wsdlLocation="http://soa11gdev:8001/soa-
  infra/services/default/HelloWorldBPEL/HelloWorldBPEL.wsdl">
  <interface.wsdl interface="http://xmlns.oracle.com
  /SOA11g/HelloWorldBPEL/HelloWorld#wsdl.interface(HelloWorld)"/>
  <binding.ws port="http://xmlns.oracle.com/
  SOA11g/HelloWorldBPEL/HelloWorld#wsdl.
  endpoint(helloworld_client_ep/HelloWorld_pt)"
    location="http://soa11gdev:8001/soa-
    infra/services/default/HelloWorldBPEL/helloworld_client_ep?WSDL"
      soapVersion="1.1">
    <property name="weblogic.wsee.wsat.transaction.flowOption"
    type="xs:string" many="false">WSDLDriven</property>
  </binding.ws>
</reference>
```

And the `Mediator1.componentType` file in the same project includes the following code snippet:

```
<reference name="HelloWorld_BPEL"
  ui:wsdlLocation="http://soa11gdev:8001/soa-
  infra/services/default/HelloWorldBPEL/HelloWorld.wsdl">
  <interface.wsdl interface="http://xmlns.oracle.com
  /SOA11g/HelloWorldBPEL/HelloWorld#wsdl.interface(HelloWorld)"/>
</reference>
```

Prior to deploying this to the test server, we first create a configuration plan `cfgplan_test.xml` with the following content:

```
<?xml version="1.0" encoding="UTF-8"?>
<SOAConfigPlan xmlns:jca="http://platform.integration.oracle
/blocks/adapter/fw/metadata"
  xmlns:wsp="http://schemas.xmlsoap.org/ws/2004/09/policy"
  xmlns:orawsp="http://schemas.oracle.com/ws/2006/01/policy"
  xmlns:edl="http://schemas.oracle.com/events/edl"
  xmlns="http://schemas.oracle.com/soa/configplan">
  <composite name="*">
    <import>
      <searchReplace>
        <search>http://soa11gdev:8001</search>
        <replace>http://soa11gtest:8001</replace>
      </searchReplace>
    </import>
    <reference name="*">
      <binding type="ws">
        <attribute name="location">
          <searchReplace>
            <search>http://soa11gdev:8001</search>
            <replace>http://soa11gtest:8001</replace>
          </searchReplace>
        </attribute>
      </binding>
    </reference>
  </composite>
</SOAConfigPlan>
```

The configuration plan replaces all references of `http://soa11gdev:8001` to the test server's equivalent `http://soa11gtest:8001`.

We finally deploy the Mediator project to the test environment attaching the configuration plan that we just created:

```
cd %ORACLE_HOME/bin
ant -f ant-sca-deploy.xml deploy -Duser=$USERNAME -Dpassword=$PASSWORD
-DserverURL=$SOAURL/soa-infra/deployer -DsarLocation=$CODE/HelloWorld_
Mediator/deploy/sca_HelloWorld_Mediator_rev1.0.jar -Dpartition=default
-Doverwrite=true -DforceDefault=true -Dconfigplan=/tmp/cfgplan_test.
xml
```

By attaching the configuration plan, the code, which was originally developed to reference development server specific URLs, is now deployed to the test server referencing test specific URLs.

Understanding and configuring composite audit levels

Setting the level of auditing tells the SOA Infrastructure how much information you want logged in order to assist in the monitoring and troubleshooting of instances. For example, if the audit level is completely `off`, the administrator will have no visibility into any composite instance. No instance data is logged and it is impossible to tell anything at that point (although instances are actually created and requests are serviced just fine). On the other hand, if the audit level is set to `development`, not only is the instance data logged, but the payload is also logged at every operation, giving the administrator complete visibility into the step-by-step execution of every instance!

Although setting the audit level to development may appear tempting, it has both performance and storage implications. Audit data is stored in the database, and if you have a large number of transactions, the database growth can be huge. One large customer of Oracle SOA Suite 11*g* has audit data that grows by nearly 10 gigabytes per day, faster than they are able to purge it! The following graphs show that as the payload size increases, the resulting database storage needs drastically increase for `development` versus `production` audit levels. For example, for a sampling of 500 messages with an average message size of 400 KB, successful transactions result in 90 MB of storage space needed for `development` audit levels versus 31 MB for `production`. For faulted transactions, it's even worse. 488 MB is needed if the `development` audit level is set versus 190 MB for `production`.

Sampling for 500 Message Invocations (0% Faults)		
	AUDIT Level	
Message Size (KB)	▲ Development (MB)	▲ Production (MB)
100	40	22
200	65	27
400	90	31
800	170	31
1500	350	35

Sampling for 500 Message Invocations (100% Faulted and Recovered)		
	AUDIT Level	
Message Size (KB)	▲ Development (MB)	▲ Production (MB)
100	314	134
200	359	169
400	438	190
800	612	220
1500	916	460

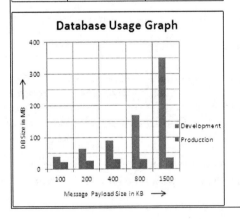

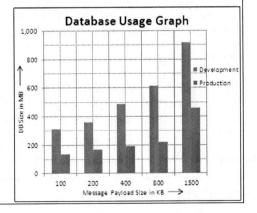

Not only are there storage concerns, as we have seen, but performance implications are severe. Enabling the `development` audit level at the SOA Infrastructure can result in approximately a 40 percent hit in composite instance performance!

Audit levels

Although audit levels can be configured in various areas, as we shall describe shortly, they mostly (but not in every case) fall under one of these four levels:

- **Off**: Absolutely no composite instance or payload information is collected. Although this is the best in terms of performance, it severely limits the visibility as no information is logged, rendering it an option that is not recommended in most cases. Instances are created, but nothing is logged to the database or displayed on the console, which may lead to difficulties in fault diagnosis and incident analysis.

- **Development**: Both composite instance and payload information are collected. Though this option provides the most detail, it is the worst performing of all the audit levels. It is recommended to set this in development environments for debugging purposes, but not in production environments, except for transactions that specifically require that degree of auditing.

- **Production**: Although composite instance information is collected, most payload details are not. This is the typical setting for production environments and provides the best balance between performance and visibility. If payload details need to be captured, it is best to consider setting the audit level to `development` only for specific composites, components, or services, as we shall describe later.

- **Inherit**: Audit levels are inherited from the parent level (we will describe this shortly).

To view the instance details, you should click on the composite on the navigator on the left, click on the **Instances** tab, then click on the instance ID. A pop-up window will reveal the details of this instance, including the audit trails. The following screenshots show the difference between the `development` and `production` audit levels:

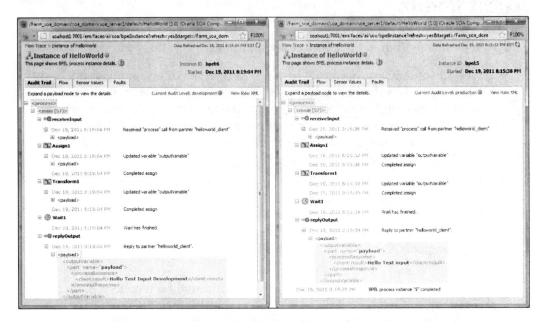

Audit levels set to `development` capture payloads throughout most activities, such as **Assign** and **Transform**. By expanding the ⊞ sign in the **Assign** activity, the payload is displayed. As you can see, the `development` audit level is advantageous and it allows you to see the changes made to the message across every activity or routing rule, but as discussed earlier, there are both storage and performance implications as a result.

Order of precedence for audit level settings

Before describing the order of precedence for audit level settings and what exactly it is, let's recap on specific terminology first:

- **Component**: Examples of components include a BPEL process, a Mediator service, or a BPMN process. Within JDeveloper, these components are the building blocks for composite applications.

- **Composite**: A composite consists of zero or more components. For example, a single composite can include a BPEL component and two Mediator components. Composite applications are packaged into a single JAR file that is deployed to the SOA Infrastructure.

- **Service engine**: Though we have not described service engines in detail yet, they are the actual engines that run the code. There are three main service engines — BPEL Service Engine, Mediator Service Engine, and BPMN Service Engine. As their names imply, the BPEL Service Engine executes the BPEL code, the Mediator Service Engine executes the Mediator code, and the BPMN Service Engine executes the BPMN code.

- **SOA Infrastructure**: The SOA Infrastructure is the underlying infrastructure, which is comprised of the service engines mentioned in the preceding section and to which the composite applications are deployed.

Why have we described these terms? Because audit levels can be manipulated across each of these. It is possible to set the audit level at the component level, the composite level, or even the service engine level. But if the audit level is set at the composite level as `development` and at the SOA Infrastructure level as `production`, which one takes precedence?

At a high level, the order of precedence is as follows:

Component > Composite > Service Engine > SOA Infrastructure

What this means is that, for example, if the audit level is set to `development` at the composite level and `production` at the SOA Infrastructure level, that the setting at the composite level overrides that of the SOA Infrastructure. If the composite audit level is set to `inherit`, it will inherit the settings from the applicable service engine. If the service engine is also set to `inherit`, it will inherit the settings from the SOA Infrastructure. As a general rule, we recommend setting all audit level settings to `inherit` and controlling it at the SOA Infrastructure level. Then, as the need for different levels of auditing are required, start manipulating the service engine, composite, and component audit levels as needed.

Unfortunately, the rules on what takes precedence are rather complicated as you start changing each of them. If auditing at the service engine is enabled and the composite audit level is set to `off`, there is no audit trail generated for this composite and its underlying components. Neither the service engine nor SOA Infrastructure audit levels take effect in this case. When the audit level of a composite is set to `inherit`, depending on what the audit levels of the service engine and the SOA Infrastructure are, either of them may take effect, which is confusing. Detailed examples of order of precedence can be found in the first chapter of the Oracle Fusion Middleware Administrator's Guide for Oracle SOA Suite 11*g* Release 1 (11.1.1).

Modifying audit levels

We had previously discussed that audit levels can be set at the component, composite, service engine, and SOA Infrastructure levels. Here, we will describe how to set each of these.

Modifying component audit levels

Component level auditing can only be manipulated for BPEL and BPMN components, but not Mediator components.

For example, developers can modify BPEL component level auditing by inserting the `bpel.config.auditLevel` property within their component reference in the `composite.xml` file of their project as shown in the following code snippet:

```
<component name="HelloWorld">
  <implementation.bpel src="HelloWorld.bpel" />
  <property name="bpel.config.auditLevel">Off</property>
</component>
```

Modifying composite audit levels

Audit levels can be changed during runtime at the composite level. To do so, perform the following steps:

1. On the navigator, expand **Farm_[Domain]** | **SOA** | **soa-infra**.
2. Expand the partition (for example, default) and click on the composite name (for example, **HelloWorld**).
3. Click on the **Settings** button.
4. Click on the **Composite Audit Level** menu item.
5. Choose between one of the four audit levels:
    - **Inherit**
    - **Off**
    - **Production**
    - **Development**

Modifying service engine audit levels

Both the BPEL Service Engine and BPMN Service Engine have a fifth audit level—minimal. The minimal audit level collects instance information, but not payload details in the flow audit trails.

To set the audit level for the BPEL Service Engine:

1. Right-click on **soa-infra** and then navigate to **SOA Administration | BPEL Properties**.
2. Set the **Audit Level** field.
3. Click on **Apply**.

To set the audit level for the BPMN Service Engine:

1. Right-click on **soa-infra** and then navigate to **SOA Administration | BPMN Properties**.
2. Set the **Audit Level** field.
3. Click on **Apply**.

To set the audit level for the Mediator Service Engine:

1. Right-click on **soa-infra** and then navigate to **SOA Administration | Mediator Properties**.
2. Set the **Audit Level** field.
3. Click on **Apply**.

Modifying SOA Infrastructure Audit Levels

The SOA Infrastructure audit level can be configured by performing the following:

1. Right-click on **soa-infra** and then navigate to **SOA Administration | Common Properties**.
2. Set the **Audit Level** field.
3. Click on **Apply**.

Summary

The focus of this chapter was to walk through key activities that enable the Oracle SOA Suite 11*g* administrator to perform various composite application functions, including basic management to deployment to auditing. Specifically, we focused on the following:

- Managing composite lifecycles, discussing the differences between startup/shutdown states and the active/retired modes.

- Understanding revisions and how to set the default revision of composites.

- Deploying, undeploying, and redeploying composites from Oracle Enterprise Manager Fusion Middleware Control.

- Understanding and managing partitions, including partition creation and deletion, as well as bulk management operations such as starting up, shutting down, and undeploying all composites in a partition.

- Setting up ant scripts for deploying, undeploying, and redeploying composite applications.

- Using ant to import and export artifacts to and from the MDS.

- Understanding the purpose of configuration plans and how to use them.

- Discuss the various audit levels, how to set them, and performance and storage implications of each.

The ant-build scripts are an important aspect that every Oracle SOA Suite 11*g* administrator should have a good handle on. Though we touched upon the more important elements of ant as it pertains to Oracle SOA Suite 11*g*, for more information, refer to *chapter 43.6.2* titled *How to Manage SOA Composite Applications with ant Scripts* in the *Oracle Fusion Middleware Developer's Guide for Oracle SOA Suite 11g* at `http://download.oracle.com/docs/cd/E12839_01/integration.1111/ e10224/sca_lifecycle.htm#sthref2497`.

The next chapter will cover the essentials of monitoring the Oracle SOA Suite 11*g* infrastructure, the service engines, and instances. We will also describe the infamous ECID, how to search BPEL and composite sensors, detail out the component and composite states, and break down the log files in an easy to understand format.

3
Monitoring
Oracle SOA Suite 11*g*

There are several tools and techniques available for administrators to continuously monitor the Oracle SOA Suite 11*g* infrastructure. Many administrators choose command-line scripting to monitor portions of the overall environment, resources, and deployments. Alternatively, there are enterprise grade monitoring products such as Oracle Enterprise Manager Grid Control, that allow for monitoring of multiple environments distributed across an organization, as well as the transactions spanning across them. However, the scope of this book is limited to various scripting techniques and the out-of-the-box Oracle Enterprise Manager Fusion Middleware Control console that provides real-time access to in-flight transactions, instance states, and performance summaries, keeping administrators well informed about the behavior of each composite. It provides a rich snapshot of important runtime data such as message payloads, throughput, response times, and fault information that can be drilled down to an individual transaction, component, or engine.

There are three main areas of monitoring that an Oracle SOA Suite 11*g* administrator will typically focus on:

- Transactions
- Instance state and performance
- Infrastructure

Quite simply, if these three areas are covered, you would probably have a good handle on monitoring your environment in general. The goal is to ensure the overall health and dependability of the infrastructure to execute transactions.

Transactional monitoring involves:

- Reviewing faulted instances to take action (retry, replay, or ignore).
- Searching log files for additional log information on faulted instances.
- Searching through composite sensors if the end user is complaining of a particular business transaction not going through and if composite sensors are implemented in the code.
- Enabling selective tracing (included with the latest version of Oracle SOA Suite 11g) that allows you to change the trace level for a defined scope. Examples of scope are a particular logged-in user, a deployed application, or a BPEL composite.

Monitoring instance state and performance involves:

- Reviewing the **Performance Summary** and **Request Processing** pages on the console to graphically display specific metrics on selected composites
- Running SQL queries to retrieve summary and detail performance information on composite instances

Infrastructure monitoring involves:

- Reviewing filesystem log files for system and application errors
- Monitoring the Oracle WebLogic Server managed servers for overall health
- Monitoring the JVM for appropriate sizing and garbage collection frequency
- Monitoring JMS destinations such as queues and topics to ensure that messages are being processed
- Monitoring data sources to preemptively identify any issues
- Monitoring threads

Once you understand all areas of monitoring, it might make sense to invest in a tool that helps with the automation of the monitoring activities—an area we do not discuss in this book as there are many options available on the market. Oracle's standard monitoring solution for Oracle SOA Suite 11g is Oracle Enterprise Manager Grid Control with the SOA Management Pack.

Transaction monitoring

When monitoring transactions, the goal is to achieve two purposes:

- Identifying transactions that have not been completed successfully to determine further action

- Ensuring that the transactions do not experience poor performance

When a payload is received by the SOA Infrastructure, it may pass through multiple components within your infrastructure and may even traverse multiple external systems as well. For example, a sales order may be received by a BPEL process, which in turns places it into a queue. Afterwards, it may be consumed by some third-party application that processes the sales order, before sending it back to another Mediator service, which routes it to the final order management application. If any one of the above steps in this particular integration fails, how can you identify where the message is? What would also be important to you is to know the time taken by each component to determine if it is inline with your predefined SLAs.

In this section, we will cover different areas and topics that provide you with the tools necessary for effective transaction monitoring.

Monitoring instances

To monitor composite instances, you should first understand a few key concepts:

- Every transaction displayed on Oracle Enterprise Manager Fusion Middleware Control is a composite instance. Each composite instance is designated a unique composite instance ID.

- Every composite may consist of one or more components (for example, BPEL, BPMN, Mediator, and so on). You must navigate to the composite instance and drill down to the component to view its details. Every component has its own component instance ID.

- The **Execution Context ID** (**ECID**) is a global unique identifier of a particular transaction. It is injected into the header of the payload when the instance is first created and is included throughout the lifecycle of the payload. Thus, the ECID may appear in multiple composites and components. The ECID should not be confused with either of the instance IDs described above.

- Every composite instance and component instance has metadata that includes the creation time, last updated time, and state of the instance.

Monitoring faulted instances

One of the more common activities an administrator performs is retrieving a list of faulted or rejected instances and getting the necessary information to troubleshoot them. This can be done through the following steps:

1. Log in to Oracle Manager Fusion Middleware Control.
2. Click on **soa-infra**.
3. Click on the **Faults and Rejected Messages** tab.
4. Click on the first instance ID. A pop-up window will appear, showing the details of the instance.
5. Review the error.
6. Repeat the steps for all faulted instance IDs.

In some cases, the fault shown on the console may not contain enough information to effectively troubleshoot the error, and a review of the log files may be necessary. Later in this chapter, we will discuss how to identify and view log file information, as well as increasing the loggers to dump more information as necessary.

Searching composite sensors

Composite sensors are added to the composite at design time by the developer(s). They provide a method for implementing trackable fields on messages. Instances that are displayed on the composite dashboard cannot be correlated to a business indicator. More often than not in the real world, it is important to know which instance corresponds to an important field in the message such as a customer ID or an order number. Composite sensors can be used to capture these business indicators at runtime and persisted in the database. These can then be searched using these composite sensors, instead of the non-meaningful instance ID via the Oracle Enterprise Manager Fusion Middleware Control console.

If the composite is not designed to capture composite sensors, you will not be able to search on them. Composite sensors are similar to variable sensors in BPEL processes and similar to trackable fields in Oracle **Enterprise Service Bus (ESB)** 10g.

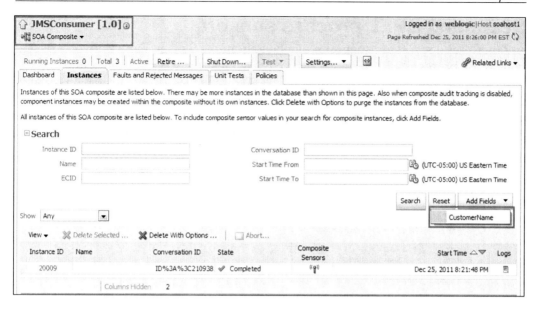

By navigating to any composite and clicking on the **Instances** tab, if the composite is designed to capture composite sensors, an **Add Fields** button appears. The preceding screenshot shows that the **JMSConsumer** composite has a **CustomerName** sensor. When chosen, a new search field is added allowing you to search by that particular composite sensor on this page. Remember, composite sensors can technically capture any type of data defined by the developer at design time. When searching by a particular composite sensor, a list of instances, which contains that particular sensor value, will be retrieved.

To view the name of the composite sensor and its value, you can click on the icon.

The screenshot in the *Understanding IDs and ECIDs* section later in this chapter also shows composite sensors in the flow trace. The screenshot displays the composite sensor with the name CustomerName having a value of "Jane Doe".

Developers are encouraged to implement composite sensors. This allows the administrator to search a particular business field such as an order number or customer ID. There is also no limit on the number of composite sensors that can be added to a composite. You can query the COMPOSITE_SENSOR_VALUE table in the database to retrieve composite sensor data.

Searching BPEL process sensors

Another useful set of information is available from the **Sensor Values** tab of
your BPEL process. BPEL sensors capture the values of activity, variable, and
fault sensors, if any, that are configured at design time. Sensors are a very important
means of instrumentation in business processes as they record key business or
process analytics information. Have a look at the following screenshot and you
will see how a Variable Sensor records the e-mail delivery acknowledgement in
the MessageId variable. Sensors are another means of making sure that business
processes are executing with all the checks and balances in place.

Oracle SOA Suite 11g is a stateful engine that requires a backend database
(also referred to as the dehydration store) to store all information about process
metadata and instance states.

The metadata information for process sensors is stored in the dehydration store
database. You can find the sensor configuration information for each type in their
corresponding dehydration store tables ACTIVITY_SENSOR_VALUES, VARIABLE_
SENSOR_VALUES, and FAULT_SENSOR_VALUES in the [PREFIX]_SOAINFRA schema.

Understanding IDs and ECIDs

To effectively perform transaction monitoring, it helps to understand the difference between the various IDs. Every composite instance has a unique composite instance ID, sometimes simply referred to as an instance ID. The instance ID is a sequential numeric identifier and is the primary means of navigating instances through the console.

The **Execution Context ID (ECID)**, on the other hand, is a global unique identifier of a particular transaction. As a message is passed from composite to composite, the ECID is passed with each message. This allows for the correlation of a message across different components even if the message leaves Oracle SOA Suite 11*g* and comes back!

An ECID is generated when the request is first processed by Oracle Fusion Middleware. If it exists, no new ECID is generated. The following is an example of an ECID:

```
cb680017c6a0acfe:-606797c4:134357968da:-8000-0000000000001736
```

In the sample integration design shown in the following screenshot, we have a BPEL process that produces a message in some external JMS queue. Afterwards, this message is consumed asynchronously by another BPEL process that passes it on to a Mediator service, which in turn invokes a final BPEL process. In this example, each of these components are in their own composite (that is, the integration consists of a total of four composites).

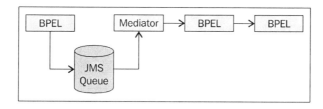

Each composite instance has its own instance ID (see instance IDs 20008, 20009, 20010, and 20011 in the flow shown in the following screenshot). Upon the instantiation of the first composite, an ECID is generated. As shown in the following screenshot, the first composite instantiated includes the BPEL component named `CustomerJMSProduce` with the composite instance ID of 20008.

This ECID, which is shown on the top-right corner of the flow trace in the screenshot, is inserted as a property with the message as it is passed on to the next composite. Thus, all composites and components within this single flow will maintain the same ECID, allowing the engine to tie the execution of the transaction into a single flow.

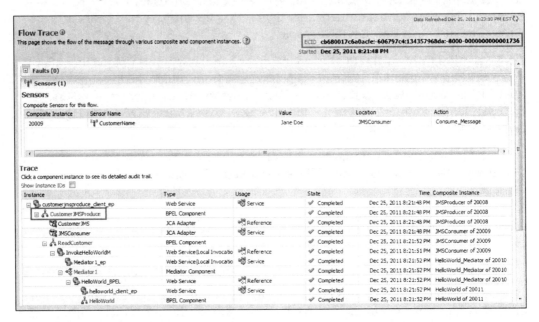

Querying the database also confirms this. We can query the COMPOSITE_INSTANCE table for this particular ECID:

```
SELECT ID, COMPOSITE_DN, STATE, CREATED_TIME, 'COMPOSITE'
FROM   COMPOSITE_INSTANCE
WHERE  ECID = 'CB680017C6A0ACFE:-606797C4:134357968
DA:-8000-0000000000001736'
```

The following screenshot shows the query response that returns four composite instances associated with this ECID:

ID	COMPOSITE_DN	STATE	CREATED_TIME	'COMPOSITE'
20012	InboundQueues/JMSProducer!1.0*soa_71b5e4d7-7b78-45a3-be31-469beb277401	1	25-DEC-11 09.29.01.593000000 PM	COMPOSITE
20013	default/JMSConsumer!1.0*soa_7af0890e-571d-44a5-8e9b-50bad870ea35	64	25-DEC-11 09.29.01.753000000 PM	COMPOSITE
20014	default/HelloWorld_Mediator!1.0*soa_ad87b6bd-5ad7-48d0-ae52-6bc036d21b18	1	25-DEC-11 09.29.04.916000000 PM	COMPOSITE
20015	default/HelloWorld!1.0*soa_8c1c8eab-c3bf-4ba8-9f7a-04f56b830c33	1	25-DEC-11 09.29.05.044000000 PM	COMPOSITE

Each of those composites has a single component. Thus, we can combine the output from the `CUBE_INSTANCE` and `MEDIATOR_INSTANCE` tables, to also retrieve a similar flow, but at the component level.

```
SELECT TO_CHAR(CMPST_ID) COMPOSITE_INSTANCE_ID, COMPONENT_NAME, STATE
COMPONENT_STATE, CREATION_DATE CREATED_TIME, 'BPEL' TYPE
FROM    CUBE_INSTANCE
WHERE   ECID = 'CB680017C6A0ACFE:-399CCED5:13477C6A1B4:-8000-
0000000000004A0D'
UNION
SELECT TO_CHAR(COMPOSITE_INSTANCE_ID) COMPOSITE_INSTANCE_ID,
COMPONENT_NAME, COMPONENT_STATE, CREATED_TIME D, 'MEDIATOR' TYPE
FROM    MEDIATOR_INSTANCE
WHERE   ECID = 'CB680017C6A0ACFE:-399CCED5:13477C6A1B4:-8000-
0000000000004A0D'
```

Once again, the query would return the four components and there instance IDs, as shown in the following screenshot:

COMPOSITE_INSTANCE_ID	COMPONENT_NAME	COMPONENT_STATE	CREATED_TIME	TYPE
20012	CustomerJMSProduce	5	25-DEC-11 09.29.01.629000000 PM	BPEL
20013	ReadCustomer	9	25-DEC-11 09.29.01.848000000 PM	BPEL
20014	default/HelloWorld_Mediator!1.0*soa_a...	0	25-DEC-11 09.29.04.971000000 PM	MEDIATOR
20015	HelloWorld	5	25-DEC-11 09.29.05.068000000 PM	BPEL

Querying the product database tables, though generally discouraged by Oracle, is perhaps the quickest and simplest mechanism to retrieve detailed instance information. *Chapter 8, Managing the Matadata Services Repository and Dehydration Store* will cover more details about the key database tables that store runtime data.

Instance states

When querying the database, it is important to understand the various states that are maintained in the product tables. We have listed the states of each of these three main database tables that you will likely be focusing on:

- `COMPOSITE_INSTANCE`: Stores composite instance data

- `CUBE_INSTANCE`: Stores BPEL and BPMN instance data

- `MEDIATOR_INSTANCE`: Stores Mediator instance data

COMPOSITE_INSTANCE

The COMPOSITE_INSTANCE table maintains composite specific information. The state is stored in the STATE column. Since composites consist of multiple components, each having its own state, there are many variations that can be expected. For example, if a composite has two components, and both have executed but one of them failed, the state of the composite would be 3. If the first component ran successfully, but the second one is still running, the state would be 0. State 32 (unknown) occurs when the **Capture Composite Instance State** setting is disabled (refer to *Chapter 4, Tuning Oracle SOA Suite 11g for Optimum Performance* for details on this), wherein the composite instance state is not captured in order to improve performance. State 64 (stale) occurs when the composite is redeployed by overwriting the previous version. The instance state of all the old instances of the previously deployed composite is set to stale, indicating that it was executed under a previous revision of the composite.

The following table lists all states in the COMPOSITE_INSTANCE table:

State	Description
0	Running
1	Completed
2	Running with faults
3	Completed with faults
4	Running with recovery required
5	Completed with recovery required
6	Running with faults and recovery required
7	Completed with faults and recovery required
8	Running with suspended
9	Completed with suspended
10	Running with faults and suspended
11	Completed with faults and suspended
12	Running with recovery required and suspended
13	Completed with recovery required and suspended
14	Running with faults, recovery required, and suspended
15	Completed with faults, recovery required, and suspended
16	Running with terminated
17	Completed with terminated
18	Running with faults and terminated
19	Completed with faults and terminated
20	Running with recovery required and terminated

State	Description
21	Completed with recovery required and terminated
22	Running with faults, recovery required, and terminated
23	Completed with faults, recovery required, and terminated
24	Running with suspended and terminated
25	Completed with suspended and terminated
26	Running with faults, suspended, and terminated
27	Completed with faults, suspended, and terminated
28	Running with recovery required, suspended, and terminated
29	Completed with recovery required, suspended, and terminated
30	Running with faults, recovery required, suspended, and terminated
31	Completed with faults, recovery required, suspended, and terminated
32	Unknown
64	Stale

CUBE_INSTANCE

The CUBE_INSTANCE table maintains BPEL and BPMN component instances. The state is stored in the STATE column. The CUBE_INSTANCE table is joined to the parent COMPOSITE_INSTANCE table via the CMPST_ID column.

The following table lists all states in the CUBE_INSTANCE table:

State	Description
1	Initiated
2	Open and running
3	Open and suspended
4	Open and faulted
5	Closed and pending cancel
6	Closed and completed
7	Closed and faulted
8	Closed and cancelled
9	Closed and aborted
10	Closed and rolled back

MEDIATOR_INSTANCE

Mediator instance information is maintained in the MEDIATOR_INSTANCE table, with the state stored in the COMPONENT_STATE column. The way states are maintained is rather different here, as a Mediator component may consist of one or more routing rules, each having its own case. The MEDIATOR_INSTANCE table is joined to the parent COMPOSITE_INSTANCE table via the COMPOSITE_INSTANCE_ID column.

This table lists all states in the MEDIATOR_INSTANCE table.

State	Description
0	No faults but still there might be running instances
1	At least one case is aborted by user
2	At least one case is faulted (non-recoverable)
3	At least one case is faulted and one case is aborted
4	At least one case is in recovery required state
5	At least one case is in recovery required state and at least one is aborted
6	At least one case is in recovery required state and at least one is faulted
7	At least one case is in recovery required state, one faulted, and one aborted
>=8 and <16	Running
>=16	Stale

Monitoring instance performance

There are several means available to help assist in viewing instance performance. You can view the details of a single instance through the console or you can rely on several out-of-the-box graphs and metrics. In this chapter, you will also have access to key SQL queries to obtain more performance metrics in addition to the metrics that are displayed in Oracle Enterprise Manager Fusion Middlware Control console.

Understanding last update time of instances

What is often misleading about the console is that most of the timestamps shown are actually the last updated time of the transaction, and not the time it was created. Keep this in mind as sometimes the timestamps may appear out of order, particularly in flows that are linked together via the ECID, and complete at different times.

 The timestamps shown on the console are the last update time of the transaction, and not the time it was created.

Let's say that you clicked on the **ReadCustomer** BPEL component in the composite flow trace sample integration design screenshot shown in the *Understanding IDs and ECIDs* section in this chapter. You will be taken to the instance flow trace of the **ReadCustomer** component detailing each of the activities that were executed in sequence. The audit trail displays a timestamp below each activity, providing the date and time of its occurrence. Timestamps can often give you a fair idea on time durations for executing specific activities. For example, the **Wait** activity shown in the following screenshot took three seconds to complete, indicated by having started at **9:32:08 PM** and ending at **9:32:11 PM** on the same day.

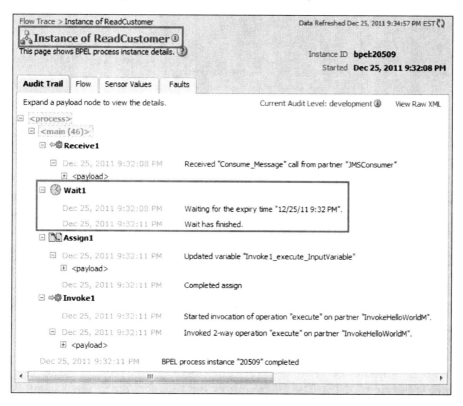

By clicking on the **Flow Trace** link on the top-left of the screen shown in the preceding screenshot, you would be taken back to the flow trace as shown in the screenshot under the *Understanding IDs and ECIDs* section in this chapter. Clicking on the Mediator component named **Mediator1** will take you to the screen shown in the following screenshot. Likewise, the difference in timestamps can give you an idea of how long a specific routing rule, transformation, or invocation has taken.

For example, the invocation to the Mediator process has taken less than one second, as indicated by the start time of **9:32:11 PM** and ending at **9:32:11 PM**. Unfortunately, the console does not display a more granular timestamp.

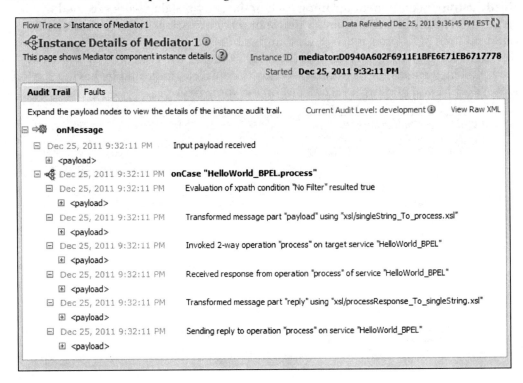

Viewing performance summary graphs and request processing metrics

Performance metrics available in Oracle Enterprise Manager Fusion Middleware Control are obtained through a JRF layer component known as the **Dynamic Monitoring Service (DMS)**. The DMS component registers a runtime MBean with each managed server's runtime MBean, collects a set of metrics for each composite running on its host server, and periodically feeds the collected information back to the DMS collection MBean on the AdminServer. The snapshot of metrics are thus collected and stored within the AdminServer's memory.

The metrics data displayed in Oracle Enterprise Manager Fusion Middleware Control is stored within the memory of the AdminServer and as such any restart of the AdminServer clears all historical metrics data.

To view instance performance summaries:

1. Go to the navigator, expand **SOA**, and right-click on **soa-infra**.
2. Navigate to **Monitoring | Performance Summary**.
3. The **Performance Summary** page is displayed, as shown in the following screenshot.
4. On the right-hand side of this page, there is the **Metric Palette** where you can pick and choose the metrics that you want displayed.
5. We have chosen the following metrics to display for the composite named **JMSConsumer**:
   - **Average processing time for successful instances**
   - **Average Incoming Messages Processing Time**
   - **Average Outbound Messages Processing Time**

As you can see in the following screenshot, the **Average processing time for successful instances** (but not failed instances) was steady at around **5** seconds, but spiked to **15** seconds at around the 9:31 PM timeframe. This was apparently due to unexpected load on the system at that time.

We can also see that the **Average Incoming Messages Processing Time**, which is the time it took for the BPEL process to consume the message from the JMS queue, peaked at around **0.6** seconds during the same timeframe.

The **Average Outbound Messages Processing Time**, which is the time the JMSConsumer component took to invoke the next **Mediator1** mediator service, ranged from **0.5** to **1.0** seconds, which is not too bad for this particular transaction. From these metrics, we can determine that during the peak time, the consumption of the message (peak **0.6** seconds) and the invocation of the target mediator service (peak **1.0** seconds) were probably not the cause of the spike of **15** seconds total end-to-end processing time of the composite.

So, there must have been something else within the composite that resulted in the poor performance under load.

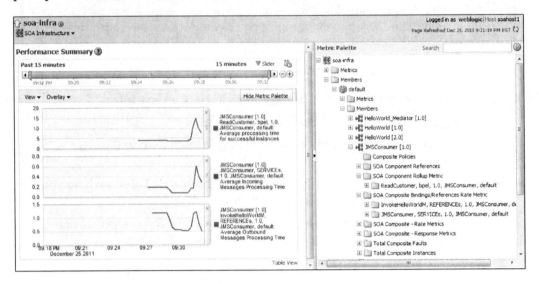

Viewing request processing metrics

To view request processing metrics:

1. On the navigator, expand **SOA**, right-click on **soa-infra**, and navigate to **Monitoring | Request Processing**.

2. The **Request Processing** page is displayed, revealing **Service Engines**, **Service Infrastructure**, and **Binding Component** metrics.

3. The following screenshot shows the **Service Engines** metrics on this page. These are high level metrics at the **Service Engine** level:

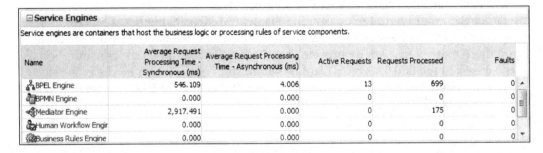

Name	Average Request Processing Time - Synchronous (ms)	Average Request Processing Time - Asynchronous (ms)	Active Requests	Requests Processed	Faults
BPEL Engine	546.109	4.006	13	699	0
BPMN Engine	0.000	0.000	0	0	0
Mediator Engine	2,917.491	0.000	0	175	0
Human Workflow Engir	0.000	0.000	0	0	0
Business Rules Engine	0.000	0.000	0	0	0

4. Clicking on the service engine name takes you to the service engine home dashboard, allowing you to drill down to statistics, instances, faults, deployed composites, and recovery.

Monitoring using SQL queries

The standard information obtained from Oracle Enterprise Manager Fusion Middleware Control might not be sufficient and adequate for fine grained monitoring. By querying some core product tables in the [PREFIX]_SOAINFRA schema such as the COMPOSITE_INSTANCE, CUBE_INSTANCE, and MEDIATOR_INSTANCE tables, you can get detailed metrics that include success/failure counts, composite instance performance, and durations of invokes as well. Here, we provide two main queries to obtain performance metrics on BPEL processes and Mediator services, specifically the duration of time that each component took. Though Oracle typically does not recommend querying the product tables directly (since the structure of the tables may change after a patch or upgrade), note that these queries below run fine on Oracle SOA Suite 11g PS3 (11.1.1.4), PS4 (11.1.1.5), and PS5 (11.1.1.6).

The following query outputs a list of all BPEL component instances, their state, average, minimum, and maximum durations, as well as counts:

```
SELECT DOMAIN_NAME PARTITION,COMPONENT_NAME,
    DECODE(STATE,'1','RUNNING','5','COMPLETED','6',
    'FAULTED','9','STALE') STATE,
    TO_CHAR(AVG((TO_NUMBER(SUBSTR(TO_CHAR(MODIFY_DATE-
    CREATION_DATE),12,2))*60*60) +
    (TO_NUMBER(SUBSTR(TO_CHAR(MODIFY_DATE-CREATION_DATE),15,2))*60) +
    TO_NUMBER(SUBSTR(TO_CHAR(MODIFY_DATE-
    CREATION_DATE),18,4))),'999990.000') AVG,
    TO_CHAR(MIN((TO_NUMBER(SUBSTR(TO_CHAR(MODIFY_DATE-
    CREATION_DATE),12,2))*60*60) +
    (TO_NUMBER(SUBSTR(TO_CHAR(MODIFY_DATE-CREATION_DATE),15,2))*60) +
    TO_NUMBER(SUBSTR(TO_CHAR(MODIFY_DATE-
    CREATION_DATE),18,4))),'999990.000') MIN,
    TO_CHAR(MAX((TO_NUMBER(SUBSTR(TO_CHAR(MODIFY_DATE-
    CREATION_DATE),12,2))*60*60) +
    (TO_NUMBER(SUBSTR(TO_CHAR(MODIFY_DATE-CREATION_DATE),15,2))*60) +
    TO_NUMBER(SUBSTR(TO_CHAR(MODIFY_DATE-
    CREATION_DATE),18,4))),'999990.000') MAX,
    COUNT(1) COUNT
FROM    CUBE_INSTANCE
GROUP BY DOMAIN_NAME, COMPONENT_NAME, STATE
ORDER BY COMPONENT_NAME, STATE
```

domain_name in the query represents the partition name shown on the console. In the following screenshot, which is the output of the preceding SQL query, we can see that there are **192** successfully completed instances of the **HelloWorld** BPEL process in the **default** partition. These 192 instances took an average of **0.068** seconds and the maximum duration took **3.900** seconds to complete.

PARTITION	COMPONENT_NAME	STATE	AVG	MIN	MAX	COUNT
InboundQueues	CustomerJMSProduce	Completed	0.378	0.000	19.800	179
default	CustomerJMSProduce	Stale	0.457	0.100	1.400	7
default	HelloWorld	Completed	0.068	0.000	3.900	192
EBS	HelloWorld	Completed	0.000	0.000	0.000	5
default	ReadCustomer	Completed	5.725	3.300	12.900	4
default	ReadCustomer	Stale	6.898	1.000	38.900	176

The following query displays a list of all Mediator component instances, their state, average, minimum, and maximum durations, as well as counts:

```
SELECT SUBSTR(COMPONENT_NAME, 1, INSTR(COMPONENT_NAME,'/')-1)
PARTITION,
    SUBSTR(COMPONENT_NAME, INSTR(COMPONENT_NAME,'/')+1,
    INSTR(COMPONENT_NAME,'!')-INSTR(COMPONENT_NAME,'/')-1) COMPONENT,
    SOURCE_ACTION_NAME ACTION,
    DECODE(COMPONENT_STATE,'0','COMPLETED','2',
    'FAULTED','3','ABORTED','4','RECOVERY
    NEEDED','8','RUNNING','16','STALE') STATE,
    TO_CHAR(AVG((TO_NUMBER(SUBSTR(TO_CHAR(UPDATED_TIME-
    CREATED_TIME),12,2))*60*60) +
    (TO_NUMBER(SUBSTR(TO_CHAR(UPDATED_TIME-CREATED_TIME),15,2))*60) +
    TO_NUMBER(SUBSTR(TO_CHAR(UPDATED_TIME-
    CREATED_TIME),18,4))),'999990.000') AVG,
    TO_CHAR(MIN((TO_NUMBER(SUBSTR(TO_CHAR(UPDATED_TIME-
    CREATED_TIME),12,2))*60*60) +
    (TO_NUMBER(SUBSTR(TO_CHAR(UPDATED_TIME-CREATED_TIME),15,2))*60) +
    TO_NUMBER(SUBSTR(TO_CHAR(UPDATED_TIME-
    CREATED_TIME),18,4))),'999990.000') MIN,
    TO_CHAR(MAX((TO_NUMBER(SUBSTR(TO_CHAR(UPDATED_TIME-
    CREATED_TIME),12,2))*60*60) +
    (TO_NUMBER(SUBSTR(TO_CHAR(UPDATED_TIME-CREATED_TIME),15,2))*60) +
    TO_NUMBER(SUBSTR(TO_CHAR(UPDATED_TIME-
    CREATED_TIME),18,4))),'999990.000') MAX,
    COUNT(1) COUNT
FROM    MEDIATOR_INSTANCE
GROUP BY COMPONENT_NAME, SOURCE_ACTION_NAME, COMPONENT_STATE
ORDER BY COMPONENT_NAME, SOURCE_ACTION_NAME, COMPONENT_STATE
```

Notice the output of the preceding query in the following screenshot to see that there are **3** successfully completed instances of the **HelloWorld_Mediator** Mediator service, which is deployed to the **default** partition. These **3** instances took an average of **1.000** seconds, a minimum of **0.200** seconds, and a maximum of **2.100** seconds to complete.

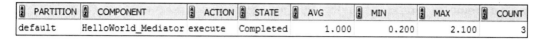

PARTITION	COMPONENT	ACTION	STATE	AVG	MIN	MAX	COUNT
default	HelloWorld_Mediator	execute	Completed	1.000	0.200	2.100	3

The DMS Spy Servlet

DMS Spy Servlet is a small web-based application that displays **Dynamic Monitoring Service (DMS)** related metrics, which are built-in metrics automatically collected by the servers. Simply navigate to the URL `http://<host>:<soaport>/dms/Spy` and log in using the administrator account (for example, weblogic).

You can retrieve an immediate snapshot on everything from running JDBC statements to JVM threads to MDS repository configuration to numerous Oracle WebLogic Server metrics.

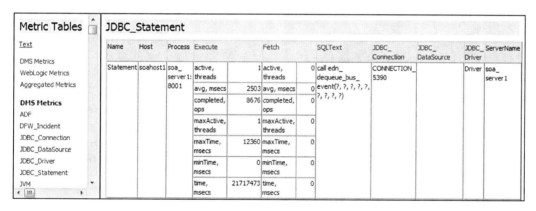

The DMS Spy Servlet is perhaps the easiest way to quickly get instant monitoring information. Additional information about DMS Spy Servlet can be found on the Oracle documentation site at `http://docs.oracle.com/cd/E15586_01/core.1111/e10108/monitor.htm#CFAHIAIB`.

Identifying and viewing log file entries

When you install Oracle SOA Suite 11g, you will likely have three types of managed servers available with the default installation—AdminServer, soa_server1, and bam_server1. These names can vary depending upon what you choose to enter while creating the domain. In a cluster, the number of managed servers may increase with incrementing numerals at the end (for example, soa_server2, bam_server2, and so on). If you use a different naming convention, these names may not be the same, but for the purpose of the book we assume that we are dealing with the default configuration. Each of these managed servers has several log files that include:

- Managed server log file (for example, soa_server1.log)
- Diagnostic log file (for example, soa_server1-diagnostic.log)
- Server startup standard out log file (for example, soa_server1.out)
- The HTTP access log (access.log)

Fortunately, Oracle Enterprise Manager Fusion Middleware Control provides the ability to access and search several of these log files. The following steps will help you to download the managed server log and diagnostic log files:

1. Log in to Oracle Manager Fusion Middleware Control.
2. Right-click on **soa-infra**, then navigate to **Logs | View Log Messages**.
3. Click on the **Target Log Files** button.
4. Select **soa_server1.log** (or any other log file), then click on the **Download** button.

In some cases, where the composite instance faults do not offer enough information to help with the troubleshooting efforts, it may be necessary to search the log file for a particular ECID to retrieve additional information. To search for a particular ECID in the log file:

1. Log in to Oracle Manager Fusion Middleware Control.
2. Right-click on **soa-infra**, then navigate to **Logs | View Log Messages**.
3. Select **Date Range** (for example, **Most Recent 1 hour**).
4. Select all **Message Types**—**Incident Error**, **Error**, **Warning**, **Notification**, **Trace**, and **Unknown**.
5. Click on the **Add Fields** button and add **ECID**.
6. Enter an ECID in the field, and click on the **Search** button.
7. Review the output.

The following screenshot shows the results of a search through the managed server log files for a particular ECID. Rows relevant to this ECID are displayed, and in this case we see that several notifications showing how a JMSAdapter was invoked and how a Mediator service was executed. This information may still not be enough, in which case the logger levels will have to be increased (we will discuss this shortly).

Unfortunately, searching log files through the console is slow and cumbersome, and we recommend accessing the log files themselves directly on the filesystem instead.

Another important mechanism available to monitor and troubleshoot information from log files is by enabling **Selective Tracing** in Oracle Enterprise Manager Fusion Middleware Control. This can be configured by expanding **Weblogic Domain**, right-clicking on your domain name, and then navigating to **Logs | Selective Tracing**. This brings you to a screen where the **Selective Tracing** session can be configured. The following screenshot shows how you can select **Option Name** to choose the scope of the trace session, trace level, duration of trace, and also specify a custom **Trace ID**.

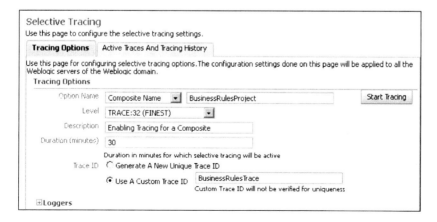

You may also select the loggers that you want to be active for the tracing session by expanding the **Loggers** icon. All loggers are enabled by default and there is the option to both sort by the available columns as well as search on them. You can enable the configured Selective Tracing session by clicking on the **Start Tracing** button.

By selecting the **Active Traces And Tracing History** tab, you will notice the tracing session being listed. If a few instances of the composite for which the tracing session is enabled are executed now, you would see that the Log Viewer presents a filtered search on the Trace ID. The following screenshot shows **Log Messages** for a trace session configured on the `BusinessRulesProject` composite. Trace entries can be exported to a new file by clicking on the **Export Messages to File** button. The trace session expires at the end of the specified duration or you may manually disable it in the **Active Traces And Tracing History** tab by highlighting the session and clicking on the **Disable** button. Selective Tracing is available only for the current domain.

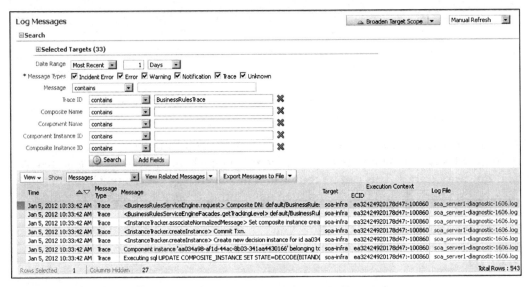

Relevant log files

In a standard installation, the key log files are located in the following locations on the filesystem:

```
$MW_HOME/user_projects/domains/[Domain]/servers/[server_name]/logs/
[server_name].log
$MW_HOME/user_projects/domains/[Domain]/servers/[server_name]/logs/
[server_name].out
$MW_HOME/user_projects/domains/[Domain]/servers/[server_name]/logs/
[server_name]-diagnostic.log
$MW_HOME/user_projects/domains/[Domain]/servers/[server_name]/logs/
access.log
```

The `soa_server1.log` file logs entries that are both infrastructure and transaction specific. In the event that an error is found in a composite instance that is unclear, locate the timeframe of that instance and search this log file. Here, for example, see the details of an error related to the initialization of `MQSeriesAdapter`:

```
####<Dec 28, 2011 10:08:00 PM EST> <Error> <Deployer> <soahost1> <soa_
server1> <[ACTIVE] ExecuteThread: '0' for queue: 'weblogic.kernel.
Default (self-tuning)'> <<WLS Kernel>> <> <cb680017c6a0acfe:58ce28
8b:13487c99be3:-8000-0000000000000002> <1325128080369> <BEA-149205>
<Failed to initialize the application 'MQSeriesAdapter' due to error
weblogic.application.ModuleException: The ra.xml <connectionfactory-
impl-class> class 'oracle.tip.adapter.mq.ConnectionFactoryImpl' could
not be loaded from the resource adapter archive/application because
of the following error: java.lang.NoClassDefFoundError: oracle/tip/
adapter/api/OracleConnectionFactory.
```

The `soa_server1.out` file is generated when you start up the managed server via Node Manager or the Oracle WebLogic Server Administration Console. Review this log for server startup issues. For example, it may include startup information such as JVM heap and the `CLASSPATH` settings as well as runtime infrastructure issues errors:

```
********************************************************
** SOA specific environment is already set, skipping...
********************************************************
.
JAVA Memory arguments: -Xms1536m -Xmx1536m -Xgcprio:throughput
    -XX:+HeapDumpOnOutOfMemoryError -XXtlasize:min=16k,preferred=128k,
    wasteLimit=8k
.
WLS Start Mode=Production
.
CLASSPATH=/u01/app/oracle/Middleware/oracle_common/modules/oracle.
    jdbc_11.1.1/ojdbc6dms.jar:/u01/app/oracle/Middleware/Oracle_SOA1/
    soa/modules/user-patch.jar:/u01/app/oracle/Middleware/Oracle_SOA1/
    soa/modules/soa-startup.jar:...

<Jan 1, 2012 2:59:42 PM EST> <Error> <oracle.sdp.messaging.engine>
<SDP-25088> <Unable to refresh the driver locator cache, due to the
following error: EJB Exception: : Local Exception Stack:
Exception [TOPLINK-4002] (Oracle TopLink - 11g Release 1 (11.1.1.5.0)
(Build 110305)): oracle.toplink.exceptions.DatabaseException
Internal Exception: weblogic.jdbc.extensions.
ConnectionDeadSQLException: weblogic.common.resourcepool.
ResourceDeadException: 0:weblogic.common.ResourceException: Could
not create pool connection. The DBMS driver exception was: IO Error:
Socket read timed out
```

The `soa_server1-diagnostic.log` file writes entries in the **Oracle Diagnostic Logging (ODL)** format. See the following screenshot that provides a prototype of a log message in the ODL format. This is a text file and entries in this file conform to an Oracle standard that includes information such as timestamp, server name, error type, component ID, user, and other log information. In the figure, you can see that the `JMSProducer` composite was deployed successfully in 15.471 seconds.

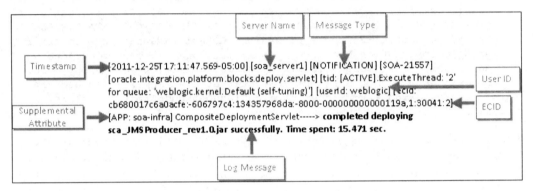

In the following log snippet, logged in ODL format, the entry shows the operation `CustomerProduce` failing, due to a connection issue while inserting a message into a JMS queue:

```
[2011-12-25T17:12:05.211-05:00] [soa_server1] [ERROR] [] [oracle.
soa.adapter] [tid: [ACTIVE].ExecuteThread: '2' for queue: 'weblogic.
kernel.Default (self-tuning)'] [userId: <anonymous>] [ecid:
cb680017c6a0acfe:-606797c4:134357968da:-8000-00000000000011fa,0:2]
[WEBSERVICE_PORT.name: CustomerJMSProduce_pt] [APP: soa-infra]
[composite_name: JMSProducer] [component_name: CustomerJMSProduce]
[component_instance_id: 12] [J2EE_MODULE.name: fabric] [WEBSERVICE.
name: customerjmsproduce_client_ep] [J2EE_APP.name: soa-
infra] JCABinding=> JMSProducer:CustomerJMS [ CustomerProduce_
ptt::CustomerProduce(opaque) ] Could not invoke operation
'CustomerProduce' against the 'null' due to: [[
BINDING.JCA-12511
JCA Binding Component connection issue.
```

Modifying logger levels

By right-clicking on **soa-infra** and navigating to **Logs | Log Configuration**, you will be taken to the page allowing you to configure the logger levels.

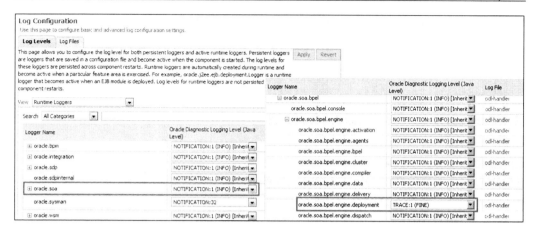

Expand **oracle.soa | oracle.soa.bpel | oracle.soa.bpel.engine | oracle.soa.bpel. engine.deployment** and set the logging level from **NOTIFICATION:1 (INFO)** to **TRACE:1 (FINE)**. Now, rerunning the `JMSProducer` composite results in considerably more information in the `soa_server1-diagnostic.log` file, including the payload:

```
[2012-01-01T22:35:56.144-05:00] [soa_server1] [TRACE] [] [oracle.
soa.adapter] [tid: [ACTIVE].ExecuteThread: '2' for queue: 'weblogic.
kernel.Default (self-tuning)'] [userId: <anonymous>] [ecid:
cb680017c6a0acfe:-3f1527ec:13487d1ea4c:-8000-0000000000000fe1,0:2]
[SRC_CLASS: oracle.integration.platform.blocks.adapter.fw.log.
LogManagerImpl] [WEBSERVICE_PORT.name: CustomerJMSProduce_pt]
[APP: soa-infra] [composite_name: JMSProducer] [component_name:
CustomerJMSProduce] [component_instance_id: 30005] [J2EE_MODULE.name:
fabric] [SRC_METHOD: log] [WEBSERVICE.name: customerjmsproduce_client_
ep] [J2EE_APP.name: soa-infra] JMS Adapter   JMSProducer:CustomerJMS
[ CustomerProduce_ptt::CustomerProduce(body) ]   JmsProducer_
execute:[default destination = jndi/CustomerJMSQueue]: Successfully
produced message.
[2012-01-01T22:35:56.256-05:00] [soa_server1] [NOTIFICATION] []
[oracle.soa.adapter] [tid: weblogic.work.j2ee.J2EEWorkManager$WorkWi
thListener@16bc6851] [userId: <anonymous>] [ecid: cb680017c6a0acfe:-
5675273b:1348cccad75:-8000-0000000000055743,0] [APP: soa-infra]
JMSAdapter JMSConsumer JMSMessageConsumer_consume: Got message with ID
ID:<458362.1325475356144.0> from destination jndi/CustomerJMSQueue

[2012-01-01T22:35:56.261-05:00] [soa_server1] [TRACE] [] [oracle.soa.
adapter] [tid: weblogic.work.j2ee.J2EEWorkManager$WorkWithListener@
16bc6851] [userId: <anonymous>] [ecid: cb680017c6a0acfe:-5675273b:1
348cccad75:-8000-0000000000055743,0] [SRC_CLASS: oracle.integration.
platform.blocks.adapter.fw.log.LogManagerImpl] [APP: soa-infra] [SRC_
METHOD: log] JMS Adapter
JMSProducer:CustomerJMS [ CustomerProduce_ptt::CustomerProduce(body)
```

```
]  XMLHelper_convertJmsMessageHeadersAndPropertiesToXML:
<JMSInboundHeadersAndProperties xmlns="http://xmlns.oracle.com/pcbpel/
adapter/jms/">[[
  <JMSInboundHeaders>
    <JMSCorrelationID></JMSCorrelationID>
    <JMSDeliveryMode>2</JMSDeliveryMode>
    <JMSExpiration>0</JMSExpiration>
    <JMSMessageID>ID:&lt;458362.1325475356144.0></JMSMessageID>
    <JMSPriority>0</JMSPriority>
    <JMSRedelivered>false</JMSRedelivered>
    <JMSType></JMSType>
    <JMSTimestamp>1325475356144</JMSTimestamp>
  </JMSInboundHeaders>
  <JMSInboundProperties>
    <Property name="tracking_ecid" value="cb680017c6a0acfe:-
    3f1527ec:13487d1ea4c:-8000-0000000000000fe1"/>
    <Property name="tracking_compositeInstanceId" value="30006"/>
    <Property name="tracking_parentComponentInstanceId"
    value="bpel:30005"/>
    <Property name="tracking_conversationId"
    value="urn:E115FC7034F211E1BF23313DB35B2981"/>
    <Property name="JMSXDeliveryCount" type="integer" value="1"/>
  </JMSInboundProperties>
</JMSInboundHeadersAndProperties>
```

The `access.log` file is generated in the event that you do not have the Oracle Web Tier installed. This log file logs all HTTP requests to the internal web server following the standard Apache HTTP Server log format. Reviewing this may help in identifying all SOAP requests that have hit your server, as this is the first touch point to the server. This is an example of an entry in the `access.log` file:

```
192.168.97.111 - - [18/Dec/2011:12:12:59 -0500] "POST /soa-infra/
services/default/HelloWorld/helloworld_client_ep HTTP/1.1" 200 466
```

Note that the same message may be duplicated across many of these log files, so as you gain better familiarity with each of them, you will know what to look for.

Monitoring service engine instances and faults

As an administrator, you may sometimes need to monitor recent instances and faults of the different components running in the SOA Infrastructure. The execution status and metrics for an instance in a particular engine can be monitored from the Oracle Enterprise Manager Fusion Middleware Control console by right-clicking on **soa-infra** and navigating to **Service Engines | [Component]**. Once you are here, you can see all the recent instances for the selected component across all the composites.

Examine the following screenshot to see a typical monitoring page for a Business Rules (Decision Service) engine. The information displayed here includes:

- Instance ID of the component
- Component name
- SOA composite application of which the component is a part
- State of the instance
- Instance start time
- Last modification time
- A Logs icon

You may also click on other tabs that display the statistics (average processing times, cache statistics, operation statistics, counts, and so on) or faults, if any, associated with the service engine. This particular information for the decision service engine is made available from the BRDECISIONINSTANCE table in the dehydration store. Alternatively, you can also query the database by joining this table and the COMPOSITE_INSTANCE table on ECID or COMPOSITE_INSTANCE_ID.

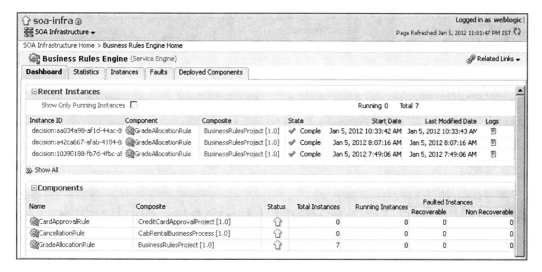

You can further drill down into an individual instance (either completed, running, or faulted) from here to see its complete audit trail. Clicking on any instance will open a new window that shows the execution report of the instance. The following screenshot shows the **Audit Trail** of an instance that has executed on the decision service engine, when **Audit Level** was set to DEVELOPMENT.

The development-level trace report displays the fact name, activated rule, as well as the pushed and popped ruleset names. The entries in the trace report of a business rules engine are explained in the following table. For BPMN and BPEL engines, you also get to see a more friendly graphical view.

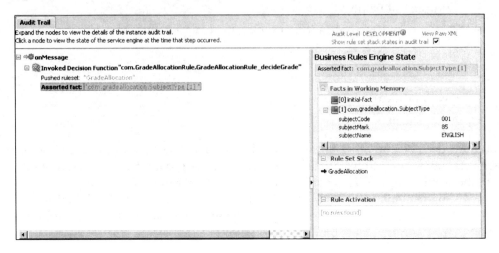

Audit Trail Part	Description
Decision Service Name	Name of the decision service component being invoked.
Asserted Fact	Fact passed to the decision service engine from other engines like BPEL, BPMN, or Mediator.
Activated Rule	Name of the rule that is activated and its corresponding fact.
Pushed Ruleset	Ruleset that is invoked when the fact is asserted.
Fired Rules in Ruleset	Name of the ruleset whose rule is executed.
Fired Rule	Rule that is being executed.

Monitoring the Event Delivery Network (EDN)

Oracle SOA Suite 11g has an out-of-the-box **Event Delivery Network (EDN)** that allows you to publish and subscribe to business events. The EDN framework creates the messaging plumbing out of the box, that is, you will not have to create any backend queues to support event delivery and consumption in the infrastructure. The default EDN is configured on the database, and this uses **Oracle Advanced Queuing (AQ)** behind the scenes. You can also have EDN based on JMS that uses the JMS API. In the development and testing stage, access to the EDN logs is of great help to identify and troubleshoot issues with your EDN implementation. EDN logging level can be changed by following the next steps:

1. Log in to Oracle Manager Fusion Middleware Control.
2. Right-click on **soa-infra**, then navigate to **Logs | Log Configuration**.
3. Expand the logger nodes to **oracle.integration.platform.blocks.event** or enter `blocks.event` in the search box and click on the **Search** button to filter the view.
4. Change log level of **oracle.integration.platform.blocks.event.saq** to **TRACE: 32**. Configuring the logging at this level will ensure that the body of the event message is available in the EDN trace.
5. Check the **Persist log level state across component restarts** box and click on the **Apply** button. This will let the log level survive managed server restarts.

In addition to configuring the EDN runtime java loggers as discussed earlier, you can also enable the debug flag when using the default EDN implementation based on the database. The value of the `ENABLED` column in the `EDN_LOG_ENABLED` table in the dehydration store can be set to `1` for making the EDN logs available for review and configuration in a browser console at `http://<host>:<soaport>/soa-infra/events/edn-db-log`.

The following screenshot shows a sample EDN log output wherein the screen displays the event payload and status (**Enqueing Event**, **Enqueing Complete**, **Dequeing Complete**, and so on). The logging is disabled by default. However, it can be enabled by clicking on the **Enable** link on the page. You can also **Clear** the debug table or **Reload** logs from the same page.

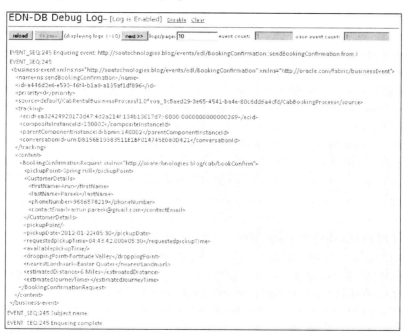

Monitoring the WebLogic Server

From an infrastructure monitoring perspective, ensuring that the Oracle WebLogic Server and all its underlying components are functioning should be your primary concern. In this section, we describe the monitoring of managed servers, JVM, JMS destinations, and data sources.

Monitoring managed servers

As long as your managed servers are reported as being healthy, usually there is not much to worry about. A warning state does not mean that the managed server is unresponsive, but the cause of the warning should be investigated. One of the key issues to managed server monitoring is ensuring the appropriate monitoring of threads.

To view the state of the managed servers:

1. Log in to the Oracle WebLogic Server Administration Console.
2. On the home page, click on **Servers**.
3. A list of all your managed servers will appear along with their state and health.

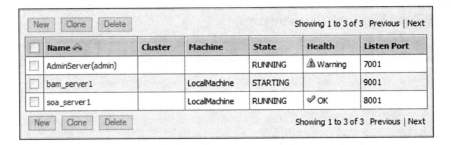

	Name ⌃	Cluster	Machine	State	Health	Listen Port
☐	AdminServer(admin)			RUNNING	⚠ Warning	7001
☐	bam_server1		LocalMachine	STARTING		9001
☐	soa_server1		LocalMachine	RUNNING	✔ OK	8001

Ensure that the managed servers are running and are in a healthy state, as designated by the green checkbox with **OK**. In *Chapter 6, Troubleshooting Oracle SOA Suite 11g Infrastructure*, we will discuss approaches in troubleshooting warning or failed managed server states.

Monitoring the JVM

Although there are too many areas surrounding JVM monitoring to describe here, three of the more important ones include ensuring that the heap allocated to the JVM is appropriately sized (that is, comparing heap versus non-heap usage), that there is not excessive garbage collection, and JVM thread performance. Perform the following steps to monitor the key JVM statistics:

1. Log in to the Oracle WebLogic Server Administration Console.

2. On the home page, click on **Servers**.

3. Navigate to the **Monitoring | Performance** tab.

4. Here, the total heap size and the percentage of free heap are displayed.

5. Click on the **Garbage Collect** button. Observe how much **Heap Free Current** is freed before and after garbage collection.

Oracle WebLogic Server 11*g* also provides a dashboard that provides real-time monitoring of many metrics, including the JVM runtime heap. This is helpful to review while there is a heavy load on the system as it allows you to view the current and free heap size.

Log in to the Oracle WebLogic Server Administration Console and click on **Monitoring Dashboard**. Select **JVM Runtime Heap** and click on the start button. The **Heap Size Current** and **Heap Free Current** are graphically displayed for all running servers as shown in the following screenshot. If the free heap hovers around zero for a considerable time, this is an indication that the heap size may be configured too small. If repeated and frequent garbage collections occur without much memory being freed up, additional JVM monitoring may be required at that point.

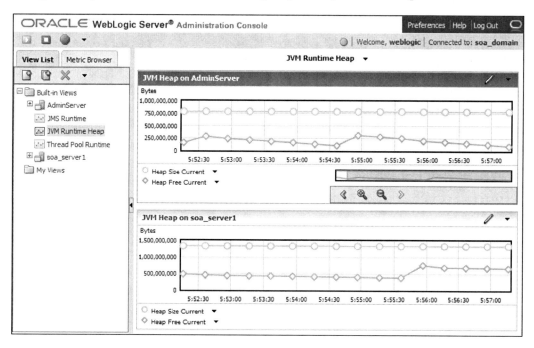

From the Oracle WebLogic Server Monitoring Dashboard, the Thread Pool Runtime can also be monitored in real-time. The key is to monitor the Hogging Thread Count and the Pending User Request Count. On a low usage environment, these should ideally be hovering around zero. From the Oracle WebLogic Administration Console, navigate to **Servers** | **[soa_server]** | **Monitoring** | **Threads** to view these important statistics along with the thread pool and the thread pool threads. Everything from **Active Execute Threads** to **Hogging Thread Count** is shown on this page. The Throughput shown on this page is a single value that denotes the mean number of requests completed per second. The higher this value, the better. But the thread pool changes its size automatically to maximize throughput, so in normal cases there is nothing you need to do aside from monitoring it to understand the behavior of your server under different types of load. This chapter provides WLST code that can be executed anytime to obtain JVM specific statistics.

Monitoring JMS destinations

More often than not, many of the integrations that run on top of Oracle SOA Suite 11g may leverage JMS destinations to support asynchronous integrations. These destinations can be JMS queues (for point-to-point integrations) or JMS topics (for publish-subscribe integrations). Oracle WebLogic Server 11g provides a way to easily create these JMS destinations that become accessible via a JNDI in the code.

As an administrator, you must be aware of all queues and topics created, as there are many reasons why you would want to monitor them:

- Ensure that messages in the queues and topics are being produced and consumed without error and/or delay.
- Ensure that poison messages, ones that have exceeded the maximum number of delivery attempts, do not remain in the queue or topic.

To monitor your JMS destinations:

1. Log in to the Oracle WebLogic Administrator Console.
2. Click on **JMS Modules**.
3. Click on the JMS module name that is hosting your queue/topic.
4. Click on the queue or topic name.
5. Click on the **Monitoring** tab. Here you will see a summary of statistics regarding your JMS destination such as current, pending, and total messages.

6. If the JMS destination already has subscribers, click on the checkbox beside your destination name, then click on the **Show Messages** button. From here, you can export some or all of the messages to an XML file, if you choose to (for either backup purposes or with the intention of importing them into a different environment).

7. Click on the JMS **Message ID**. The following screenshot displays the result of this. Details of the message are displayed as part of the JMS header, including ECID, composite instance ID, as well as the payload of the message:

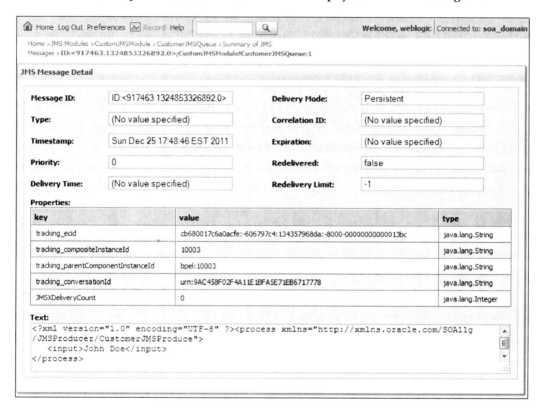

Monitoring data sources

For data source monitoring, as long as the connection pool configuration is valid (that is, there are no connectivity issues to the database) and the number of active connections do not approach or exceed the maximum configured connections, then that is usually all that is needed.

To check the JDBC DataSource Runtime Statistics:

1. Log in to the Oracle WebLogic Administrator Console.

2. Click on **Data Sources**.

3. Click on the **Monitoring** tab. Here, the state of the data sources (for example, running), as well as the average, current, and high active connections count are displayed.

4. Click on **Customize this table**. From **Column Display Available**, select **Current Capacity, Leaked Connection Count, Number Available**, and **Active Connections Current Count**, and move them under **Chosen Column**.

5. Click on **Apply**.

6. The **Monitoring** tab of the data source will look like that shown in the following screenshot. The key is to ensure that the sum of **Active Connections Current Count** and **Leaked Connection Count** do not exceed the connection pools' **Current Capacity**. If they do, it is either time to fix the leaked connections or increase the pool capacity.

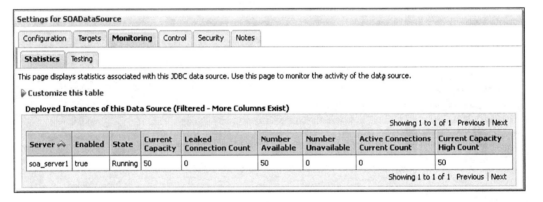

7. To get the maximum capacity to determine how to appropriately size your connection pool:

   ° Click on the data source name (for example, **SOADataSource**).

   ° Navigate to **Configuration | Connection Pool**.

   ° Note the setting of the **Maximum Capacity** parameter.

In cases where the database may not be accessible or is down, the database password used for the connection pool has expired or reset, network related issues occur, or data source related errors begin to appear in the logs, it may be worthwhile to test and ensure that the data source is working properly by performing the following steps:

1. Log in to the Oracle WebLogic Administrator Console.

2. Click on **Data Sources**.

3. Click on the data source name (for example, **SOADataSource**).

4. Navigate to **Monitoring | Testing**.

5. Select the radio button and click on the **Test Data Source** button.

6. If the connection is working (that is, the data source is able to access the database at the host, port, database name, username, and password), the following message will appear on the top of the page:

   Test of [DataSource] on server [soa_server] was successful.

Monitoring from the console may involve too many navigation steps and be cumbersome at times. You may want to consider creating scripts that can be executed on the go to obtain the health of all the data sources running on the infrastructure. For proactive monitoring purposes, you may even create a cron job to regularly check your data source statistics, since any failure of the data source will eventually lead to the failure of the entire infrastructure.

OEM Grid Control and the SOA Management Pack

The latest **Oracle Enterprise Manager** (**OEM**) Grid Control 12*c* is Oracle's monitoring and management product of choice for the majority of Oracle software and applications. By leveraging OEM Grid Control, you can monitor and manage all your Oracle and non-Oracle software through a single, centralized console. OEM Grid Control is licensed separately from Oracle SOA Suite.

OEM Grid Control should not be confused with Oracle Enterprise Manager Fusion Middleware Control or other consoles such as Oracle Enterprise Manager Application Server Control (included with older versions of the Oracle Application Server).

An agent (specifically, the Oracle Management Agent) is installed on every server you wish to monitor, and data on the installed server and operating system is collected and reported back to the central repository (specifically, the Oracle Management Server) at regular intervals. It is through the **Oracle Management Server** (**OMS**) that you can log in to view server status, performance, configure alerts, and perform administrative tasks.

For environments with a large number of applications, systems, and servers, we recommend a monitoring tool such as OEM Grid Control to simplify the monitoring and management functions of the administrator. Some key benefits of OEM Grid Control include:

- Centralized monitoring and management of both Oracle and non-Oracle applications and software
- Pre-configured alerts
- Out-of-the-box support for targets such as applications (for example, Oracle E-Business Suite and Oracle Fusion Applications), middleware (for example, Oracle WebLogic Server and Oracle SOA Suite), database, operating systems (for example, Windows, Linux, AIX, and Solaris), virtual machines, and more
- Ability to perform administrative functions such as startup/shutdown, patching, cloning, provisioning, capturing diagnostic information, and much more

The Oracle SOA Management Pack Enterprise Edition extends OEM Grid Control to provide additional functionality such as visibility into complex SOA orchestrations, monitoring of security policies, performance monitoring of Oracle SOA Suite and Oracle Service Bus, and trace end-to-end transactions across tiers. Imagine performing these functions for all your environments from a single, centralized console!

Summary

As an Oracle SOA Suite 11g administrator, you must be comfortable with monitoring both the infrastructure as well as transactions. In this chapter, we covered the following:

- Composite instance monitoring
- Performance of composite instances through the console and SQL queries
- Reviewing and understanding relevant logs, using selective tracing and structure of a log entry
- Oracle WebLogic Server and infrastructure monitoring of managed servers, JVM, messaging queues and topics, and data sources

In *Chapter 6, Troubleshooting Oracle SOA Suite 11g Infrastructure*, we will see how to go about troubleshooting and resolving various errors, faults, and exceptions that you may find during your monitoring activities.

Now that you have learnt how to manage and monitor Oracle SOA Suite 11g, the next chapter focuses on methods to improve the performance of your infrastructure.

4

Tuning Oracle SOA Suite 11*g* for Optimum Performance

As an Oracle SOA Suite 11*g* administrator, when managing highly visible and mission critical business process application of your enterprise, one of the most important ongoing activities that you will engage in is performance tuning the infrastructure. Considerations like scalability, performance, and reliability of the underlying infrastructure are paramount. Pre-configured default settings are not optimal or may require tuning for performance and production environments, and this is where optimization is required to extract the best performance out of your environment.

In this chapter, you will learn details of specific areas that you need to focus on to improve your infrastructure performance. The key to optimization is to understand why you require optimizing in the first place, and knowing the ramifications of the changes you are making.

Many recommendations and suggested settings throughout this chapter have resulted in considerable performance improvements in real production environments, but may not be applicable for all types of implementations as hardware sizing, operating system choice, code design patterns, and other factors all contribute to choosing optimal settings. Please exercise caution when making any change.

Performance tuning is challenging as often it is difficult to know where to begin. Also equally important is to understand the interdependencies that various tuning configurations may have, so as to avoid undesirable runtime behavior. In order to maximize performance, you will need to understand, monitor, analyze, and tune all of the components that make up your infrastructure. There are a lot of factors that may come into play that degrade the performance of your infrastructure. For example, inadequate hardware that runs your infrastructure, improper code design, impeding endpoint applications, and network clogging are just some of the many factors that undermine the effectiveness of any enterprise system. However, when you are confident that these problems are not interfering with the performance of your infrastructure, it is time to look towards tuning your SOA environment. As an administrator, it is important for you to roadmap your performance planning, as optimization is normally a tradeoff between performance, reliability, environmental complexity, maintainabililty, and security, and decisions have to be made after carefully weighing the pros and cons and priorities.

The first step is to review your existing infrastructure and applications followed by devising a tuning strategy accordingly. There are a few things to remember and act on when embarking on any performance tuning exercise:

- Ensure that you follow change control. Make backups before you try to tune the existing infrastructure so that you can revert to a previous state should it prove necessary. See *Chapter 9, Backup and Recovery*, for further details on backup and recovery.

- Benchmark your tuning by taking a baseline of the performance before and after changing any settings. This is the only way you will know whether your changes have had any impact on performance or not.

- Make sure you understand key tuning areas and plan the tuning exercise. If it is unclear precisely where the problem lies and where to begin, it is even more important to plan a performance tuning regime before approaching it. You will shortly see a methodology to do so.

- It is also necessary to document the changes made and their impact on performance. This will help in understanding why a change was made and give a clearer picture on the performance of the system.

As mentioned earlier, you need to first develop a performance tuning plan for your environment. You should also be aware that tuning and optimization can only take you to a certain extent in meeting your overall performance standards. When you have exhausted optimization techniques, or when the optimizations themselves compromise factors essential to your infrastructure, such as security, it may be time to upgrade your hardware or scale out. *Appendix A, Advanced Administration Topics*, describes how to achieve high availability and scalability with your Oracle SOA Suite 11g infrastructure through clustering.

The following diagram provides you with a descriptive overview of an effective first-hand methodology for performance tuning that you, as an administrator, can plan, present, and execute:

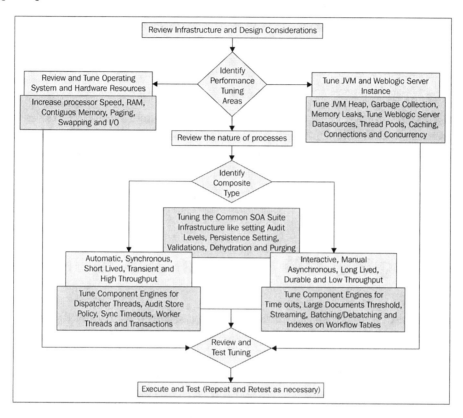

After having planned and identified the key performance tuning areas of your infrastructure, it is then time to apply effective optimization at several levels.

Your tuning exercise needs to be comprehensive, wholesome, and iterative, and should consider the following areas:

- Tuning of the Java Virtual Machine (JVM)
- Tuning the underlying application server (Oracle WebLogic Server, IBM WebSphere, and so on)
- Tuning the SOA Infrastructure
- Correct design of composite applications
- Tuning the Oracle Enterprise Manager Fusion Middleware Control console
- Tuning of the underlying dehydration store database schemas
- Tuning the Linux operating system

Tuning of the Java Virtual Machine (JVM)

Oracle SOA Suite 11*g* in simplified form is just a Java application that runs on a J2EE compliant application server such as Oracle WebLogic Server 11*g*, IBM WebSphere, or Red Hat JBoss. Although you can choose any of the supported application servers for your Oracle SOA Suite 11*g* infrastructure, this book will focus on the more commonly used Oracle WebLogic Server. The full list of certified application servers for Oracle SOA Suite 11*g* can be accessed at `http://www.oracle.com/technetwork/middleware/downloads/fmw-11gr1certmatrix.xls`.

Currently, there are two JVMs that are supported for Oracle WebLogic Server 11*g* — Sun JDK and JRockit JDK. Our performance tests have shown that using JRockit with an Oracle SOA Suite 11*g* installation on Linux results, on average, in a 32 percent performance improvement when compared to using Sun JDK. It is, thus, our recommendation for any installation running on Microsoft Windows and Linux operating systems (but not Oracle Solaris), including development instances, to use JRockit instead.

Switching the JVM from Sun JDK to JRockit JDK

In the event that you have already configured to use Sun JDK, follow these instructions, which are intended for 64-bit Linux operating systems, to use JRockit instead. We almost always recommend a 64-bit operating system and a 64-bit JVM to allow for larger memory allocation:

1. Download and install Oracle JRockit JDK (latest version currently 28.2.0):

    ° Download JRockit for Linux x86-64 from `http://www.oracle.com/technetwork/middleware/jrockit/downloads/index.html`.

    ° Execute the following command to change permissions and start the installer:

      ```
      chmod 750 jrockit-jdk1.6.0_29-R28.2.0-4.1.0-linux-x64.bin
      ./jrockit-jdk1.6.0_29-R28.2.0-4.1.0-linux-x64.bin
      ```

    ° On the **Welcome** prompt, press *Enter*.

    ° On the **Choose Production Installation Directory** prompt, enter a directory such as `/u01/app/oracle/jrockit1.6.0_29`, to install JRockit and press *Enter* twice.

    ° On the **Optional Components 1** prompt, press *Enter* to accept the default (which is not to install Demos and Samples).

- ○ On the **Optional Components 2** prompt, press *Enter* to accept the default (which is not to install Source Code).
- ○ On the **Installation Complete** prompt, press *Enter* to exit the installer.

2. Log on to the Linux server hosting your Oracle SOA Suite 11*g* installation as the oracle user.

3. Stop the `AdminServer` as well as all managed servers.

4. Stop the Node Manager.

5. Edit the file `$MW_HOME/wlserver_10.3/common/bin/commEnv.sh` and replace the following two entries as follows:

```
OLD:  JAVA_HOME="/u01/app/oracle/jdk1.6.0_26"
NEW:  JAVA_HOME="/u01/app/oracle/jrockit1.6.0_29"
OLD:  JAVA_VENDOR=Sun
NEW:  JAVA_VENDOR=Oracle
```

6. Edit the file `$MW_HOME/user_projects/domains/[Domain]/bin/setDomainEnv.sh`, and replace the following two entries as follows:

```
OLD:  BEA_JAVA_HOME=""
NEW:  BEA_AVA_HOME="/u01/app/oracle/jrockit1.6.0_29"
OLD:  SUN_JAVA_HOME="/u01/app/oracle/jdk1.6.0_26"
NEW:  SUN_JAVA_HOME=""
```

7. Edit the domain configuration file `$MW_HOME/user_projects/domains/[Domain]/bin/setSOADomainEnv.sh`, and replace the following entry as follows:

```
OLD:  PORT_MEM_ARGS="-Xms768m -Xmx1536m"
NEW:  PORT_MEM_ARGS="-Xms1536m -Xmx1536m -Xgcprio:throughput
-XX:+HeapDumpOnOutOfMemoryError
```

8. Start up the Node Manager.

9. Boot up the `AdminServer` and all managed servers back again.

The version of the JDK being used is outputted in multiple places. You can view the type and version information either from the admin server log file located at `$DOMAIN_HOME/servers/AdminServer/logs/AdminServer.log` or by simply logging on to the Oracle WebLogic Server Administration Console and performing the following:

1. Navigate to **Servers | [soa_server] | Monitoring**.

2. Click on **Dump Thread Stacks**.

3. You should see a string similar to the following under FULL THREAD DUMP:

```
Oracle JRockit(R) R28.2.0-79-146777-1.6.0_29-20111005-1807-
linux-x86_64
```

Optimizing JVM settings

PORT_MEM_ARGS, in the setSOADomainEnv.sh(.cmd) script, controls most JVM related configuration settings. The following JVM settings for JRockit are proven to be good in most environments:

```
PORT_MEM_ARGS="-Xms1536m -Xmx1536m -Xgcprio:throughput
-XX:+HeapDumpOnOutOfMemoryError -XXtlasize:min=16k,preferred=128k,was
teLimit=8k"
```

We will describe each of these arguments in detail.

-Xms and -Xmx

These are the **minimum heap size** (-Xms) and **maximum heap size** (-Xmx). We recommend setting both of these to the same value as it prevents the JVM from trying to expand the heap (effectively fixing the heap size), which improves performance. For small environments, a value of 1536 MB tends to be acceptable, for medium environments, a value of 4 GB is acceptable, and larger implementations should start at 6 GB, but can go up to 16 GB if needed.

Note that bigger is not always better. On a 64-bit operating system, even though the memory addressing is much larger, if possible, set the maximum heap size below 4 GB to take advantage of JRockit's compressed references to reduce memory usage. The size of the heap you require will depend on multiple factors:

- The number of SOA composites deployed to the server.
- The number of MDS artifacts referenced in your code. When an SOA composite imports a schema from the MDS (for example, oramds:/apps/CustomMetaData/schema/HelloWorld.xsd), this is automatically loaded into memory. The more artifacts from the MDS that are referenced by your code, the more memory is going to be required to store them.

A general rule of thumb is to consider that for every 100 MB of MDS artifacts referenced in the deployed SOA composites, increase your JVM by 1 GB. This is sometimes very difficult to calculate, so consider basing your estimates on the entire size of the artifacts in the MDS. Use the ant command described in *Chapter 2, Management of SOA Composite Applications*, to export the entire contents of the MDS and get an estimate on the sizing after extracting its contents.

-Xgcprio:throughput

This uses the default dynamic garbage collection mode, which, in JRockit JVM R27.3.0 and later versions, is optimized for throughput and will dynamically set the nursery size to an approximate optimal value. Thus, there is no need to manually set the nursery size (via the -Xns argument) in most cases.

-XX:+HeapDumpOnOutOfMemoryError

Although this is not a performance setting, we recommend setting it to dump the heap to an hprof file when java.lang.OutOfMemoryError exceptions are thrown. This is useful for later analysis and troubleshooting.

-XXtlasize:min=16k,preferred=128k,wasteLimit=8k

We recommend increasing the **thread local area** (**TLA**) size in multi-threaded applications such as Oracle SOA Suite 11*g* where each thread allocates a lot of objects, or if the average size of these objects is large. Avoid increasing it to a value that is too high, as it may result in fragmentation and more frequent garbage collections. The minimum value of 16k and preferred value of 128k have proven to be good in most environments. The wasteLimit of 8k sets the limit of how much of a TLA can be wasted when trying to get memory for an object.

Additional JVM performance tuning documentation from Oracle can be found at:

- http://docs.oracle.com/cd/E23943_01/web.1111/e13814.pdf
- http://docs.oracle.com/cd/E15289_01/doc.40/e15060.pdf

Tuning the underlying WebLogic Application Server

The second level of tuning is done at the application server level. Tuning the application server will not only improve the overall messaging performance, but also other factors like reliability, manageability of transactions, and faster velocity of **Message Driven Beans** (**MDB**).

In this section, you will learn how to tune Oracle WebLogic Server, which serves as the backbone of your SOA infrastructure for:

- Tuning transactions and timeouts
- Logging, I/O, and connection buffering
- Data source connection availability

- Thread allocation
- Resource adapter connection pools
- EJBs and SOA Infra deployments

Tuning transactions and timeouts

Handling transaction timeouts is one of those tasks that are generally left to the last moment. However, on the SOA infrastructure where composite applications may be involved in transacting with numerous endpoints, good timeout handling is critical. Managing response times is directly linked to your system's **Quality of Service (QoS)**. Badly behaved external systems may go offline and leave the WebLogic Server threads locked or overloaded systems may stall, causing a network client to block indefinitely. For these and numerous other reasons, it is absolutely necessary to detect and handle network timeouts where participating clients are part of a transaction. The matter is further worsened when we have long running business processes that may even span over multiple days, weeks, or months.

Composite instances may fail due to timeout errors for various reasons. A typical instance, running on the Oracle SOA Suite 11*g* infrastructure, interacts with many internal and external components, all of which have their own timeout behavior. For this reason, it is sometimes difficult to isolate the specific setting that is causing a particular timeout error. This chapter starts with describing why timeouts occur and also provides the necessary tuning settings required at various levels to overcome them.

A timeout occurs when an instance does not complete within a predefined amount of time, the timeout period or threshold. The default timeout period of Oracle SOA Suite 11*g* infrastructure is generally set to a low value. Components such as the application server itself or a particular service engine has preset timeout settings defined to prevent long-running processes from holding resources over an extended period of time. When a component's timeout is reached, it returns an error to the instance, causing it to fail with a specific error message and free up any resources held.

Having the right timeout settings depends on requirements such as how long it is acceptable to wait for responses from end systems and the nature of business processes that are running. Some environments require a longer timeout period than others. For example, if all processes within a specific application server depend on access to a slow, remote web service, it may make sense to increase the overall timeout period for the application server. On the other hand, applications that prefer a rapid response and high throughput might benefit from lowering the timeout, enabling them to react faster to a connection failure.

Similarly, it may be necessary to have different timeout values for separate applications or components within a single environment. Consider a scenario where there is a long running business process deployed on the BPEL and BPMN engine, requiring the overall application server timeout to be set at a higher value to accommodate its processing window, while an all synchronous composite application may require shorter timeout periods.

Oracle Enterprise Manager Fusion Middleware Control and Oracle WebLogic Server Administration Console allow you to set timeout thresholds at different levels within the infrastructure. Here are some of the typical timeout error messages that you, as a system administrator, will encounter in your infrastructure:

```
An exception occurred during transaction completion: nested exception
is
javax.transaction.RollbackException: Timed out
```

Or

```
oracle.fabric.common.FabricInvocationException: org.springframework.
transaction.UnexpectedRollbackException:JTA transaction unexpectedly
rolled back (maybe due to a timeout) Transaction timed out after 31
seconds
```

There are primarily four types of timeout parameters which are responsible for the majority of timeout errors. Tuning the transaction timeout parameters correctly will take care of most of the troublesome timeout issues. These timeout parameters can be tuned at the:

- Application server level
- EJB level
- Component engine level
- HTTP level (discussed later under the *Tuning Composite Application* section)

Tuning transactions at the application server level

In this section, you will see a short list of recommendations to help you optimize your application's ability to manage transactions and timeouts optimally. These tuning techniques are applicable to nearly all application servers that we may use, but for the scope of this book, we will limit ourselves to Oracle WebLogic Server.

Tuning Java Transaction API (JTA)

Oracle WebLogic Server's EJB container includes a global transaction handling mechanism that provides begin/commit/rollback functionality for applications that need to explicitly demarcate transaction boundaries.

The following diagram shows how Oracle WebLogic Server internally handles transactions between different transactional as well as non-transactional applications. Clients may participate in a transaction by handling over the commit and rollback responsibility to the server's EJB Container that contains a deployment descriptor to automatically manage transactions. The global transaction object provides objects' simple begin/suspend/resume functionalities for applications that need to explicitly demarcate transactional boundaries.

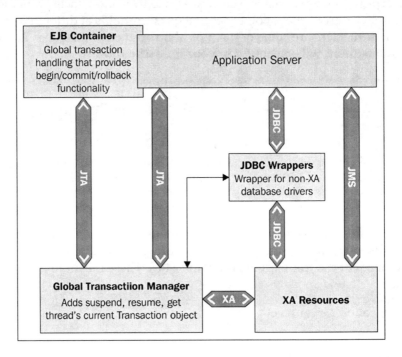

Transactions enlisted in JTA are subject to timeouts. The JTA transaction timeout errors can be identified by the following error found in the engine logs:

```
Unexpected exception while enlisting XAConnection java.sql.
SQLException: Transaction rolled back: Transaction timed out after 301
seconds
```

The default maximum time that an instance can be enlisted in a transaction is 30 seconds. The above error is likely due to the fact that a particular transaction took more time than the maximum time specified.

Tuning of the JTA is of utmost importance for one or all of the following reasons:

- Automatic activities, such as service tasks and invokes in BPMN or BPEL processes, may overshoot the minimum timeout threshold

- High concurrency may lead to low performance databases, queuing systems, and/or external endpoints that may keep the transactions alive for more than the specified timeout setting
- Improper transaction handling in the design of composite applications that may accidentally lead to long running transactions without a proper dehydration

To tune the underlying Oracle WebLogic Server's JTA, log in to the Oracle WebLogic Server Administration Console. From the landing page, navigate to **Services | JTA** and override the default value for the Timeout Seconds parameter with the tuned value as described in the following table:

Parameter Name	Default Value	Tuned Value	Remarks
Timeout Seconds	30	3600	Default number of seconds for transaction timeout, unless overridden by the EJB container. Setting a higher value than default will allow more time for long running global transactions to complete.
Abandon Timeout Seconds	86400	3600	After X number of seconds, stop trying to resolve branch(es) of a committed transaction and log an error.
			This should never happen unless the resource dies during commit processing and does not come back.
			Tuning this to a lower level is necessary to free resources in the transaction manager during the second phase of a two-phase commit.
Maximum Duration of XA Calls	120000	1200000	This should be tuned to a higher value to support very long running instances that may span multiple days.

Tuning the JTA, as demonstrated in the preceding table, will adequately handle your long running transactions and prevent server timeouts. However, in case you notice faulty transactions, server resources may still linger on. To prevent losing server threads to these faulty XA resources, Oracle WebLogic Server JTA has an internal resource health monitoring mechanism. A resource is considered active if either there are no pending requests or the result from any of the XA resource pending requests has not failed. If an XA resource is not active within two minutes, the Oracle WebLogic Server transaction manager declares it dead and any further requests to it are shunned.

The two minute interval can be configured by using the `MaxXACallMillis` JTA MBean attribute. It is currently not exposed through the Oracle WebLogic Server Administration Console. You can, however, configure `MaxXACallMillis` through Oracle Enterprise Manager Fusion Middleware Control. Follow these steps to tune this property:

1. Log in to Oracle Manager Fusion Middleware Control.
2. Navigate to **WebLogic Domain | [Domain]**.
3. Right-click on **AdminServer** and select **System MBean Browser**.
4. Expand **Configuration MBeans | com.bea | JTA** and click on your domain.
5. On the right-hand side, you will see additional information about the entire configuration MBean for JTA. Override the default value for the **Read Write (RW)** MBean `MaxXACallMillis` to a value of `240000`.
6. Click on the **Apply** button to save this new setting.

Tuning data sources

Oracle SOA Suite 11g predominantly runs stateful processes. It utilizes a database to store metadata and instance data during runtime. This data is stored in what is known as the dehydration store. Oracle SOA Suite 11g leverages the dehydration store database to maintain long-running asynchronous processes and their current state information while they wait for asynchronous callbacks. We will cover management and monitoring of the dehydration store schema in detail in *Chapter 8, Managing the Metadata Services Repository and Dehydration Store*. The connection to this underlying dehydration store is maintained through data source configurations on the application server. Hence, every application in the SOA infrastructure constantly uses database connections to dehydrate and rehydrate instance data. More often than not, database performance is impacted by insufficient resources on the application server side. The overall performance of the infrastructure is immediately affected, if enough connections are not available in the Oracle WebLogic Server connection pool, and as such, tuning and optimizing your backend database connections for Oracle SOA Suite 11g is essential. Otherwise, you may end up seeing the following messages in your diagnostic loggers:

```
Internal error: Cannot obtain XAConnection weblogic.common.
resourcepool.ResourceDisabledException: Pool is suspended, cannot
allocate resources to applications
```

This problem can be encountered by increasing the connections or correctly dimensioning your data source connection pools to match the free sessions/processes that your database can handle:

1. Log in to Oracle Manager Fusion Middleware Control.

2. Expand **WebLogic Domain**, right-click on your domain name, and click on **JDBC Data Sources**.

3. From the list of all available data sources, click on **SOADatasource** (which is the default transactional data source to connect to instance dehydration store) and click on the **Connection Properties** tab.

4. Override the default values for connection pool with the tuned value as shown in the following table. Some of the settings are available by further drilling down in the **Advanced** section.

Parameter Name	Default Value	Tuned Value	Remarks
`oracle.net.CONNECT_TIMEOUT`	`10000`	`20000`	You may receive many connection pool timeout errors such as `weblogic.common.resourcepool.ResourceDeadException` or `weblogic.common.ResourceException: Got minus one from a read call` in scenarios where multiple instances use multiple connection threads. When these errors occur, the database terminates its connection. The `oracle.net.CONNECT_TIMEOUT` property, defined for `SOADataSource`, should be set to a larger value to overcome these exceptions.

Parameter Name	Default Value	Tuned Value	Remarks
Initial Capacity	5	50	Establishing a JDBC connection with a DBMS can be very slow. If the application requires database connections that are repeatedly opened and closed, this can become a significant performance issue. It is good to start with a high value of Initial Capacity, so that connections are opened and available to all clients when the server is first started.
Maximum Capacity	50	200	The MaxCapacity attribute of the JDBCConnectionPool element sets the maximum number of physical database connections that a connection pool can contain. Tuning this to a higher value means that if the connections available run out of the initial capacity, more are added. The database must be configured to support these number of processes. Note that these are the number of connections from each SOA server in your cluster. So, setting it to 200 in a 4-node cluster may potentially result in 800 simultaneous connections to the database.
Capacity Increment	5	10	Capacity Increment should be tuned to a higher value than the default, so that every time a connection is needed, adequate connections are provisioned.
Inactive Connection Timeout	0	90	This property applies in the case of leaked connections (connections that are not properly returned to the connection pool in the data source). Oracle WebLogic Server will recover the connection after the time set here lapses. The default value of 0 sets this feature off.

5. Apply these changes and then click on the **Transaction Properties** tab.

6. Tune the default value of the XA parameters as shown in the following screenshot.

7. Click on the **Apply** button to save the changes.

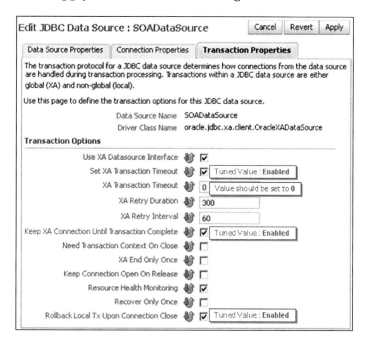

The following table describes the settings shown in the preceding screenshot in more detail:

Parameter Name	Default Value	Tuned Value	Remarks
Set XA Transaction Timeout	False	True	This will ensure that Oracle WebLogic Server will time out the transaction based on the value for XA Transaction Timeout. Make sure to set Use XA Datasource Interface to true (default setting). This attribute is only applicable for XA-compliant drivers.

Parameter Name	Default Value	Tuned Value	Remarks
XA Transaction Timeout	0	0	Make sure XA Transaction Timeout is enabled and XA Transaction Timeout is set to 0 seconds for all configured XA data sources. It will default to the container's JTA transaction timeout.
Keep XA Connection Until Transaction Complete	False	True	Sometimes errors may occur when a local transaction using an XA pool was either not committed or not rolled back and a global transaction is started. This behavior can be avoided by setting the value of KeepXAConnTillTxComplete to true.
Rollback Local Tx Upon Connection Close	False	True	This would always roll back any local transaction which is not committed or rolled back before starting a global transaction.

These instructions provided in the preceding table enabled you to tune SOADataSource. There are other data sources in the Oracle SOA Suite 11g infrastructure that might also need tuning for high performance. Depending upon the usage of these data sources, they can also be tuned in a similar way to that which we saw earlier. A few of the other data sources include:

- BAMDataSource
- EDNDataSource
- EDNLocalTxDataSource
- mds-soa
- SOALocalTxDataSource

Note that any change in the data source configuration that mandatorily requires a server restart is denoted by the 🌸 icon.

Please make sure you bounce the admin and managed servers on which the data sources are deployed for the changes to take effect.

Alternatively, you can also tune the data sources from the Oracle WebLogic Server Administration Console by navigating to **Services | JDBC | Datasources** and selecting the appropriate data source.

Tuning Resource Adapter connection pools

Most of the integration needs in your deployed composites would require interaction with the database. Did you even know that the threads required to process your application instance at runtime are allocated from the database connection pool?

Oracle SOA Suite 11*g* includes a native Database Adapter, which forms the core of any **Enterprise Information System (EIS)**, to interact with databases. You can use the database adapter in conjunction with BPEL, BPMN, and Mediator components for any interactions with a backend database. The Database Adapter would require a JNDI connection to be created on the Oracle WebLogic Server. Performance of the Database Adapter is directly related to the number of round trips to the database and the network cost of each trip.

Follow the next few highlighted steps to tune the database resource adapter setting from the Oracle WebLogic Administration Server Console:

1. On the Oracle WebLogic Server Administration Console home page, click on **Deployments**.

2. From the list of deployments, click on **DbAdapter** and then navigate to the **Configuration | Outbound Connection Pools** tab.

3. Clicking on **javax.resource.cci.ConnectionFactory** will open the **Settings** page to configure the connection pool and transactional setting of the resource adapter.

4. Click on the **Connection Pool** tab.

5. Increase **Initial Capacity** to **50**, **Max Capacity** to a higher value (for example, 200-1500, depending upon whether the installation is medium or large), and **Capacity Increment** to **10**, and save.

6. Click on the **Transaction** tab.

7. Set **Transaction Support** to **XA Transaction** and save. This is required to enable rollbacks in XA based transactions.

8. From the **Properties** tab, you can update several settings, notably the `dataSourceName` that you want the `DbAdapter` to use.

9. Save the changes and update the DbAdapter deployment plan (`Plan.xml`).

10. Activate the changes.

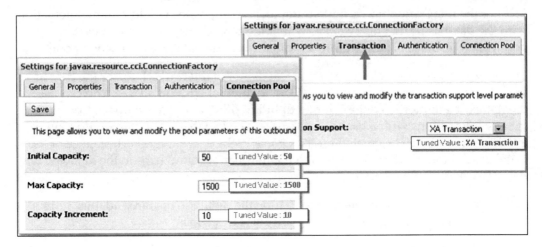

The JNDI and connection properties of a database adapter are present inside a .jca file of a composite. This dot JCA (.jca) file of the adapter in the composite application project code can also be edited for limiting the number of thread, batching, sequencing, and polling. This is necessary because Work Managers cannot be configured for adapter deployments. Furthermore, the properties set in the .jca file at design time can be overridden at runtime from Oracle Enterprise Manager Fusion Middleware Control.

Tuning database for XA Transaction Timeout

The next step to tune transactional behavior at the infrastructure level is to verify the distributed_lock_timeout value in the database. It specifies the amount of time for distributed transactions to wait for locked resources. The value for this database parameter should be set to a value greater than XA Transaction Timeout. To see and alter this value in the database, follow these steps:

1. Connect to the Oracle SOA Suite 11g database sys schema table as sysdba.

2. Execute this SQL command to see the default value of the distributed_lock_timeout parameter in seconds:

   ```
   SQL>SHOW PARAMETER DISTRIBUTE_LOCK_TIMEOUT;
   ```

3. The default value of the parameter is 60 seconds and to increase it run the following statement:

   ```
   SQL>ALTER SYSTEM SET DISTRIBUTE_LOCK_TIMEOUT=3600 SCOPE=SPFILE;
   ```

4. Shut down and then restart the database.

5. In the event that you are connecting to an Oracle **Real Application Cluster (RAC)**, set this parameter to the same value for all the nodes in the RAC cluster.

> A general rule to follow is to make sure that the Oracle WebLogic Server JTA timeout is set to a lower value than the shortest timeout value configured for a participating XA resource (for example, XA Transaction Timeout for Oracle XA JDBC connections). Not doing so can lead to an unexpected and inconsistent distributed transaction outcome, that is, a participating XA Resource timing out before Oracle WebLogic Server JTA as the distributed transaction coordinator. The timed out XA Resource may take action to resolve its own part of the distributed transaction before Oracle WebLogic Server can take action. This will lead to heuristic error messages at the time when the Oracle WebLogic Server transaction manager tries to prepare/commit the distributed transaction.

Tuning EJB timeouts for long running transactions

Oracle SOA Suite 11*g* contains an **Enterprise Java Bean (EJB)** set that forms a part of the SOA Infra (`soa-infra`) application in the Oracle WebLogic Server. Each of these EJB objects has a pre-defined timeout setting that overrides the one set at the infrastructure. By default, this is set to `300 seconds`. Timeout errors could occur in the case of long running processes slowing down the overall SOA system. The following EJBs will, therefore, have to be tuned in order to participate in global transactions and avoid timeouts:

- `BPELActivityManagerBean`
- `BPELDeliveryBean`
- `BPELDispatcherBean`
- `BPELEngineBean`
- `BPELFinderBean`
- `BPELInstanceManagerBean`
- `BPELProcessManagerBean`
- `BPELServerManagerBean`
- `BPELSensorValuesBean`

Changing timeouts of these EJBs is fairly simple. The following few steps highlight how to change the EJB timeout parameter from the Oracle WebLogic Administration Console for `BPELActivityManagerBean`. The same steps need to be followed to tune each one of them:

1. Open the Oracle Weblogic Server Administration Console, and click on **Deployments**.

2. Click on the **soa-infra** deployment.

3. Locate and click on **BPELActivityManagerBean**.

4. Click on the **Configuration** tab.

5. You can now reset the **Transaction Timeout** value for this MBean from here by overriding the default value of **300** to **600** (in seconds).

6. After all the changes are saved, you need to update the deployment plan of `soa-infra` and activate the changes for these changes to take effect.

The following screenshot shows the screen that you will see while following the preceding steps:

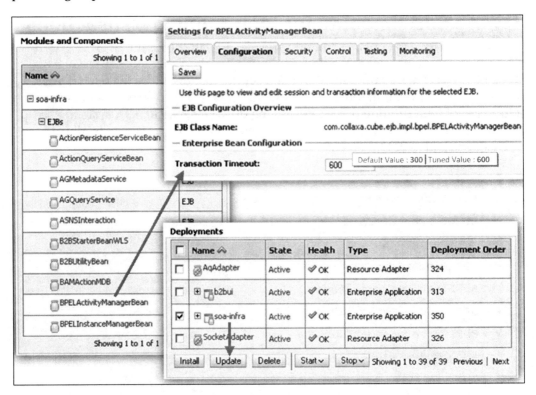

Before changing the EJB timeout settings, the SOA managed server(s) should be shut down. Otherwise, you will receive errors while activating the changes. Furthermore, `Plan.xml` for the SOA Infra would have to be copied to all managed servers (if not on shared storage) and the managed servers would have to be restarted.

The plan file can be located in your middleware installation folder at `$MW_HOME/Oracle_SOA1/soa/applications/Plan.xml`. Ensure that no other file is named `Plan.xml` as the same file may be used for changes made to resource adapters. A standard convention is to use `DBPlan.xml` for DB Adapter, `JMSPlan.xml` for JMS, `MQPlan.xml` for MQ Adapter, and so on, so that the plan files are not overwritten as the adapters are configured.

Tuning connection backlog buffering

More often than not, your SOA infrastructure will be exposing high throughput, low latency, and synchronous composite applications. If client applications invoking your composite endpoints complain of getting **Connection Refused** messages, when trying to access your endpoints, and no other messages appear in the server logs, then your **Accept Backlog** value may need to be tuned.

The **Accept Backlog** tunes the number of TCP connections that the server instance can buffer in the wait queue. Raise the **Accept Backlog** value from the default by 25 percent to 30 percent to overcome connection refusals. Continue increasing the value by 25 percent until the messages cease to appear. For example, increase the default value of 300 to around 400. This can be changed in the **Tuning** tab available under **Environment | Servers | [soa_server] | Tuning**.

Tuning the SOA Infrastructure

After the underlying Oracle WebLogic Server has been tuned for performance, the SOA infrastructure becomes the next area to optimize where different service engines, audit store configuration, persistence settings, and threads can be optimized. In this section, you will learn how to tune the following:

- SOA Infrastructure properties to lower audit levels and disable payload validation.
- Service Engine threads for BPEL and BPMN engines.
- Mediator Service Engine threads for parallel processing, re-sequencing concurrency, and sleep intervals.
- JCA Adapter properties for threads, transactions, streaming, batching, and timeouts.

Since all the tuning covered here is done by overriding the default server MBeans, this chapter also includes a few WLST scripts that updates them. The scripts are general purpose, and understanding how to execute them will allow you to modify any server level MBeans.

Adjusting the log level

Oracle SOA Suite 11g writes standard out and log information in flat files on the filesystem. The logs typically reside under `$MW_HOME/user_projects/domains/[Domain]/servers/[soa_server]/logs`. Set the log levels to `SEVERE` across the board. This will reduce the amount of information logged and will give a slight improvement on performance. These log levels can be adjusted and enabled to higher levels of auditing at runtime, if additional debugging information is ever required. To set the log levels:

1. Log in to Oracle Enterprise Manager Fusion Middleware Control.
2. Right-click on **soa-infra** and navigate to **Logs | Log Configuration**.
3. Select the dropdown **View With Persistent Log Level State**.
4. Apply the following **Log Configuration** settings:

```
Log Levels - oracle.bpm              ERROR: 1 (SEVERE)
Log Levels - oracle.integration      ERROR: 1 (SEVERE)
Log Levels - oracle.sdp              ERROR: 1 (SEVERE)
Log Levels - oracle.sdpinternal      ERROR: 1 (SEVERE)
Log Levels - oracle.soa              ERROR: 1 (SEVERE)
Log Levels - oracle.sysman           ERROR: 1 (SEVERE)
Log Levels - oracle.wsm              ERROR: 1 (SEVERE)
```

Optimizing logging through audit store tuning

When enabling production level auditing of composite instances, the application performance is impacted significantly as compared to when auditing is fully enabled. Changing the audit level from **Development** to **Production**, and further to **Off**, greatly improves the performance of the SOA infrastructure.

In the Oracle Enterprise Manager Fusion Middleware Control navigator, right-click on **soa-infra** and navigate to **SOA Administration | Common Properties**. Set the **Audit Level** to **Production** unless required otherwise (see *Chapter 2, Management of SOA Composite Applications*, for a more detailed explanation of the audit levels). Uncheck **Capture Composite Instance State** and **Payload Validation**. The following screenshot shows how instance id **20707** was executed with **Capture Composite Instance State** enabled while instance id **30001** was not.

Although when viewing a list of instances, it is a lot better to know the state of the instance (versus a question mark), disabling it results in a 24 percent performance improvement! Likewise, **Payload Validation** should only be enabled in development environments, if needed.

Instance ID	Composite	Conversation ID	State	Start Time △▽
30001	HelloWorld [1.0]		❓ ---	Dec 29, 2011 9:44:46 PM
20707	HelloWorld [1.0]	urn:324D23902F79:	✔ Completed	Dec 25, 2011 11:22:18 PM

 Performance testing has shown that disabling **Capture Composite Instance State** results in, on average, a performance improvement of 24 percent of your composite instances.

By default, audit data is logged to the database synchronously. This means that instances will remain active until the audit information is committed to the database. This does not perform ideally under load. By switching the audit policy to **deferred**, all audit operations are invoked asynchronously, resulting in performance comparable to setting the audit level to **off**. This is huge! Note that **Capture Composite Instance State** must be disabled when using **deferred** for this to take effect.

 Perhaps the largest composite instance performance gain can be attained by setting the audit policy to **deferred**, which results in all audit data being committed to the database asynchronously.

Set composite instance auditing to **deferred** by following these steps:

1. Log in to Oracle Enterprise Manager Fusion Middleware Control.
2. Right-click on **soa-infra** and navigate to **SOA Administration | Common Properties | More SOA Infra Advanced Configuration Properties**.
3. Click on **Audit Config**.
4. Set the audit parameters as shown in the following table:

Parameter Name	Tuned Value
AuditConfig/policies/Element_0/isActive	False
AuditConfig/policies/Element_0/name	Immediate
AuditConfig/policies/Element_1/isActive	True
AuditConfig/policies/Element_1/name	Deferred

5. All other settings are defaulted to reasonable values, so no additional changes are required.

Tuning of Service Engines

Oracle BPEL Process Manager provides several property settings that can be configured from Oracle Enterprise Manager Fusion Middleware Control to optimize performance for response times, throughput, and concurrency. The BPEL Service Engine can be tuned at either the domain level or the process level.

It is absolutely essential to know the nature of processes that are to be executed in your infrastructure, for you to be able to tune it. Processes can be categorized by the nature of their interfaces, for example, asynchronous, push based, or synchronous. They can also be durable (long running) or transient (short lived). Again, in any of these processes, there may be activities that are idempotent (retryable, such as the Assign and Invoke activities) or invocations that are non-blocking (happening in parallel). A process can also have a breakpoint wherein its state is saved in the dehydration store or the state is not stored at all. All these factors have to be taken into consideration when tuning the service engines.

The following diagram elaborates on the different types of processes that you may have and how you can optimize the runtime execution infrastructure for them. The diagram explores the various considerations to keep in mind while setting infrastructure level properties such as **idempotency**, **dispatcher threads**, **nonBlockingInvoke**, **completionPersistPolicy**, and **completionPersistLevel**. For example, for an asynchronous and a durable process, caller threads are allocated for each instance and all messages are persisted as the instance dehydrates at multiple breakpoints. These kinds of processes would need a different tuning than synchronous and transient processes that do not persist instances. These properties are discussed in more length in a later section of this chapter, when we will discuss tuning at the composite application level.

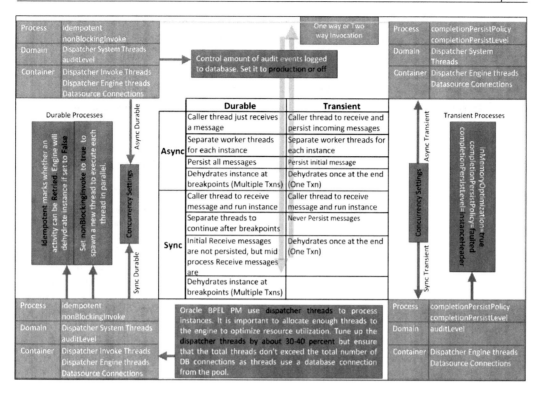

		Durable	Transient
Async		Caller thread just receives a message	Caller thread to receive and persist incoming messages
		Separate worker threads for each instance	Separate worker threads for each instance
		Persist all messages	Persist initial message
		Dehydrates instance at breakpoints (Multiple Txns)	Dehydrates once at the end (One Txn)
Sync		Caller thread to receive message and run instance	Caller thread to receive message and run instance
		Separate threads to continue after breakpoints	Never Persist messages
		Initial Receive messages are not persisted, but mid process Receive messages are	Dehydrates once at the end (One Txn)
		Dehydrates instance at breakpoints (Multiple Txns)	

Tuning the BPEL Service Engine

You can tune the BPEL Service Engine from Oracle Enterprise Manager Fusion
Middleware Control by right-clicking on **soa-infra** and navigating to **SOA
Administration | BPEL Properties**.

Apply the settings shown in the following table to tune the BPEL Service Engine. Some properties are accessed by clicking on the **More BPEL Configuration Properties** link. Make sure you click on **Apply** to save your changes.

Parameter Name	Default Value	Tuned Value	Remarks
Audit Trail Threshold	50000	20000	This property sets the threshold for saving message payloads in the AUDIT_TRAIL dehydration table. Messages with values greater than this threshold are saved in the AUDIT_DETAILS table.
			Audit trail with string messages greater than this value are not loaded in the console, but are linked. Hence, if you have processes with large payloads saving them to AUDIT_TRAIL table may severely degrade the performance.
Large Document Threshold	100000	2000000	Any document with a size more than 100 KB will be dehydrated by the BPEL engine. To minimize the frequent round trips to the database, tune this to a significant value, if your processes deal with large documents.
Dispatcher System Threads	2	10	These threads do the cleaning and housekeeping work for the engine.
Dispatcher Engine Threads	30	100	Threads allocated to process messages generated by the engine during an activity must be processed asynchronously. Once instances are received and hydrated, these threads are responsible for picking and processing them.
			If there are lots of processes with many dehydration points, tuning this MBean to a higher value will increase your performance.

Parameter Name	Default Value	Tuned Value	Remarks
Dispatcher Invoke Threads	20	70	Invoke threads are used to instantiate new instances in the engine. You would need to tune it to a higher value if there are multiple branches/flows in the process to achieve faster processing.
			This property throttles the load setting of your BPEL engine and hence impacts the performance of all the receive activities in the domain.
Disable BPEL Monitors and Sensors	False	True	You can choose to disable this in case you do not use BPEL monitors and sensors, and use an alternate mechanism such as the BAM Adapter.
AuditStorePolicy	SyncLocal Transaction	AsyncsyncLocal Transaction	Setting this to AsyncsyncLocal Transaction will change the audit data storage strategy to save audit data asynchronously, using a separate local transaction.
SyncMaxWaitTime	45	300	The SyncMaxWaitTime property determines the timeout for request-response operations and has to be tuned up in case you have message processing scenarios where participating processes/services overshoot the default value of 45 seconds.

Tuning the BPMN Service Engine

You can also tune the BPMN engine in the same way as you have tuned your BPEL engine. To tune it, right-click on **soa-infra**, navigate to **SOA Administration | BPMN Properties**, and make the same changes to the BPMN engine MBeans. The only other MBean that you can tune specifically for the BPMN engine is `DispatcherMaxRequestDepth`, which determines the maximum number of internal messages the engine will process. We recommend setting it to a value of `1000`.

Tuning the Mediator Service Engine

There are two main areas that impact Mediator performance. Those include:

- Choosing between sequential and parallel routing rules at design time
- Mediator Service Engine properties related to throughput

Before discussing the main Mediator Service Engine properties, it is important to understand the execution behavior of Mediator routing rules.

Choosing among routing rules

Mediator executes routing rules either sequentially or in parallel. Even if a Mediator service is designed as a one-way service and a sequential routing rule is used, it behaves similarly to a synchronous transaction (that is, the client holds onto the request until the request is completed, and faults are propagated back up to the client). Thus, despite their superior performance, sequential routing rules should not be used for true asynchronous transactions.

On the other hand, by using parallel routing rules, services can be designed to be truly asynchronous. However, the service engine executes these requests in a rather unique fashion.

Let's say you have five Mediator services deployed to your SOA server and each of these has a single parallel routing rule. Let's say that the average time it takes to complete execution of each service is one second. If you receive 10 requests on the first Mediator service and the Mediator Service Engine is configured with 10 threads, you would expect all requests to be completed within one second. That is not the case.

The Mediator Service Engine loops through every composite, which has a parallel routing rule every X seconds, where X is the **Parallel Locker Thread Sleep** setting. In our example, the service engine will loop through the five Mediator composites, one at a time, and see if there are any requests to process from the composite's internal queue. It processes only one request from that composite, then moves on to the next composite. It finds no request, so it moves on to the next, and the next, until it loops back to the first composite, where it would then process its next request. The engine behaves this way by design in order to prevent starving of threads caused by load on a single composite. What the engine wants to avoid is that, if you have a Mediator service that has received hundreds of thousands of requests and another one having received two requests, each service is given a fair amount of time to be serviced, otherwise the two requests may have to wait for hours to execute.

Thus, the three settings to consider in asynchronous Mediator services are the following:

- The **Parallel Locker Thread Sleep** setting, which is defined at the Mediator Service Engine level
- The number of threads allocated to the Mediator Service Engine, defined by the **Parallel Worker Threads** parameter
- The **Priority** property, which is set at design time and applicable only to parallel routing rules

Mediator Service Engine properties

To tune the Mediator Service Engine settings, right-click on **soa-infra**, then navigate to **SOA Administration | Mediator Properties**.

Consider setting **Metrics Level** to **disabled** unless DMS metrics collection is explicitly required. **Parallel Worker Threads** should be set to around **4** for smaller environments and **20** for larger ones. Also, consider setting **Parallel Maximum Rows Retrieved** to **200** for smaller environments and **600** for larger ones. Always set **Parallel Locker Thread Sleep** to **1**, which is the lowest setting, as this will impact the time the engine waits before looping through subsequent services.

Using scripting (WLST) to modify component engine MBeans

All this while you have seen how you can tune the Service Engines from Oracle Enterprise Manager Fusion Middleware Control by navigating their respective MBeans. As an administrator, you should ideally automate this activity, so that you can replicate the change across environments easily. To your relief, you can use **WebLogic Scripting Tool (WLST)** to hierarchically navigate through the domain and server MBeans. Upon connecting to the server runtime from WLST, you can browse the SCA component engines and composite MBeans by changing your location to a custom writable tree.

Setting up WLST

To set up WLST, perform the following:

1. Open a prompt and execute the following command:

    ```
    $MW_HOME/wlserver_10.3/common/bin/wlst.sh
    ```

2. This will set your environment and all libraries in CLASSPATH.

3. Execute the following sequence of commands in the wls prompt to navigate and update, for example, the DispatcherEngineThreads property in the BPEL engine:

    ```
    connect('<username>','<password>','<soahost>:<soaport>')
    custom()
    cd('oracle.as.soainfra.config/oracle.as.soainfra.config:name=bpel,
    type=BPELConfig,Application=soa-infra')
    get('DispatcherEngineThreads')
    print "Tuning it to a value of 100"
    set('DispatcherEngineThreads', 100)
    get('DispatcherEngineThreads')
    exit()
    ```

The following screenshot shows the output of executing the TuneBPELEngine.py script, which updates various BPEL component engine related MBeans. The folder structure on the left of the screenshot shows the navigation hierarchy within the MBean path.

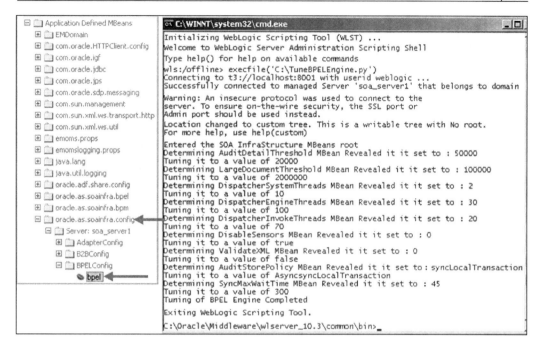

The chapter contains a `ReadMe.txt` file detailing how to set up your environment and sample scripts that can be used to tune the various service engines, and even retrieve and update composite application properties at runtime through WLST scripting.

Tuning composite applications

The tuning covered in this chapter will give your SOA Infrastructure the performance boost that is required by the composite applications running on it. However, there are composite application design time considerations that should be addressed, otherwise improperly designed composites may degrade the overall performance regardless of how tuned your infrastructure is. As an administrator, having fundamental knowledge of these design time considerations is recommended.

BPEL persistence

Over the life cycle of a BPEL instance, the instance with its current state of execution might be saved in the database multiple times. This can incur considerable overhead. There are roughly two cases leading to an instance getting stored in the database:

- When the instance is waiting for an event (wait, onAlarm, pick, and so on), the instance is dehydrated to the database. Later when the event happens (alarm expires or the message comes in), the instance is rehydrated and resumes execution.

- When an instance encounters a non-idempotent activity. The instance in this case is persisted in the database as it may have to be retried after the non-idempotent activity.

At the composite level, there are three persistence properties that can be tuned to optimize the process performance. Proactively, you should also try to set the instance persistence levels at design time itself. They are:

- `inMemoryOptimization`: This property is used to indicate to the engine that the process does not need to save in-flight instance in the database. The engine will keep the instances of this process in memory during the course of execution. The default value of this is `false` and can be overridden to true to optimize transient processes.

- `completionPersistLevel`: After an instance has completed its execution, it is persisted in two dehydration store tables named CUBE_INSTANCE and CUBE_SCOPE. The CUBE_INSTANCE table stores the header information of the instance, while CUBE_SCOPE stores the state of the instance. By default, both tables are used to store information on a completed instance. The `completionPersistLevel` can be used to fine tune what part of the instance is used. The default value can be overridden with an `instanceHeader` switch that will save only the header part of the instance. `completionPersistLevel` can only be used when `inMemoryOptimization` is set to be `true`.

- `completionPersistPolicy`: `completionPersistPolicy`, as the name implies, decides if the composite instance will be retained in the database upon completion. However, it can only be used when `inMemoryOptimization` is set to be `true`. Override the default value of this property to either `off` (no instance data saved) or `faulted` (only faulted instances are saved) for significant performance.

Since transient processes do not save any information to the dehydration store, setting `inMemoryOptimization` to `true` is useful for request-response style processes, if no trace of the instance is needed afterwards. In another example, to improve performance and reduce auditing, you may opt to persist only faulted instances and their variable values by setting `inMemoryOptimzation` to `true`, `completionPersistPolicy` to `faulted`, and `completionPersistLevel` to `all`, as shown in the following snippet:

```
<BPELProcess src="YourProcess.bpel" id="YourProcess">
  <configurations>
    <property name="inMemoryOptimization">true</property>
    <property name="completionPersistPolicy">faulted</property>
    <property name="completionPersistLevel">all</property>
  </configurations>
</BPELProcess>
```

HTTP timeouts in references

Composites can make external web service calls via references. Sometimes these external services may take some time to respond, particularly if they themselves are poor performing. This usually has nothing to do with the performance of your SOA Infrastructure, however, a thread continues to be dedicated to this composite until the external target service responds. As the load increases on this particular composite, the number of threads required increases. This is usually not a problem until you run out of threads! At that point, the SOA server would no longer be able to service new requests, all because of the slow performance of some target service.

This is a scenario where the use of HTTP timeout settings on the reference may be needed.

Developers can add HTTP timeout settings at design time by adding two properties in the reference section of `composite.xml`:

```
<reference name="Register">
  <interface.wsdl
  interface="http://ns.com/RegisterWS/#wsdl.interface(IRegisterWS)"/>
  <binding.ws
    port="http://tempuri.org/#wsdl.endpoint
    (RegisterWS/BasicHttpBinding_IRegisterWS)" soapVersion="1.1"
    location="RegisterWS.svc.wsdl"
    streamIncomingAttachments="false"
    streamOutgoingAttachments="false">
    <property name="weblogic.wsee.wsat.transaction.flowOption"
    type="xs:string" many="false">WSDLDriven</property>
    <property name="oracle.webservices.httpReadTimeout"
```

```
        type="xs:string" many="false">10000</property>
        <property name="oracle.webservices.httpConnTimeout"
        type="xs:string" many="false">10000</property>
    </binding.ws>
</reference>
```

The **HTTP Read Timeout** setting, denoted by the `oracle.webservices.httpReadTimeout` property, defines how long (in milliseconds) the reference should wait until the target service completes servicing its request. Setting this depends on the maximum length of time that you expect the target service to respond to your request. If the read timeout is reached, the HTTP socket abandons the request.

The **HTTP Connection Timeout** setting, denoted by the `oracle.webservices.httpConnTimeout` property, defines how long (in milliseconds) the reference should wait until it is able to establish a connection with the target service. Set this to a realistic value, such as 30 seconds or less. There is usually no need for your composite to keep trying unsuccessfully for minutes to establish a connection with a service that may already be down!

These values can be changed at runtime on a composite-by-composite basis as follows:

1. Log in to Oracle Enterprise Manager Fusion Middleware Control.

2. Expand **soa-infra**.

3. Expand the partition and click on the composite name that you want to update.

4. On the composite **Dashboard**, scroll down to the **Services and References** section.

5. Click on the **Reference** name.

6. Click on the **Properties** tab.

7. Update the following two HTTP Timeout settings and click on **Apply**:
    ◦ **HTTP Read Timeout (ms)**
    ◦ **HTTP Connection Timeout (ms)**

Service and Reference properties are described in more detail in the next section.

Tuning technology adapter services and references

Adapters are live wires of any middleware or integration based system that connects your application processes to backend informational systems (such as FTP, JMS, web services, databases, and so on). Oracle SOA Suite 11*g* creates and maintains connections to these various technology adapters that may be requested by an executing process instance.

With the growing need for business process optimization, efficient integration with existing backend applications will eventually determine the success of your SOA applications as well as your infrastructure. Imagine the stress that your infrastructure needs to handle when there are hundreds of composite applications, and each in turn interacts with multiple technology and resource adapters in its processing logic.

Adapters can be used in a composite application either as a Service (acting as an entry point to the composite) or as a Reference (dealing with outbound invocations) and define Activation Specifications for Inbound Actions (Service) and Interaction Specifications for Outbound Actions (Reference). You, as an Oracle SOA Suite 11*g* administrator, can breathe easy as each of these adapter connections can be individually managed and tuned at runtime from Oracle Enterprise Manager Fusion Middleware Control. The key properties that you should aim to tune are payload/message size, concurrency, transactions, threads, timeouts, batching, and streaming. It is essential to know how these adapter properties can be tuned to achieve optimal performance and what effect one has on the other. You can tune the adapters as described here:

1. Log in to Oracle Enterprise Manager Fusion Middleware Control.

2. Right-click on **soa-infra**, navigate to **SOA Infrastructure | Services**, and **References**.

3. Depending upon the nature of your adapter, you can either locate it by clicking on the **Services** or **References** tab.

4. The type column indicates the nature of adapter used by the service or reference (**JCA**, **Web Service**, **Direct Binding**, and so on).

5. The adapter properties can be viewed from the **Properties** tab and edited by overriding their default values in the corresponding textbox.

6. You can also add more properties by clicking on **Add | Search | Select**.

7. Click on **Apply** to save your changes.

The following screenshot shows how you can tune adapter properties at runtime from Oracle Enterprise Manager Fusion Middleware Control for different services and references created in composites.

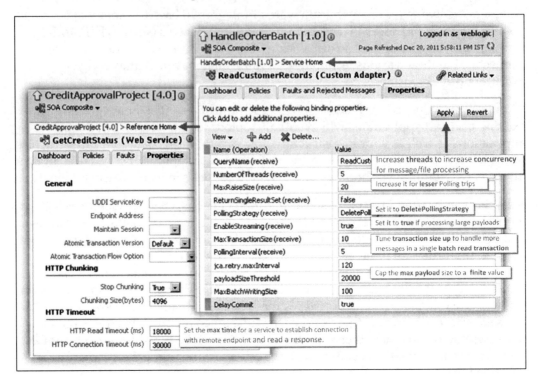

A few of the properties that you may have to consider for tuning are described in the following table:

Property Name	Default Value	Tuned Value	Remarks
NumberOfThreads	1	5	The value of this property determines the number of polling threads that are made available at any point in time when the activation is initiated. Increasing this value will increase the concurrency of your application and enable more instances to be instantiated.

Property Name	Default Value	Tuned Value	Remarks
MaxRaiseSize	1	20	This property specifies the maximum number of rows an adapter reads for processing each XML message in each polling cycle.
			Increasing this value in cases where message batching is enabled will ensure that rows within an XML document are not read one by one. Setting it to 0 will make the reading unbounded, which may have its own repercussions.
PollingStrategy	blank	DeletePolling Strategy or LogicalDelete PollingStrategy	The best practice for polling, using resource adapters, is to use either the DeletePollingStrategy or LogicalDelete PollingStrategy.
			LogicalDelete PollingStrategy involves updating an available column for each processed row and updating the WHERE clause at runtime to filter out processed rows. It mimics the logical delete, wherein a database row is not deleted after it is read, but instead a status column isDeleted is set to true.
			DeletePollingStrategy is more optimal (from a performance standpoint) as it deletes the row read without having to perform an additional update operation.

Property Name	Default Value	Tuned Value	Remarks
EnableStreaming	False	True	Enabling this property will direct your engine to stream the payloads to database rather than manipulating them in the runtime memory.
			Consider setting the property to true when your adapter is processing large files/messages and you want to offload some processing out of your infrastructure.
MaxTransactionSize	10	10	Setting a properly dimensioned MaxTransactionSize in a distributed polling scenario will balance the processing load by not greedily allowing threads to pick all unprocessed rows by themselves. This implies that at a time, a thread will only fetch at most that many rows as set by MaxTransactionSize. The message throughput is also determined by a simple calculation around this setting, that is, (NumberOfThreads **X** MaxTransactionSize)/ PollingInterval
payloadSizeThreshold	Infinite	20000	Due to finite system resources and restraint on the component engines, the payload size threshold must be set to avoid OutOfMemory errors in case your infrastructure cannot handle incoming requests.
			Setting this threshold allows you to reject messages that exceed the threshold limit.

Property Name	Default Value	Tuned Value	Remarks
Distributed	False	True	Setting this property to true will append SELECT FOR UPDATE SKIP LOCKED to the polling query. This is absolutely necessary in scenarios where concurrent threads will each try to select and lock the available rows, but the locks are only obtained on fetch. If an about to be fetched row is already locked, the next unlocked row will be locked and fetched instead. It is recommended to set this to true in a distributed environment.

In addition to the changes described here, you can also enable batch reading and writing while using resource adapters for databases. Batching greatly improves database performance by sending groups of insert, update, or delete statements to the database in a single transaction, rather than individually.

Tuning the Oracle Enterprise Manager Fusion Middleware Control console

You have now reached a stage where you have highly tuned and optimized your infrastructure. However, you might sometimes still see that logging on to Oracle Enterprise Manager Fusion Middleware Control takes a long time. This might happen when you have a large number of composite applications deployed into the infrastructure and subsequently a large number of instances for each of them. It should be a good idea to tune the page load times by enabling lazy loading and on demand instance fetching.

Simply right-click on **soa-infra**, navigate to **SOA Administration | Common Properties**, and tune the display options by checking the two checkboxes under **Data Display Options** as illustrated in the following screenshot. Set the duration details to a reasonable value such as **12 hours** (or higher), depending on how much data you want retrieved by default.

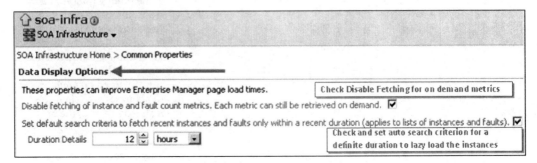

Tuning the dehydration store database schema

The performance of the Oracle SOA Suite 11g platform is directly dependent on the performance of the underlying dehydration store database and, hence, it becomes vitally important to tune this database for optimal performance.

Most importantly, you need to ensure that the underlying database is configured to handle adequate processes and sessions to support the infrastructure. The database must also be tuned so that it has enough memory for caching, **Program Global Area (PGA)**, and **System Global Area (SGA)**, and has an adequate number of open and shared cursors and processes.

The following table provides a few generic changes that you should consider making to your Oracle database to improve the response time and throughput of your SOA infrastructure. Ultimately, Oracle database tuning is a vast topic and tuning parameters are not universal, so engage your Oracle DBA during your load and performance tests to assist in providing optimal settings. These changes are part of the database initialization parameters and are made to the init[SID].ora file. The SQL queries can be found in the attached chapter code.

Parameter Name	Default Value	Tuned Value	Remarks
AQ_TM_PROCESSES	0	1	This property controls processing of messages with delay and expiration properties specified. It is strongly recommended not to set AQ_TM_PROCESSES to 0. If it is set to 1, a one time manager process is created to monitor the messages.
FILESYSTEMIO_OPTIONS	NONE	SETALL	Oracle recommends setting this to SETALL to enable both asynchronous and direct I/O on file system files where possible.
NLS_SORT		BINARY	Specifies the collating sequence for ORDER BY queries and setting to BINARY requires less system overhead.
OPEN_CURSORS	300	1000	OPEN_CURSORS specifies the maximum number of open cursors a session can have at once. It is important to have the value of OPEN_CURSORS set high enough to prevent your application from running out of open cursors.
PLSQL_CODE_TYPE	INTERPRETED	NATIVE	PL/SQL compilation mode of NATIVE is typically faster than INTERPRETED.
TRACE_ENABLED	TRUE	FALSE	Setting this to FALSE may result in minimal performance improvement, but you may lose valuable diagnostic information in the event of a database error.
UNDO_RETENTION	900	0	By setting UNDO_RETENTION to 0, you enable auto tuned retention. That is, as long as your tablespace can autoextend, you are less likely to get an ORA-01555.

Parameter Name	Default Value	Tuned Value	Remarks
PROCESSES	150	3000	Sets the maximum number of processes that can be started by an instance. This is one of the more important primary parameters to set and tuned to a higher value, as many other parameter values are deduced from this.
SESSIONS	150	3000	The default value of SESSIONS is derived from PROCESSES. If you alter the value of PROCESSES, you may want to adjust the values of these derived parameters.
SGA_MAX_SIZE	5G/10G	15G	**SGA** includes Shared Pool, Database buffer cache, and Redo Log buffer. Since Oracle SOA Suite heavily depends upon the underlying database for continuous huge updates and inserts, the SGA_MAX_SIZE should be around 40 percent of your physical RAM.
SGA_TARGET	5G/10G	15G	This parameter reflects the total size of memory footprint an SGA can consume. SGA_MAX_SIZE and SGA_TARGET should be tuned to the same value.
PGA_AGGREGATE_TARGET	1G	5G	PGA_AGGREGATE_TARGET specifies the total amount of session PGA memory that Oracle will attempt to allocate across all sessions. Tune it to around 30 percent of your SGA.
CURSOR_SHARING	EXACT	SIMILAR	Oracle uses a shared SQL area when applications send similar SQL statements to the database. The sharing of SQL by setting CURSOR_SHARING to SIMILAR reduces memory use on the database server, thereby increasing system throughput.

Parameter Name	Default Value	Tuned Value	Remarks
INITRANS (for table)	1	20	The INITRANS setting controls **Initial Transaction Slots (ITLs)**. A transaction slot is required for any session that needs to modify a block in an object. The contention for ITL can be reduced by increasing the INITRANS storage parameter of the table and indexes.
INITRANS (for indexes)	2	40	
SHARED_POOL_SIZE	45	300	SHARED_POOL_SIZE has to be tuned to provide more room for new cursors and query blocks. It has to be tuned up, if cursors are being aged out due to lack of free space.
DB_BLOCK_CHECKSUM	TYPICAL	OFF	Checksums allow Oracle to detect corruption caused by underlying disks, storage systems, or I/O systems. If your application is I/O intensive and you are short on CPU capacity, you should disable it.
SESSION_CACHED_CURSORS	50	1000	The SESSION_CACHED_CURSORS parameter is used to reduce the amount of parsing with statements and cursors. If your cursors are being paged-out of the library cache, increasing SESSION_CACHED_CURSORS up to the value of OPEN_CURSORS improves the performance.

Apart from the preceding changes, the tablespaces for the [ENV]_SOAINFRA and [ENV]_MDS schemas should be auto-extended by around 100 MB each time. Apply these changes to the sp file to persist them after database restart. Shutdown and restart your database for these changes to take effect. Once again, the suggested settings described in this section are guidelines and may not be applicable to all environments.

Tuning the Linux operating system

If Oracle SOA Suite 11g is installed on a Linux operating system, consider increasing the ulimit for environments with large load. This is to avoid the following error, which appears in the `/var/log/messages` log under heavy load:

```
Dec 25 20:53:22 soahost1 sshd[22480]: fatal: setresuid 10000: Resource
temporarily unavailable
```

As the root user, perform the following:

1. Add the following in `/etc/security/limits.conf` (assuming the product is installed by the oracle Unix user):

   ```
   oracle soft nproc 16384
   oracle hard nproc 63536
   oracle soft nofile 16384
   oracle hard nofile 63536
   ```

2. Add the following in `/etc/profile` (for 32-bit operating systems):

   ```
   if [ $USER = "oracle" ]; then
     if [ $SHELL = "/bin/ksh" ]; then
       ulimit -p 16384
       ulimit -n 65536
       # Use the following for 64-bit operating systems instead
       # ulimit -Su 16383
       # ulimit -Hu 16383
       # ulimit -Sn 63535
       # ulimit -Hn 63535
     else
       ulimit -u 16384 -n 65536
       # Use the following for 64-bit operating systems instead
       # ulimit -Hn 63535 -Sn 63535 -Hu 16383 -Su 16383
     fi
   fi
   ```

3. Add the following to `/etc/pam.d/login`:

   ```
   session required /lib/security/pam_limits.so
   ```

You must log out of your current session and log back in before restarting your SOA server for these changes to take effect.

Summary

In this chapter, we have seen many options available for tuning Oracle SOA Suite 11*g* and provided guidelines and recommendations on how to improve performance of your application infrastructure, covering areas of Oracle WebLogic Server, Service Engines, code considerations, Oracle database tuning, and operating system recommendations.

It is also critically important to understand the role that your infrastructure and application design decisions can have on the performance you desire, and to ensure that these areas are not neglected when attempting to tune the system.

To summarize, in this chapter you have learned the following:

- Reviewing your existing infrastructure, having the right strategy in place before diving into performance planning, and effectively planning an optimizing technique for your Oracle SOA Suite 11*g* environment.

- The key areas and levels of your infrastructure that need to be performance tuned via the JVM, application server, infrastructure, and underlying database.

- How transactions are handled and various ways to overcome transactional timeouts.

- Provision ample threads and connections to different components such as data sources and component engines.

- The importance of correct composite application design and how significant performance can be achieved by tuning their persistence settings.

- How to use Oracle Fusion Middleware Enterprise Manager Control to locate system MBeans and dimension them appropriately to meet your required performance standards.

- Setting up WLST and creating reusable scripts that can capture all your environment changes pertaining to performance tuning. This will help you to achieve automation while tuning in higher up environments.

- Tuning technology adapters used inside composites for handling large message sizes, concurrency, and transactions.

- How performance of your infrastructure is directly impacted by the underlying dehydration store and the different database parameters that need to be tuned.

Optimal tuning ultimately depends on your hardware sizing as well as the nature of applications running on your infrastructure. There cannot be a one-size-fits-all strategy for tuning, and many of the recommendations provided in this chapter have been proven to yield considerable optimization in actual production environments. You should now be knowledgeable in enough areas to realize a highly performing environment. Remember that performance tuning is an iterative exercise. It is important that you get in to the habit of measuring, tuning, testing, and repeating.

In the next chapter, you will learn how to configure and administer common tasks in your Oracle SOA Suite 11g platform in detail.

5
Configuring and Administering Oracle SOA Suite 11*g*

Once you have learned to monitor and tune your infrastructure, it is time to look closely into configuring and administering various components that are part of your Oracle SOA Suite 11*g* environment. Depending upon the type of composites deployed to the runtime, you as an administrator would need to manage both the composite instances and the service engines they execute on.

The Oracle SOA Suite 11*g* infrastructure provides an access to all deployed composite applications, service engines, service components, business events, notifications, and other management objects. You can also perform a range of administrative tasks, such as managing composites and their individual instances, taking corrective actions for faulted and rejected messages, securing composites or components within them by attaching/detaching security policies, and much more.

As one of the larger chapters of this book, we will cover a huge amount of topics surrounding the configuration and administration of Oracle SOA Suite 11*g* here which include:

- Starting up and shutting down the infrastructure
- Enabling log rotation
- Navigating to key administration areas
- Configuring infrastructure properties
- Configuring and administering binding components and JCA Adapters
- Configuring and administering BPEL Service Engine and components

- Administering the Mediator Service Engine
- Administering the User Messaging Service
- Administering the Human Workflow Service Engines
- Administering and configuring Oracle Business Activity Monitoring
- Administering and configuring event engine and business events
- Administering domain value maps and cross references
- Configuring infrastructure resources for developers

Starting up and shutting down the infrastructure

The SOA Infrastructure can be started up and shut down in several ways — through the console, through WLST, or through shell scripts. All approaches are valid and depend on your preference. However, our recommendation is to use a set of scripts, which are available with this chapter, to make this repetitive process less cumbersome.

Regardless of the approach you follow, be aware of a few points. You should ideally start up Node Manager first. Node Manager serves multiple purposes — it can automatically restart a managed server that has crashed, it provides you with the ability to start up managed servers remotely, and it is required for clustered installations. In a clustered installation, `AdminServer` is started up on only a single physical server per cluster.

Using scripts

The instructions mentioned in the following sections describe how to start up and shut down the SOA Infrastructure in Linux by using the bash shell.

Disabling prompt of WebLogic password

When you start up any managed server, you will be prompted for the username and password that were used to create the domain. To disable prompting of these credentials at startup, edit the `boot.properties` file on all managed servers. This is a one-time step that is recommended to be done on every managed server on each node of your cluster.

Prior to starting up the SOA and BAM managed servers, perform the following steps:

1. Set the environment (refer to the *Setting the environment* section below).

2. Create a `boot.properties` file on the SOA managed server:

```
cd $MW_HOME/user_projects/domains/soa_domain/servers/[managed_
server]/security
echo "username=weblogic" > boot.properties
echo "password=<password>" >> boot.properties
```

3. Repeat steps 1 and 2 on all servers in the cluster.

Now that you have created the `boot.properties` file, after you start up the managed servers, both the username and password will be encrypted in this file.

Setting the environment

Setting up the environment simplifies subsequent commands and allows for more efficient scripting. To set the environment, customize the values highlighted in the following code snippet to reflect your environment:

```
export DOMAIN=[soa_domain]
export MW_HOME=/u01/app/oracle/Middleware
export DOMAIN_HOME=$MW_HOME/user_projects/domains/$DOMAIN
```

Starting up Node Manager

Node Manager should be started up once per physical server.

```
nohup $MW_HOME/wlserver_10.3/server/bin/startNodeManager.sh &
```

Starting up AdminServer

`AdminServer` should be started only in a single server in the cluster.

```
nohup $DOMAIN_HOME/bin/startWebLogic.sh &
```

Starting up the SOA and BAM managed servers

Start up the SOA and BAM managed servers on each node of the cluster, update the highlighted managed server name, hostname, and port to reflect your environment as follows:

```
cd $MW_HOME/user_projects/domains/$DOMAIN/bin
nohup ./startManagedWebLogic.sh soa_server1 http://soahost1:8001 &
nohup ./startManagedWebLogic.sh bam_server1 http://soahost1:9001 &
```

Repeat the preceding command for other nodes in the cluster. For example, in a two-node cluster, start up the second node on the second server as follows:

```
cd $MW_HOME/user_projects/domains/$DOMAIN/bin
nohup ./startManagedWebLogic.sh soa_server2 http://soahost2:8001 &
nohup ./startManagedWebLogic.sh bam_server2 http://soahost2:9001 &
```

Shutting down Node Manager

Unfortunately there is no way to gracefully shutdown the Node Manager and it has to be force killed. To kill Node Manager, simply run the following command to obtain the process IDs of the Node Manager processes and kill them:

```
ps -ef | grep NodeManager | grep -v grep | awk '{print $2}' | xargs
kill -9
```

Shutting down AdminServer

Shutting down `AdminServer` involves simply executing the `stopWebLogic.sh` script as shown:

```
cd $DOMAIN_HOME/bin
./stopWebLogic.sh
```

Shutting down the SOA and BAM Managed Servers

To shut down the SOA and BAM managed servers, simply run the following commands:

```
cd $DOMAIN_HOME/bin
./stopManagedWebLogic.sh soa_server1 t3://soahost1:8001
./stopManagedWebLogic.sh bam_server1 t3://soahost1:9001
```

In a clustered installation, you must repeat these steps on each server in the cluster. For example, on the second node, the commands would be:

```
cd $DOMAIN_HOME/bin
./stopManagedWebLogic.sh soa_server2 t3://soahost2:8001
./stopManagedWebLogic.sh bam_server2 t3://soahost2:9001
```

The chapter code contains all these shell scripts and more that you can keep handy to start, stop, and control servers in your infrastructure.

Enabling log rotation

By default, the log rotation size for each managed server in Oracle SOA Suite 11*g* is set to a small value. This log file rotation value should be increased to reduce I/O contention associated with debug messages and the switching of log files at frequent intervals.

In the Oracle WebLogic Server Administration Console, the **Rotation file size** parameter can be altered by navigating to **Environment | Servers | [soa_server] | Logging**. Ensure that the rotation file size is set to 5000 KB or higher. Alternatively, you may choose to rotate the log file by date, by setting the **Rotation type** to **By Time** instead.

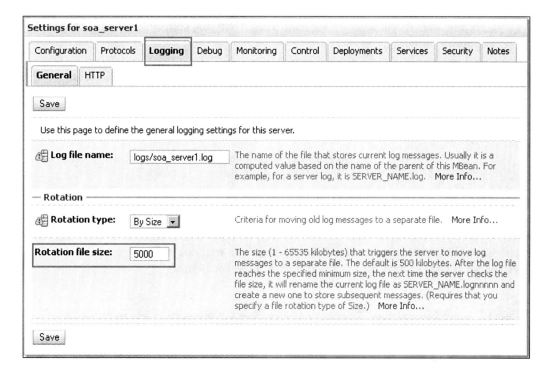

Unfortunately, the WebLogic Server log rotation affects only the `soa_server1.log` file but not the `soa_server1.out` file, which is generated when you use Node Manager to start up and shut down the SOA managed server. To enable log rotation of the `soa_server1.out` log file on a Linux-based system, perform the following steps:

1. Ensure that you have the `logrotate` binary installed on your operating system:

   ```
   ls /usr/sbin/logrotate
   ```

2. Create a `logrotate` configuration file (for example, under `/home/oracle/scripts/logrotate.conf`) with the following contents, setting `[Domain]` to your domain name:

```
/u01/app/oracle/Middleware/user_projects/domains/[Domain]/servers/
soa_server?/logs/soa_server?.out {
   missingok
   copytruncate
   compress
   rotate=5
   size=5M
}
```

3. Create a `logrotate` status file (for example, under `/home/oracle/scripts/logrotate.status`) with the following contents, setting [Domain] to your domain name:

```
logrotate state -- version 2
"/u01/app/oracle/Middleware/user_projects/domains/[Domain]/
servers/soa_server1/logs/soa_server1.out" 2012-1-1
```

4. Add a new `crontab` entry by typing `crontab -e` and adding the following line:

```
0,15,30,45 * * * * /usr/sbin/logrotate -s $HOME/scripts/logrotate.
status $HOME/scripts/logrotate.conf
```

This will check every 15 minutes to see if it is necessary to rotate the `soa_server1.out` standard out file based on the rules defined in the `logrotate.conf` configuration file. If new log files are added, you must ensure that they are added to the status file or they will not be rotated. This can be repeated for other managed servers as necessary.

Navigating to key administration areas

To perform the common management tasks related to your infrastructure, we begin by describing the various administrative pages and consoles within Oracle Enterprise Manager Fusion Middleware Control.

The Oracle Enterprise Fusion Middleware Control landing page is divided into the navigator (left pane) and the dynamic content dashboard (right pane). You can expand the navigator tree to configure and manage the WebLogic domain, admin and running managed servers, the SOA infrastructure, metadata repositories, and many more. The next screenshot shows an expanded navigator view. Clicking on the **SOA Infrastructure** target menu reveals a host of common administration and configuration activities that you can perform. These activities include:

- Monitoring **Performance Summary** and **Request Processing** statistics for binding components, service infrastructure, and service engines

- Viewing and editing **Log Configuration** for runtime loggers

- Managing composite deployments and their configuration plans from the **SOA Deployment** link

- Managing running and faulted instances of deployed composites by expanding **Service Engine** and clicking on a particular engine

- Administering endpoint and adapter properties post composite deployment from the **Services and References** link

- Configuring and managing business events, current event subscribers, and event fault details from the **Business Events** link

- Configuring engine properties for service components, which make up the Oracle SOA Suite 11*g* runtime, by expanding **SOA Administration**

Many other **SOA Infrastructure** configurations and properties are made available to edit at runtime by clicking on **System MBean Browser** under **Administration**.

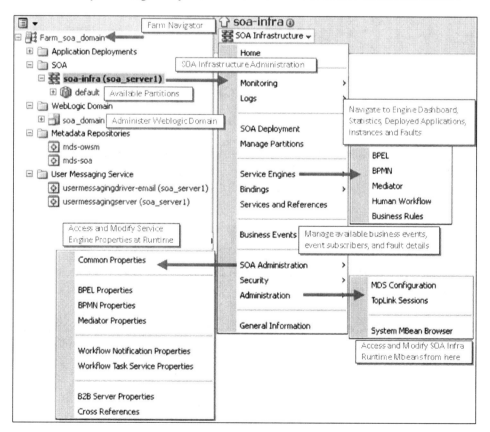

Oracle Enterprise Manager Fusion Middleware Control also provides further drill down into a context specific administration panel to manage and administer individual composites and their instances within the infrastructure. You can directly navigate to administration tasks for a specific composite from the navigator by expanding the partition it is deployed to. The following screenshot shows the **Dashboard** view of a **CabRentalProcess** composite along with information about recent instances, faults, and rejected messages belonging to this composite.

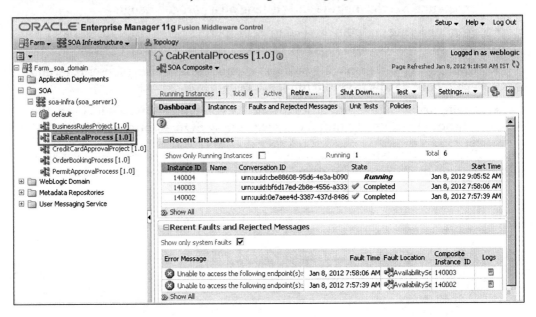

The administration activities specific to the current composite are available from the **SOA Composite** menu appearing below the **CabRentalProcess** composite. Some of the common and important ones are described here and are also highlighted in the next screenshot:

- The **SOA Deployment** menu allows you to undeploy the composite from the partition or replace it with a newer version through the **Redeploy** action.

- Select the **Export** action to export the composite along with all post deployment changes to a JAR file that can then be used to promote the composite to other environments.

- Expanding the **Test Service** link lists all service bindings that are part of the composite and enables you to manually initiate an instance of this composite through the **Test Web Service** page.

- The **Unit Tests** option allows you to run test cases that simulate interaction between the composite and its references before deployment to a production environment.

- **Oracle Web Service Manager** (OWSM) based policies for authentication, authorization, message integrity, identity propagation, and so on, can be attached or detached at runtime from the **Policies** link to either services, references, or components in a composite.

- A composite is typically comprised of exposed services and external references that are bound to change at runtime after the composite is deployed to the infrastructure. Runtime properties of binding components can be updated by expanding the **Service/Reference Properties** section.

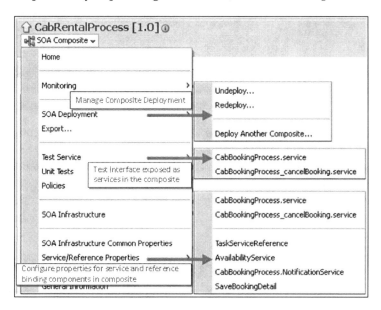

The composites and service engine dashboard also includes a **Related Links** menu providing relevant additional links, depending on the current context. The following screenshot shows the **Related Links** menu on the **Mediator Service Engine** page from where you can navigate directly to the **SOA Infrastructure Home** page, the **Mediator Properties** page to configure engine properties, the Oracle WebLogic Server Administration Console, or the page to view Mediator engine log files.

All service engines, SOA Infrastructure Common Properties, and business event dashboards provide access to **WebLogic Server Console** under the **Related Links** list. Clicking on the icon will take you to the login console of the WebLogic Server in a new tab or browser window.

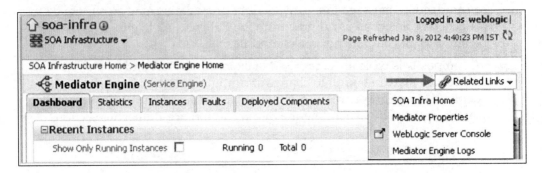

Having familiarized yourself with navigating to key administration dashboards within the Oracle Fusion Middleware Enterprise Manager Control console, it is time to get ready to execute key management tasks available from these pages.

As an administrator of Oracle SOA Suite 11g, your responsibility to manage the infrastructure and lifecycle of SOA composites is greatly simplified by the fact that a composite is composed of various components and bindings that execute on individual service engines. Rather than searching places to manage, you can zero in on a specific engine and administer the instances that have been executed on it. In the forthcoming sections of this chapter, you will see exactly how to achieve this.

Configuring infrastructure properties

Infrastructure property settings are properties that apply to all composites running on the SOA Infrastructure. Configuring these properties ensures that you have some sort of global setting applied to your environment. You can configure them from the Oracle Enterprise Manager Fusion Middleware Control console by navigating to **Administration | System MBean Browser | Application Defined MBeans | oracle. as.soainfra.config**. Infrastructure properties can be altered at runtime by entering a value in the **Value** textbox for the read-write MBeans. There is an option to even validate your modifications by invoking the validate function from the **Operations** tab. These properties are persisted in the database and each managed server, when started, loads them from the database (golden copy). Whether a server needs to be started or not, once a property is changed, is indicated by an icon adjacent to it. Once a property change has been applied, all new instances in the infrastructure are executed against it. Key infrastructure properties that can be configured from the MBeans include:

- Global logging levels, audit, and cache configuration
- Callback server endpoint and dehydration data source JNDI
- JMS or database-based mode for **Event Delivery Network (EDN)** framework
- Global transactions and fatal connection retry settings
- Universal schema validation
- UDDI registry and HTTP server connections
- Infrastructure keystore locations
- Search criteria for the retrieval of recent instances and faults

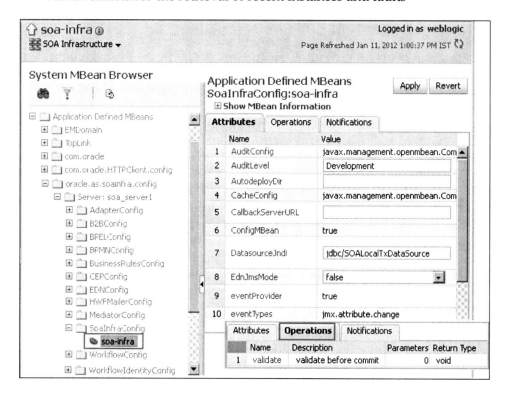

Apart from configuring the System MBeans from a web browser, their default configuration override can also be scripted with the help of the **WebLogic Scripting Tool (WLST)**. This is helpful when you are in charge of managing multiple SOA Infrastructures and want similar configurations applied all across by executing a handful of scripts. These WLST scripts can be executed in an offline mode (`wls:/offline>`) by running `wlst.sh` (or `wlst.cmd` in Windows) located under the `$MW_HOME/wlserver_10.3/common/bin` directory. Configuration properties for the SOA Infrastructure are available as part of a custom tree.

The following WLST script connects with a running SOA server, enters its custom tree, and changes the existing directory to `oracle.as.soainfra.config`. All MBeans under this directory can be viewed by executing the `ls()` command. The common infrastructure properties can be changed by simple `set([propertyName], [propertyValue])` statements. For example:

```
connect('<username>','<password>','<soahost>:<soaport>')
custom()
cd('oracle.as.soainfra.config/oracle.as.soainfra.config:name=soa-infra
,type=SoaInfraConfig,Application=soa-infra')
ls()
set('ValidateSchema',true)
exit()
```

Configuring and managing the infrastructure properties is just the beginning of a long journey. To make sure you have a better grasp of learning to manage and administer the lifecycle of an Oracle SOA Suite 11g environment in production, this chapter introduces a brief case study of a composite (having multiple services, references, and components) that is deployed to the infrastructure of which you, as the SOA administrator, are responsible for all of its management. The following screenshot shows a typical composite developed to automate processing of sales orders. The composite can be invoked over a standard web service protocol or over **Remote Method Invocation (RMI)**. Provision is also made such that it can read batches of orders stored in some file-based directory. Once the composite receives an order or an order collection in any of the described ways , its execution is initiated. It requests additional details for the order from backend systems, runs a set of fulfillment and approval rules, publishes status updates, and eventually sends out an e-mail notification. The approval rules determine whether a particular order should be processed automatically or needs manual approval, in which case human intervention is sought.

Now, imagine that you are relied upon to manage this critical business process in your organization and need to ensure that you have a good handle on configuring and administering the various engines that instances of this composite run on. It may also be required of you to manage or bulk manage live/completed instances, handle faulted messages, set up manual and automatic retries, configure notification channels, ensure that the external references are not timing out or unavailable, allow for business rules to change dynamically at runtime, and so on and so forth. Don't feel lost! This chapter will, in step-by-step detail, arm you with sufficient knowledge to handle all these tasks with ease and effectiveness.

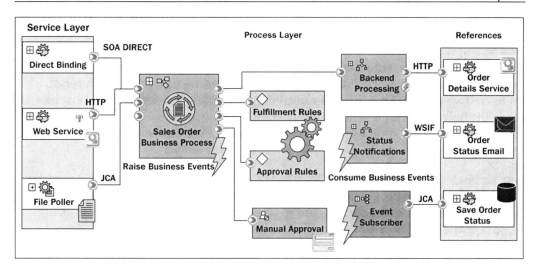

Configuring and administering binding components and JCA Adapters

After deploying the composite to the SOA Infrastructure (see *Chapter 2, Management of SOA Composite Applications* for details regarding deployment), one of the main things to address is how to manage and configure properties for binding components packaged inside them. Binding components are network protocols and mechanisms connecting your composite to external services, applications, and technologies (such as messaging queues, databases, web services, and so on). Binding components in Oracle SOA Suite 11*g* are of two kinds:

- **Services**: Services provide an entry point to the composite and advertise their capabilities to external applications by exchanging their service metadata information through a WSDL file. The service bindings define how a client application can invoke a composite. Examples of service bindings from the sales order composite in the preceding screenshot are an HTTP-based web service, JCA-based file polling service, and a Direct Binding service.

- **References**: References enable message exchanges between composites and externally deployed services. Examine the sales order composite diagram in the preceding screenshot to see how an HTTP-based third party web service, JCA-based database adapter, and **Web Service Invocation Framework (WSIF)** type notification service act as reference bindings in the composite assembly.

Configuring and managing service bindings

Oracle Enterprise Manager Fusion Middleware Control allows you to perform service binding administration tasks such as attaching policies, managing errored out messages, and setting binding properties. Depending upon your preference, there are two available mechanisms to configure binding properties. The property configuration screen for a service (SalesBookingBusinessProcess.service) in a composite application (OrderBookingComposite) is shown in the following screenshot.

Service binding properties can be accessed by either navigating to **SOA Composite | Service/Reference Properties | [Service] | Properties** or through **Application Defined MBeans** from **oracle.soa.config | Server: soa_server1 | SCA Composite | [Composite] | SCAComposite.SCAService | [Service]**. The **System MBean Browser** dashboard enables you to modify some advanced properties that aren't available under the **Properties** tab.

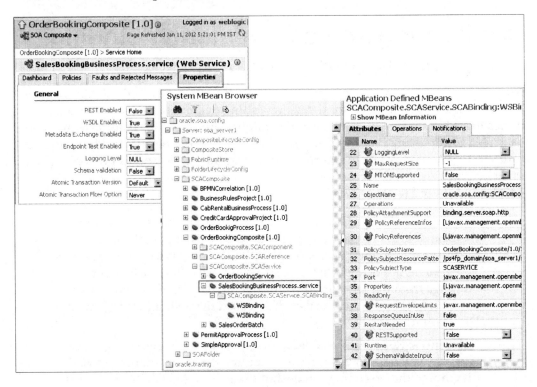

You can configure activation specifications of service binding components such as enabling REST support, enabling or disabling its WSDL, support for **MTOM** (**Message Transmission Optimization Mechanism**) (a method of efficiently sending binary data to and from web services), setting finer logging levels, and enabling incoming message semantic validation, among other configurations. You can read more about MTOM at `http://ww.w3.org/TR/soap12-mtom/`.

That's not all. If you wish to save yourself from the painful navigation on the consoles, use the WLST commands provided here to navigate to the parent MBean in order to modify service binding properties. Execute an `ls()` command to view all the RW MBeans under the parent MBean. Once you know which MBean property to alter, simply execute the `set('<mbeanName>','<mbeanValue'>)` command to change its value.

```
connect('<username>','<password>','<soahost>:<soaport>')
custom()
cd('oracle.soa.config/oracle.soa.config:name=SalesOrderBatch,revi
sion=1.0,partition=default,wsconfigtype=WebServiceConfig,SCAComp
osite="OrderBookingComposite",label=soa_d0bcfad1-1d7e-4bff-b4ae-
53b5fefb5394,j2eeType=SCAComposite.SCAService,Application=soa-infra')
ls()
get('MetadataExchange')
set('MetadataExchange','0')
set('ExposeWSDL','0')
exit()
```

In case you are wondering where to get the directory path to the MBean, the following screenshot shows how it is made available by expanding the icon beside **Show MBean Information**:

Application Defined MBeans: SCAComposite.SCAService:SalesBookingBusinessProcess.service
⊟ Hide MBean Information
MBean Name oracle.soa.config:name=SalesBookingBusinessProcess.service,revision=1.0,partition=default,wsconfigtype=WebServiceConfig,
            SCAComposite="OrderBookingComposite",Location=soa_server1,label=soa_d0bcfad1-1d7e-4bff-b4ae-53b5fefb5394,
            j2eeType=SCAComposite.SCAService,Application=soa-infra
Description SCA Service

Our case study has multiple entry points to the composite. The business process, in here, is also initiated when a certain file is available in a certain polling directory. It is quite common that the nature of the file being polled, or the polling directory itself, needs to be changed upon composite deployment. Let's assume that the **PhysicalDirectory** path specified by the developer was `C:\soa\salesorder\file` (in a Windows-based development environment), which might need to be changed once the composite is deployed to a Linux machine.

One way to do this is by overriding the polling directory location during composite deployment, using a configuration plan as discussed in *Chapter 3, Monitoring Oracle SOA Suite 11g*. Another way is to modify properties for the JCA File Adapter in the **OrderBookingComposite**, from under the **Properties** tab, at runtime. You can manually edit the adapter binding properties to change the polling directory, polling frequency, batch size, whether or not to delete the file once it is read and many other properties related to adapter activation specification. Depending upon the JCA adapter (File, Database, JMS, and so on), different properties are displayed for configuration. Apart from what is displayed on the screen, you can also add more properties by clicking on the ✚ icon. This will pop up additional properties for the selected service binding.

Configuring and managing reference bindings

In *Chapter 4, Tuning Oracle SOA Suite 11g for Optimum Performance* we explained the importance of tuning performance of endpoint applications effectively. Administering reference bindings is absolutely vital as impeding or slowly responding endpoints can induce latency in your entire infrastructure. It is often better to configure a timeout setting with a scheduled retry when interacting with external systems as there is little or no control over them. If the endpoints are unavailable or perform poorly, discontinue processing the instance rather than keep the thread hanging. Such faulted instances can then be recovered automatically or manually when the external systems are up and running again.

In our case study the `OrderBookingComposite` application interacts with an external web service and a database. You can administer interaction specifications (for references) and endpoint properties such as timeouts, thresholds, retry intervals, and more for the JCA-based database adapter and web service bindings. The reference **Properties** tab even has an **Endpoint Address** property field. Setting a value of an endpoint here will override the one configured in the WSDL. The next screenshot shows the **Reference Home** configuration page to override this and other properties. There are, however, a few important things to keep in mind while configuring these properties:

- If `jca.retry.*` based endpoint properties are added or removed, the composite application containing them needs to be redeployed for changes to take effect.

- If the non-registered JCA binding level properties are manually added in the `composite.xml` file, these and other registered properties for that reference cannot be edited from Oracle Enterprise Manager Fusion Middleware Control.

- There are no restrictions on adding, removing, or changing JCA endpoint properties at runtime, if not specified at design time. Adapters get notified of the changes automatically and the composite does not require redeployment.

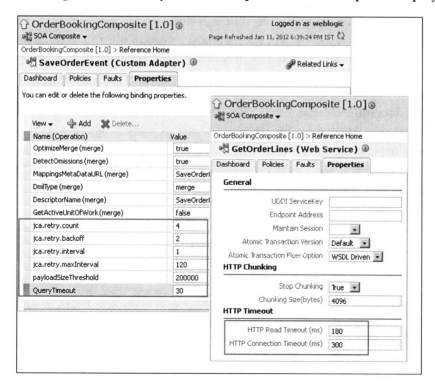

Resource adapters are defined and deployed at the domain creation/configuration stage and by default always start up within the J2EE container on the relevant target. All resource adapters barring the File Adapter are referenced from a composite by way of a JNDI location that is part of its design-time configuration. This JNDI location references the WebLogic Server layer via JCA. At runtime, the deployment descriptor of an adapter must associate the JNDI name with configuration properties (such as the host and port of a socket adapter, the channel and host of an MQ Server or the data source information for a database adapter) required by the adapter to access the backend information source.

Our order booking composite saves order events in a database through a Database Adapter. After the composite is deployed to the SOA Infrastructure, the adapter JNDI needs to be associated with a valid data source configured for a database. To do so follow these steps:

1. Log in to Oracle Weblogic Server Administration Console.
2. Click on **Deployments** under the **Your Deployed Resources** section.
3. From the list of all available deployments, click on **DbAdapter** and navigate to **Configuration | Outbound Connection Pools**.
4. Click on the **New** button and create a new outbound connection instance. Remember, the JNDI name that is used here should be the same one that was defined for the reference at design time.
5. Expand **javax.resources.cci.ConnectionFactory** to see all the JNDI names that are configured for the adapter to communicate with databases. Click on the one that was created in step 4.
6. In the **Properties** tab, you would see properties such as **xADataSourceName** and **dataSourceName**. Enter the name of the actual data source that has a connection defined for the database in any of these properties.
7. Save the changes.
8. From the list of deployments, select **DbAdapter**, and click on **Update**. This propagates the resource adapter changes to be persisted in the deployment properties (saved in the Plan.xml files).

It is important that you specify only one data source for the DbAdapter JNDI property. If an XA compliant data source is created, your adapter's outbound connection pool JNDI location should define the value under the xaDataSourceName property and the dataSourceName property should be left blank. Otherwise, you are most likely to see the following exception while saving your changes:

```
javax.resource.spi.InvalidPropertyException: Duplicate
Property Values Exception.
```

After the JNDI for the adapter reference is created, it is wise to review and test the connection to ensure that it does not run into problems later. The **Testing** tab can be accessed by navigating to **DbAdapter | Monitoring | Current Connections**. From here you can test all outbound connection threads in the adapter outbound connection pool. The following screenshot shows the JNDI name of a reference database adapter being updated to point to a transactional data source and subsequently tested from the Oracle Weblogic Server Administration Console.

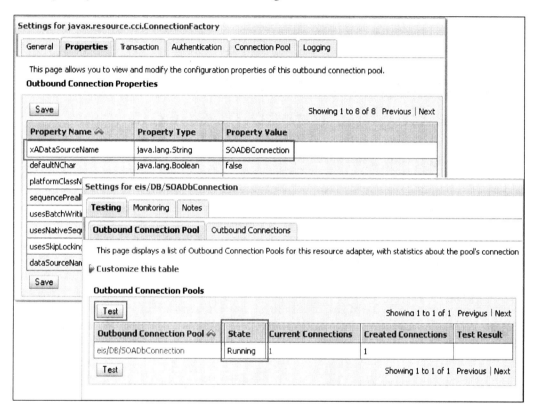

Configuring GlobalInboundJcaRetryCount

While working with JCA Adapters of all sorts, it is particularly important to briefly mention the `GlobalInboundJcaRetryCount` attribute. This attribute defines the number of retries an inbound adapter will perform, when an error is returned from the downstream service engine. It is recommended to set its value other than the default value of `-1`, which designates an indefinite number of retries.

To modify `GlobalInboundJcaRetryCount`, do the following:

1. Log in to Oracle Enterprise Manager Fusion Middleware Control.
2. Right-click on **soa-infra** and navigate to **Administration | System MBean Browser**.
3. In **System MBean Browser**, expand **Application Defined MBeans | oracle. as.soainfra.config | [soa_server] | AdapterConfig | adapter**.
4. Set the **GlobalInboundJcaRetryCount** attribute from the default value of **-1** to a positive value (for example, **5**).

Configuring and administering BPEL Service Engine and components

The Oracle BPEL Service Engine is a container providing standards for assembling, developing, and executing synchronous, as well as asynchronous, services into end-to-end business processes in the SOA Infrastructure. When the `soa-infra` application is started, it initializes the BPEL engine in a stateless manner and loads composites from the MDS repository. If the composite contains any BPEL components, it targets them to the BPEL engine. At runtime, the BPEL engine waits for requests from different channels, such as messaging sources, databases, and web services. It uses a **Dispatcher Module** that maintains an in-memory logical queue containing units of work to process incoming messages from these binding components. The BPEL Service Engine saves the process execution state in the dehydration store through a persistence module based on **Oracle TopLink** and hence there is no in-memory state replication required. The **Audit Framework** continuously audits the work being processed by storing process execution information in the database.

Managing BPEL Service Engine and components

Oracle Enterprise Manager Fusion Middleware Control allows you to perform key administration tasks such as monitoring instances, recovering from faults, manually recovering (BPEL) failed messages, and configuring properties for the BPEL Service Engine. It also provides useful statistics and performance monitoring metrics for the engine. A typical BPEL Engine Home landing page that can be accessed by navigating to **SOA Infrastructure | Service Engines | BPEL**, is shown in the following screenshot. Examine the page closely to notice that this engine executes the **OrderNotificationProcess** and **OrderProcessing** components that are both part of the **OrderBookingComposite** application and provides a summarized view of all instances, components, and faults.

The **Dashboard** tab allows you to click on any instance and view its execution trail. The **Logs** column provides specific logs to access filtered messages specific to an instance of the component. Key administration tasks performed from the BPEL Service Engine dashboard are as follows:

- Monitoring request and thread statistics for all BPEL components running on the service engine from the **Statistics** tab.

- Searching, managing, and monitoring all BPEL component instances running on the service engine by clicking on the **Instances** tab. These instances can be part of separate composites.

- Getting details such as component name, current status along with total, and running and faulted instances for deployed composites with BPEL components, clicking on **Deployed Components** tab.

- Searching and recovering faulted instances that are marked for recovery from the **Faults** tab.

- Performing a bulk manual recovery of undelivered invokes or callback messages due to a transaction rollback in the process instance for asynchronous BPEL processes by clicking on the **Recovery** tab.

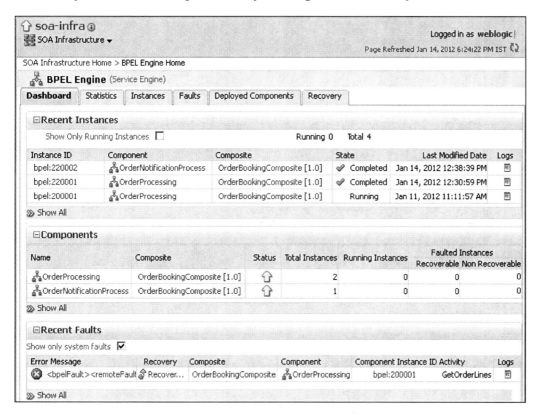

The **Recent Instances** panel displays all instances that are part of the BPEL Service Engine sorted by the most recent ones first. Click on any component **Instance ID** to further investigate its flow trace from the runtime audit trail of message flow listing all the activities, services, references, and components that the instance executed in its lifetime. If the **Audit Level** is set to **development**, a lot more information such as detailed message payload for each stage is also available. Another significant feature of Oracle SOA Suite 11g is its ability to show graphical flow displaying the instance execution path, which is exactly similar to how the process was designed initially. A graphical flow trail of **OrderNotificationProcess**, designed in BPEL, is shown in the following screenshot. Clicking on any activity opens a pop up displaying the message payload that is a result of executing that particular activity.

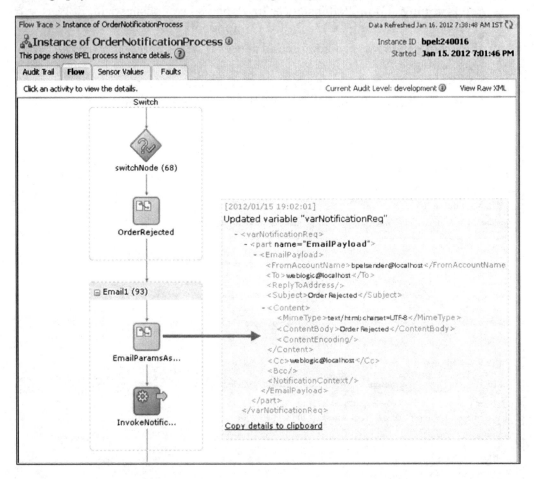

If you don't wish to see the payload of individual activities one by one, you can click on **View Raw XML** to get entire audit trail in the format of a raw XML message.

Administering BPEL Service Engine properties

The main configurable BPEL Service Engine settings are highlighted in the following list. There are three main groups of properties available to configure within the BPEL Service Engine:

- **Logging**: Affects audit and log related settings
- **BPEL Service Engine**: Affects engine-specific settings, which likely impacts throughput and performance
- **Instance Behavior**: Affects runtime behavior of instances

In Oracle Fusion Middleware Control, after right-clicking on **soa-infra** and navigating to **SOA Administration | BPEL Properties**, you are taken to the **BPEL Service Engine Properties** page. The following table describes each of the main configurable properties available:

Property	Category	Description
Audit Level	Logging	Setting this property to **Inherit** will use the same audit level settings as the SOA Infrastructure. In all other cases, this property overrides the value of the global SOA Infrastructure audit level property.
Audit Trail Threshold	Logging	This specifies the maximum size (in bytes) an audit trail details string can be before it is stored separately from the main audit trail.
Large Document Threshold	Logging	This specifies the maximum size (in bytes) to which a BPEL variable can grow before it is stored in a separate location from the rest of the instance scope data.
Dispatcher System Threads	BPEL Service Engine	This specifies the total number of threads used for general cleanup tasks. A small number of threads are required to handle the number of system dispatch messages generated during runtime. The default value is **2**.
Dispatcher Invoke Threads	BPEL Service Engine	This specifies the total number of threads allocated to process invocation dispatcher messages. Improved performance may be achieved by increasing the number of invoke threads, particularly if the majority of requests are instance invocations (as opposed to instance callbacks), However, higher thread counts may cause greater CPU utilization. The default value is **20**.

Property	Category	Description
Dispatcher Engine Threads	BPEL Service Engine	This specifies the total number of threads allocated to process engine dispatcher messages and impact activities that are processed asynchronously. Improved performance may be achieved by increasing the number of engine threads, particularly if the majority of processes are durable with a large number of dehydration points (midprocess receive, onMessage, onAlarm, and wait activities). However, higher thread counts may cause greater CPU utilization. The default value is **30**.
Payload Validation	Instance Behavior	When this property is enabled, validation of incoming and outgoing messages in the engine is performed. Payload data that fail schema validation are displayed as faulted. This is usually disabled in production environments.
Disable BPEL Monitors and Sensors	Instance Behavior	When this property is enabled, all monitors and sensors in the BPEL service engine are forcibly disabled. Monitors and sensors cannot be enabled at the composite level when this is selected.

Clicking on the **More BPEL Configuration Properties** link on the bottom of this page displays the full list of configurable properties. One common property that is typically updated is the SyncMaxWaitTime property, which is the maximum time a synchronous operation should take before timing out (default value is 45 seconds). For example, if many of your BPEL processes are timing out in 45 seconds while synchronously invoking to an external service (say, if the external service is poorly performing), two courses of action are available as a remedy. The first is to convert your BPEL process to an asynchronous one, which may not always be feasible. The second is to consider increasing SyncMaxWaitTime to a higher value so that it does not time out in 45 seconds. Setting this to a value greater than 300 is not recommended. Another property worth noting is BpelClasspath, which is the extra classpath specified when compiling BPEL generated java sources.

Administering BPEL instances and faults

The **Faults** tab in the instance detail page displays error messages in BPEL component instances, whether instances are recoverable from the fault or not, the timestamp of the fault occurrence, and the activity in which a given fault has occurred.

This is also the best way to handle individual faults needing recovery action, providing a degree of fault recovery granularity not available elsewhere. The 🎯 icon indicates a fault being marked for manual recovery with any one of the available **Recovery Actions** from the drop-down list:

- **Retry**: This action immediately retries the instance from the point of failure.
- **Abort**: Terminates the entire instance and marks the instance as **Terminated**.
- **Replay**: Replays again the entire scope activity in which the fault occurred.
- **Rethrow**: Rethrows the fault and propagates it to BPEL fault handlers (that is, catch branches). By default, all exceptions are caught by the fault management framework unless an explicit rethrow fault policy is provided.
- **Continue**: Ignores the fault and continues processing (marks the faulted activity as successful).

Managing BPEL component faults

The following screenshot shows a faulted instance of the **OrderProcessing** BPEL component that failed due to a remote exception (endpoint unavailable) and was marked as **Recoverable**. Once the target system is available, the fault can be recovered by retrying it. The **Retry Recovery Action** will let the instance retry and complete its execution. There is a certain limitation with this approach as the recovery is limited to an individual faulted instance. As such bulk fault recoveries cannot be performed at this level.

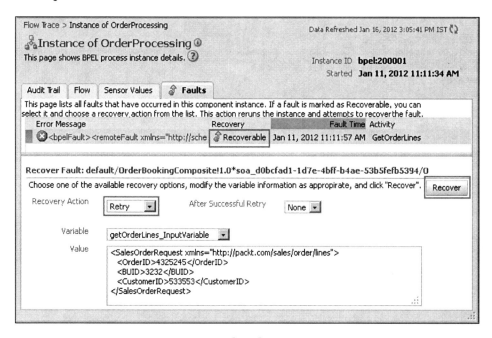

The message recovery information available on the instance's **Flow Trace** page depends upon the `AuditConfig` property set for the environment. Accessing this MBean from the **Common Infrastructure MBean properties** page will reveal that the default value of element `bpelRecoveryStatus` is set to `All`. This is how recovery information is made available. To prevent it from being displayed, set the `bpelRecoveryStatus` key to `Off`.

Bulk managing BPEL Service Engine faults

So far you saw how individual faulted instances can be recovered from the audit trail page. Managing and recovering individual faulted instances would prove to be cumbersome and time consuming. Oracle Enterprise Manager Fusion Middleware Control allows you to perform both manual and automatic bulk recovery of faulted and recoverable messages. Navigate to the **Faults** tab from the BPEL Service Engine homepage to see a list of all faulted messages and whether they are recoverable or not. For BPEL process faults to be identified as recoverable, a fault policy (using `fault-policies.xml`) must be defined at design time and bound to the composite (`fault-bindings.xml`). The fault policy should be able to categorize faults and bubble them up to the Enterprise Manager console for manual recovery by specifying the `ora-human-intervention` action. In the absence of any fault policies, the fault takes its standard course and it is left to the judgment of the BPEL engine to determine whether it is recoverable or not. You can select the faulted and recoverable instances of all BPEL components deployed to the service engine and perform a remedial action such as retrying, replaying, aborting, or ignoring them.

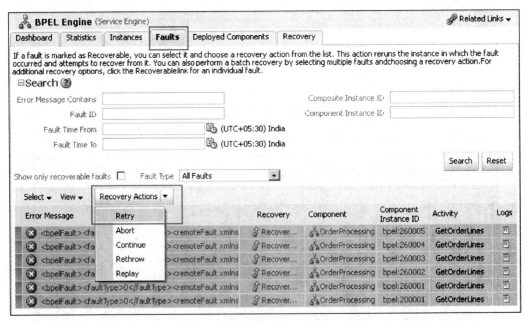

Manual message recovery in the BPEL Service Engine

You can also perform a manual recovery of undelivered invoke or callback messages for asynchronous BPEL processes that have their transactions rolled back for any reason. This is also applicable to recoverable activities that have failed and can be recovered. The sales order booking composite in our case study uses a File Adapter to read a batch of order records to be processed asynchronously. If the system fails while these instances are being processed, a manual recovery can be performed when the server restarts to ensure that all message records are recovered. To ensure that automatic recovery is not attempted multiple times for messages that fail after automatic recovery attempts by the BPEL Service Engine, they are placed in the exhausted state. The **Message State** can either be **Resolved** or **Undelivered** from the **Message State** drop-down list. Messages in these two states can be recovered by redelivering them into the BPEL engine for consumption. From here, you can perform one of the following actions on these messages:

- Hit the **Reset** button to return selected messages to the automatic recovery queue.

- Never attempt a recovery on them again by clicking on the **Mark Cancelled** button.

- Attempt to recover them immediately from the **Recover** button, as shown in the following screenshot:

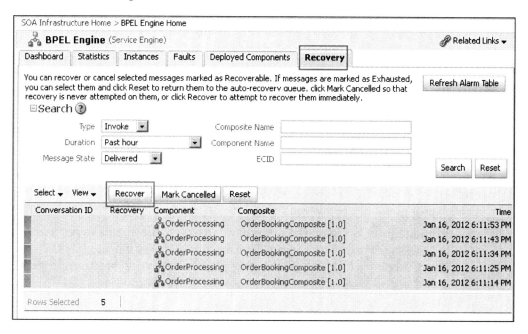

It is important to exercise caution while using message recovery since recovery of undelivered invocation messages always creates a new instance. This new instance may run to completion with no exception, albeit you continue to see the older instance as faulted. Once a message is submitted for recovery, the BPEL Service Engine may take time to complete the action. During this time, the message remains visible in the **Recovery** page. Duplicate attempts to recover the same message in the interim period are ignored.

> When the number of instances to be displayed on the Oracle Enterprise Manager Fusion Middleware Control dashboard swells, it is recommended to add an index on the DLV_MESSAGE.ECID column of the [PREFIX]_SOAINFRA.DLV_MESSAGE table to improve query performance when searching messages for a specific ECID value.

Automatic message recovery in the BPEL Service Engine

The next logical thing for you to do as an administrator would be to automate the fault recovery process. The BPEL Engine has some auto-recovery features that are buried in an MBean property allowing recovery of messages either at the time of restarting the SOA server or scheduling a recovery during off-peak hours. Messages being recovered can be throttled by limiting the number of messages picked up on each run. The **RecoveryConfig** configuration dashboard in **System MBean Browser** along with the property settings to schedule automatic recovery is shown in the next screenshot and the steps to configure the MBean are as follows:

1. Log in to Oracle Enterprise Manager Fusion Middleware Control.
2. Right-click on **soa-infra** and navigate to **SOA Infrastructure | SOA Administration | BPEL Properties | More BPEL Configuration Properties**.
3. Click on the **Recovery Config** MBean.
4. The **RecurringScheduleConfig** MBean allows configuring a time window, preferably non-peak production hours, wherein automatic recovery through retry can be scheduled. The **maxMessageRaiseSize** property controls the number of messages recovered in one go.
5. **StartupScheduleConfig** on the other hand instructs the engine to recover faulted messages on server startup. The amount of time allocated by the engine for recovery is determined by the **startupRecoveryDuration** property.

However, it is not always possible to recover everything automatically. Auto-recovery is subject to some conditions. Consider the following two scenarios:

- **Scenario 1**: If the BPEL component uses a fault policy and fault is handled using the `ora-human-intervention` action, fault is marked as **Recoverable** and the instance state is set to **Running**. In this scenario, such faults marked as **Recoverable** cannot be auto-recovered.

- **Scenario 2**: If the fault policy applied to a BPEL component catches a fault and rethrows it using the `ora-rethrow-fault` action, the fault is marked as **Recoverable** and the instance state set to **Faulted**—provided the fault is a recoverable one (for example, in the case of a destination system not being available). In this scenario, such recoverable faults can be auto-recovered on server startup and/or pre-scheduled recovery.

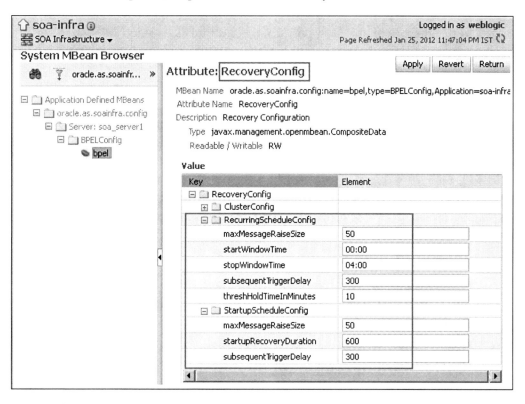

Administering Mediator Service Engine

In *Chapter 4, Tuning Oracle SOA Suite 11g for Optimum Performance* we described certain settings to optimize the performance of the Mediator Service Engine. As for bulk managing Mediator engine faults, the approach is essentially identical to managing BPEL engine faults, which is as follows:

- Navigating to the **Faults** tab of the Mediator Service Engine allows you to see a list of all faulted messages and whether they are recoverable or not
- For Mediator service faults to be identified as recoverable, a fault policy (`fault-policies.xml`) must be defined at design time and bound to the composite (`fault-bindings.xml`)
- You can select multiple faulted and/or recoverable instances and recover them
- In the absence of any fault policies, the fault takes its standard course and it is left to the judgment of the Mediator engine to determine whether it is recoverable or not

 It may be worthwhile to remember here that `fault-policies.xml` can only catch Mediator faults if the routing rule under **Static Routing** is set to **Parallel**.

All configurable Mediator Service Engine settings are highlighted in the following list. There are five groups of properties available to configure within the Mediator Service Engine:

- **Logging**: Affects log related settings
- **Mediator Engine**: Affects engine specific settings, which likely impacts throughput and performance
- **Custom**: Specifies custom properties
- **Health Check**: Affects the frequency with which the heartbeat framework checks and announces the availability of the server
- **Resequencing**: Affects all resequencing functionality, which is the ability of Oracle Mediator to resequence incoming messages in a user-specified order

In Oracle Fusion Middleware Control, after right-clicking on **soa-infra** and navigating to **SOA Administration | Mediator Properties**, you are taken to the **Mediator Service Engine Properties** page. The following table describes each of the configurable properties available:

Property	Category	Description
Audit Level	Logging	Setting this property to **Inherit** will use the same audit level settings as the SOA Infrastructure. In all other cases, this property overrides the value of the global SOA Infrastructure audit level property.
Metrics Level	Logging	This property determines if **Dynamic Monitoring Service (DMS)** metrics should be collected for Mediator services. DMS metrics are used to measure the performance of application components. See *The DMS Spy servlet* section in *Chapter 3, Monitoring Oracle SOA Suite 11g* for more details.
Parallel Worker Threads	Mediator Engine	This property sets the number of outbound threads for parallel processing. This does not impact sequential services.
Parallel Maximum Rows Retrieved	Mediator Engine	This property specifies the number of rows to retrieve per iteration for parallel processing. Oracle documentation recommends setting this value to **50** to **100** times the **Parallel Worker Threads** property. Setting this too high can result in increased memory consumption.
Parallel Locker Thread Sleep	Mediator Engine	This property specifies the idle time (in seconds) between two successive iterations for retrieving rows, when there is no message for parallel processing. We almost always recommend setting this to **1**. See *Chapter 3, Monitoring Oracle SOA Suite 11g* for further explanation.
Error Locker Thread Sleep	Mediator Engine	This is similar in concept to the **Parallel Locker Thread Sleep** property, except that it is specific to errored out messages.

Property	Category	Description
Parameters	Custom	This specifies custom configuration properties. For example, in resequenced messages, it is possible to configure the buffer window for the time window in best effort resequencing by adding the `buffer.window=20` custom parameter, which means that 20 percent of the length of the time window is added as a buffer.
Container ID Refresh Time	Health Check	This is the interval (in seconds) in which the heartbeat thread checks the status of the Mediator Service Engine and announces its presence to other servers in the cluster. This is internally accomplished by updating the timestamp of the unique identifier maintained in each Mediator Service Engine. The default value is 60 seconds.
Container ID Lease Timeout	Health Check	This is the interval (in seconds) in which the heartbeat thread checks if there are other unique identifiers that have not been updated.
Resequencer Locker Thread Sleep	Resequencing	This specifies the sleep time (in seconds) for a deferred locker when there is no message in the database.
Resequencer Maximum Groups Locked	Resequencing	This specifies the maximum number of group rows retrieved for each locking cycle.
Resequencer Worker Threads	Resequencing	This property specifies the number of resequencer threads.

Clicking on the **More Mediator Configuration Properties** link at the bottom of the **Mediator Service Engine Properties** page displays the full list of configurable properties.

Administering User Messaging Service

Oracle **User Messaging Service (UMS)** enables two-way communication between actors in processes such as human users, automatic activities, and deployed applications. UMS has support for a variety of messaging channels, such as e-mail, IM, SMS, and text-to-voice messages. Any process components, such as BPEL/ BPMN, Human Workflow, or BAM can leverage UMS to send notifications and alerts to user mailboxes. The Oracle SOA Suite 11*g* UMS infrastructure provides a range of features such as:

- Support for multiple messaging channels such as e-mail, **instant messaging (IM)**, **Extensible Messaging and Presence Protocol (XMPP)**, **short message service (SMS)**, and voice. Actionable e-mail messages can also be delivered to a process user's inbox.

- Two-way messaging allows sending messages from applications to users (referred to as outbound messaging) who can then initiate messaging interactions (inbound messaging).

- User messaging preferences provide process users with a web interface to define preferences for how and when they can receive messaging notifications allowing applications to become immediately more flexible. Rather than deciding whether to send to a user's e-mail address or IM client, the application can simply send the message to the user, and let UMS route the message according to the user's preferences.

Describing UMS architecture and components

UMS in Oracle SOA Suite 11*g* is made up of a layer of clients, servers, and drivers.

The following diagram shows a typical architecture of UMS. The UMS server consists of EJB interfaces, standard web services, and a stateless session bean to provide business logic to client applications. The UMS architecture heavily relies on JMS queues used to buffer content between clients, servers, and drivers. The UMS server layer has JAX-WS servlets to implement web services and also simple Oracle ADF Faces UI component for managing end user messaging preferences. UMS drivers contain JCA Resource Adapters to interface with external gateways. There is also a database wherein the UMS messaging states are stored.

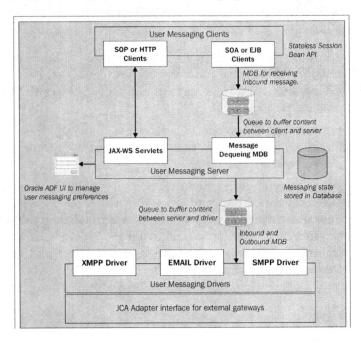

Configuring UMS for Human Workflow and BPEL process components

The `OrderBookingComposite` that we are entrusted to manage in the infrastructure has to send status e-mails to process users configured to receive notifications. All that developers need to worry about is to add an **Email Activity** in a BPEL process and populate e-mail message details or enable **Actionable Notifications** for Human Worfklow tasks. It is your job as an administrator to configure e-mail drivers to both send and receive messages. E-mail drivers send messages over SMTP and use either IMAP or POP3 for receiving incoming messages.

Configuring the e-mail messaging driver and notifications

In the following section, you will learn how to configure and set up e-mail driver properties by specifying connection parameters of the e-mail messaging server (as shown in the next screenshot).

1. Log in to Oracle Enterprise Manager Fusion Middleware Control.
2. On the navigator, expand **User Messaging Server**.
3. Right-click on **usermessagingdriver-email** and navigate to **Email Driver Properties**.
4. For outgoing notifications, enter `OutgoingMailServer` and `OutgoingMailServerPort` properties of your SMTP server as well as `OutgoingDefaultFromAddress`, `OutgoingUsername`, and `OutgoingPassword`.
5. Click on **Apply** and restart the SOA managed server.

> Note that UMS properties are not propagated across the cluster members and hence the UMS setup needs to be done individually on all the member servers of a cluster. In a cluster, these steps must be repeated for all the SOA and BAM managed servers.

You may also subscribe to incoming notifications from the e-mail server by setting up the POP server in a similar way. The only thing to take care of would be to provide the correct host and port addresses of the POP mail server.

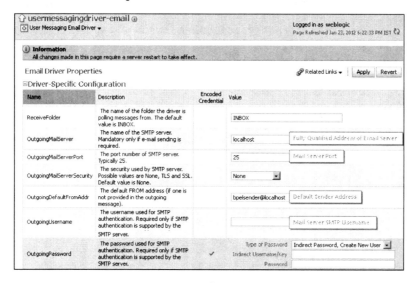

For Human Workflow components to send notification through UMS, the workflow notification setting will also have to be configured. For this purpose follow these steps:

1. Right-click on **soa-infra** and navigate to **SOA Infrastructure | SOA Administration | Workflow Notification Properties** to be able to see the configuration screen.

2. Change the **Notification Mode** to **All** or **Email**.

3. Enter the **From Address, Actionable Address,** and **Reply To Address** of your mail server.

4. Click on **Apply** and then restart all servers on which the UMS drivers are targeted. In a cluster, these properties are automatically propagated to the other servers.

In the absence of DNS, the hostnames and IP addresses of both the inbound (IMAP) e-mail server and outbound (SMTP) e-mail server that are configured for UMS should be added to the /etc/hosts file of the server on which Oracle SOA Suite 11g is running. A restart of all managed servers on which UMS is targeted is necessary for the setting to take effect.

If you are responsible for administration of just one such infrastructure, navigating to the MBean and configuring the MBeans is good enough. However, in all practical scenarios, you will have multiple farms of SOA Infrastructure. It is wise to have these configurations scripted in a WLST script that can be executed by just connecting to the required instance. The following WLST script does what we did just before:

```
connect('<username>','<password>','<soahost>:<soaport>')
custom()
cd ('oracle.as.soainfra.config/oracle.as.soainfra.config:name=human-wo
rkflow,type=HWFMailerConfig,Application=soa-infra')
   set('ASNSDriverEmailFromAddress', 'bpelsender@localhost')
   set('ASNSDriverEmailReplyAddress','bpelreceiver@localhost')
   set('ASNSDriverEmailRespondAddress','weblogic@localhost')
   set('HWFMailerNotificationMode','ALL')
disconnect()
```

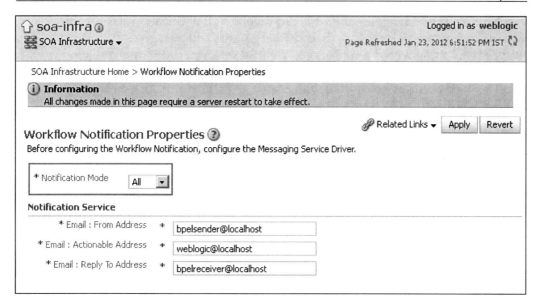

Testing UMS from Oracle Enterprise Manager Fusion Middleware Control

This is it! You have now configured UMS Email Driver and Workflow Notification to integrate with the e-mail server. To test if e-mail notifications are working use the UMS testing functionality from Oracle Enterprise Manager Fusion Middleware Control console by following these steps:

1. Log in to Oracle Enterprise Manager Fusion Middleware Control.

2. Right-click on **soa-infra** and navigate to **Service Engines | Human Workflow**.

3. Click on the **Notification Management** tab and then click on the **Send Test Notification** button.

4. Enter a valid **Send To** e-mail address and set **Channel** to **Email**.

5. Click on the **Send** button to send a mail to the given e-mail address.

Have look at the **Notification Management** dashboard and the result of testing the e-mail driver configuration via the **Send Test Notification** button, shown in the following screenshot. If the e-mail is sent successfully, a **SENT** response output is shown immediately.

The **Notification Management** dashboard displays all notifications sent from various components along with their delivery status and also gives an ability to retry/resend undelivered notifications. You can select an individual outgoing notification and click on the **Resend** button to resubmit it. Optionally, you can also select a single notification column with **Status** as **Failure** and click on **Resend All Similar Notifications** to resubmit all such kinds in one go.

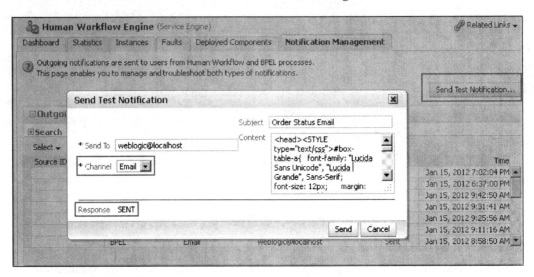

The UMS queues that are used to store messages intermittently can be managed from the WebLogic Server console by navigating to **JMS Modules | UMSJMSSystemResource**. The database schema used to store UMS messaging state is [PREFIX]_ORASDPM. Connect to this schema and execute the following query to get a list of all UMS messages that are in the faulted state along with the fault reason:

```
SELECT S.TYPE, M.CHANNEL,M.SENDER, M.STATE, S.CONTENT FROM STATUS
S, (SELECT A.VALUE SENDER, A.DELIVERY_TYPE CHANNEL, D.DELIVERY_
STATE STATE, D.ADDRESS_ID FROM ADDRESS A, DELIVERY_ATTEMPT D WHERE
A.ADDR_ID =D.ADDRESS_ID) M WHERE S.ADDRESS_ID=M.ADDRESS_ID AND
M.STATE<>'SUCCESS';
```

The following screenshot shows an example of the output of the preceding query:

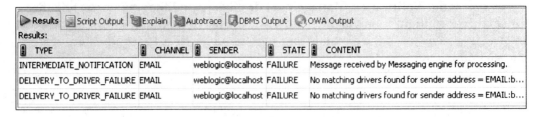

Configuring multiple send addresses with UMS

Most definitely there will be practical scenarios where e-mail notification needs to be distinguished based on **From Address** of e-mail. To understand this better, assume there is one order confirmation BPEL process sending e-mails with the **From Address** set as `OrderStatus@yourcompany.com`, whereas a customer rewards process may need to send e-mails with a different **From Address** such as `Customerservice@yourcompany.com`.

You must have observed that there is just one default **From Address** configured for the e-mail driver on the infrastructure. Configuring multiple send addresses is tricky but you may do it by following these steps (also illustrated in the next screenshot):

1. Log in to Oracle Enterprise Manager Fusion Middleware Control.
2. Right-click on **soa-infra** and navigate to **Administration | System MBean Browser**.
3. Expand **Application Defined MBeans | oracle.as.soainfra.config | Server: server_name | HWFMailerConfig | human-workflow**.
4. Click on the **Operations** tab and then on **setASNSDriver**.
5. The **propertyName**, **propertyValue**, and **driverName** values have to be entered in the form. Enter `EmailFromAddress`, `OrderStatus@yourcompany.com` (replace with actual e-mail address), and `OrderStatus`, respectively, in these fields.
6. Click on the **Invoke** button to add the entry. Repeat steps 4 to 6 to add another set of properties (for the Customer Service From Address).
7. The **ASNSDriver** attribute will show all the accounts that you created in the previous steps, invoking the **getCustomNSDriverPropertyValue** operation that returns the addresses being used for each of the drivers.
8. Log in to Oracle WebLogic Server Console and install multiple UMS e-mail drivers, one for each **From Address**.
9. You will now have to configure each e-mail driver to use the required **From Address** for sending outgoing e-mails.

10. Now, in order to use these different sender addresses, the value specified in the `driverName` attribute has to be used in the **From Account** field of **Email** activity during design time. For example, if you need to send an e-mail from the `OrderStatus@yourcompany.com` account name, the **From Account** field needs to have a value of `OrderStatus`.

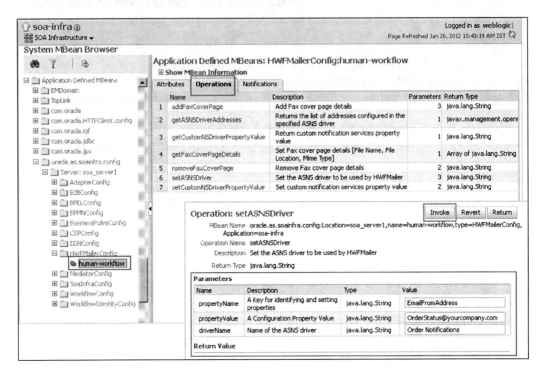

Administering the Human Workflow Service Engine

The Human Workflow Service Engine runs as a separate engine in the Oracle SOA Suite 11g service infrastructure providing human task execution functionalities to both BPEL and BPMN processes. The Human Workflow component consists of a number of services that handle various aspects of human interaction with a business process such as task approvals, rejections, reassignments, delegation, and so on.

An instance on the Human Workflow Service Engine can be initiated by an invocation from another service component such as BPEL or BPMN engine. The message is routed to the engine by the SOA Service Infrastructure and is persisted by the workflow engine in dehydration store schema.

Once an invocation transaction is committed, the instance becomes available for human interactions through a thin client such as a browser or mobile-based user interface. Each update on the instance or the runtime state through a user action is then handled by the engine in a separate transaction.

Describing Human Workflow components and applications

The Human Workflow engine allows defining to-do tasks that can be assigned to users or groups of users, giving business users more flexibility and a centralized approach for task management. Workflow tasks can be assigned to application roles and then at runtime, real users or groups from your enterprise repository defined within your organization can be mapped to these application roles. In this section, you will learn ways to integrate your company's directory server with the service infrastructure and pull organizational users to associate them with application or logical business process roles.

An important feature of the Human Workflow Service Engine is a **worklist** application built on top of ADF rich client components. The worklist application can be accessed over a thin client, giving business users a common look and feel and developers a standardized approach for building user interfacing applications that are flexible and customizable. Business process users can define their own work queues and share these views with other users and groups. All Human Workflow data definitions and custom task views can be shared across members within an organization. Logging in to the worklist application is role-based and the interface is accessible at the URL `http://<host>:<soaport>/integration/worklistapp`.

The Human Workflow engine leverages the UMS framework deployed in the infrastructure for its notification needs. The UMS engine allows process participants to customize their messaging channels and even set preferred mechanisms of being notified. These preferences, such as the mode by which to receive notifications (for example, e-mail, sms, and so on) and which devices need to be used, can all be configured from the address `http://<host>:<soaport>/sdpmessaging/userprefs-ui`.

Administration of human task instances, workflow service engine configuration, notification setup, and fault management are performed from the Oracle Enterprise Manager Fusion Middleware Control console. It also provides a mechanism to detect and handle auto-reply messages, poisoned responses, and spams in the workflow engine.

Managing workflow task configuration at runtime

Part of Oracle SOA Suite 11*g*'s ideology is to allow for as much flexibility and agility to different components such as business rules, domain value maps, and certain aspects of Human Workflow task configurations to be edited at runtime. The onus is then on you—as the administrator—to edit task assignment and routing policies, manage approval groups, change business rules responsible for dynamic task allocation, and so on, on-demand without going through the pains of software lifecycle management procedures to enable a change request. Once you have deployed human task components, to change task configuration at runtime, perform the following steps:

1. Log in to SOA Composer at `http://<host>:<soaport>/soa/composer`.

2. Click on the **Open** icon and then **Open Task**.

3. A task selection pop up opens wherein you can select the composite containing human workflow component and click on the **Open** button.

4. The following screenshot highlights the assignment/routing policy and notification settings within the task configuration page. This page allows for runtime changes to task routing policies, expiration, and escalation policies and notification settings for a human task after it is deployed to the infrastructure.

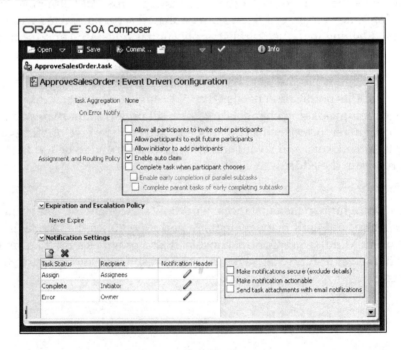

5. Click on the Edit icon to change these configurations. In order to persist the changes made on the browser, click on **Commit** for them to take effect.

Managing human task service component address

A human task component in a composite has an associated user defined task details interface executing on the worklist application. Configuration of the human task service component task detail application URI, like editing, adding, or removing, can be performed from the Oracle Enterprise Manager Fusion Middleware Control console. This configuration page is different for each Human Workflow component. Access this by navigating to a specific composite and selecting the human task service component under the **Component Metrics** table. Click on the **Administration** tab to edit the **Host Name**, **HTTP Port**, or **HTTPS Port** of the URI, or even to add a new one by using the **Add URI** button.

There are primarily two reasons that you might need to change the default entries as depicted in the next screenshot:

- When the SOA managed server in the infrastructure is SSL enabled, you must manually enable SSL by changing the workflow task display URL to use the correct protocol and port number. To enable the use of the SSL (HTTPS) URL, ensure that the **HTTP Port** setting is left blank.

- If there is a clustered setup with multiple managed servers servicing incoming requests, **Host Name** and **HTTP Port** will have to be substituted with the frontend host and port of cluster, or the load balancer address, if there is one configured. If there is more than one independent managed server, click on **Add URI** to enter details of them.

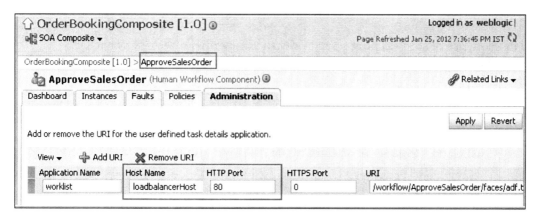

Seeding organizational users and groups

When human task flow components are created at design time, they are simply mapped to logical or application roles. Upon deployment to the Human Workflow Service Engine, you need to assign real human users to participate and act on workflow tasks. During runtime, participants can act on tasks from the worklist application, such as approve/reject a sales order, delegate approvals, provide feedback on a help desk request, and so on. To engage real users, it is necessary to integrate a directory service, maintaining your organization's users and groups, such as an LDAP server, with the infrastructure running your composites.

By default, the underlying Oracle WebLogic Server identity service uses an embedded LDAP server as the default authentication provider. The following screenshot shows the visual steps to change your default authentication provider in an existing security realm to an existing LDAP-based directory server:

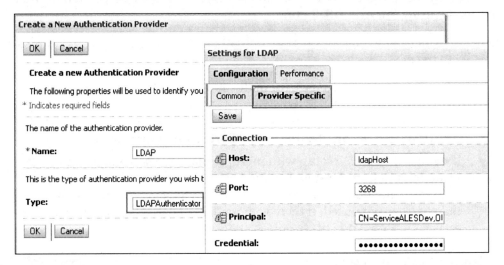

The sequence of steps to plug your infrastructure with a directory service is described here:

1. Log in to the Oracle WebLogic Server Administration Console.
2. Click on **Security Realms** under the **Your Application's Security Settings** pane.
3. Click on the name of a realm in the list (**myrealm** is the default realm).
4. Navigate to **Providers | Authentication** and click on the **New** button.
5. When the **Create a New Authentication Provider** page appears, type a name for the provider (for example, LDAP) and from the **Type** dropdown select **LDAPAuthenticator**.

6. Clicking on **OK** will create the authentication provider, but you will have to configure it to point it to an actual LDAP server.

7. Click on the authentication provider that you just created.

8. From the **Control Flag** drop-down list, choose **SUFFICIENT** (do the same for all other authenticators too) and click on **Save**. This flag instructs the WebLogic Server to accept authentication from this authenticator and not to invoke additional authenticators. If the authentication fails, the server attempts to authenticate a user by using the next authenticator in the hierarchy list.

9. Next, go to the **Provider Specific** tab where you have to specify connection parameters of the authenticator server. See the following table for an explanation of the additional attributes for the LDAP authenticator:

Provider Specific Property	Remarks
Host	This is the hostname or IP address of the authenticator (for example, `ausdcx641dap.packt.com`).
Port	This is the port number on which the authenticator server is running. Default value is `389`.
Principal	This is **Distinguished Name** (**DN**) of the authentication server user that WebLogic Server should use when connecting to it. An example principal is `CN=ServiceLDAP,OU=Service Accounts,DC=packt,DC=com`.
Credential	The credential property is usually a password used to connect to the authenticator server.
User Base DN	This is the base DN of the tree in the LDAP directory that contains users (for example, `'DC=packt,DC=com'`).
Group Base DN	This is the base DN of the tree in the LDAP directory that contains groups.
Use Retrieved User Name as Principal	This property specifies whether or not to use the user name retrieved from the LDAP server as the principal in the subject.
User Name Attribute	This is the attribute of an LDAP user object class that specifies the name of the user (for example, UID, CN, MAIL). An example User Name Attribute could be `sAMAccountName`.

10. Enter the provider-specific information about the authentication provider, check the **Use Retrieved User Name as Principal** checkbox, and click on **Save**.

11. These properties are sufficient to connect to an LDAP server. Use default settings for the rest of the fields in case you don't have valid values for them.

12. Click on **Security Realms | Providers | Authentication** to return to the list of authentication providers and click on **Reorder** to move the new provider to the top.

13. After reordering, **DefaultAuthenticator** should appear at the bottom of the list. This action enables the system to handle logins such as weblogic that are not typically in an LDAP directory, but still must be authenticated to start the server.

14. Once these changes are saved and activated, a restart of both the admin and all managed servers is required.

After the restart, under the **Users and Groups** tab in **Security Realms** you would see all of your organization's users and groups listed alphabetically. By default, Oracle WebLogic Server displays only a maximum of 1000 users and groups. Click on **Customize this table** and use the filter to limit the results.

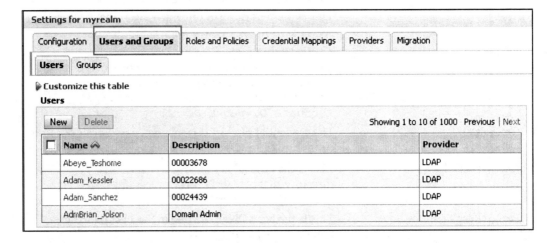

If multiple authentication providers are configured, authentication falls through all of them, according to the control flags set. The **Java Portlet Specification (JPS)**, however, provides authorization against only the first entry in the hierarchy list of providers. An alternative LDAP authentication provider can be configured for the worklist application, but **Oracle Platform Security Services (OPSS)** does not support multiple authenticators. The provider to be used for Human Workflow authentication must be the first one listed in the order of authentication providers.

The chapter contains a `Readme.txt` file along with WLST scripts to be used to connect your WebLogic Server with an LDAP authentication provider.

By default, only user names in human tasks are case agnostic (case insensitive). This behavior is controlled by the value of the `caseSensitive` property in **System MBeans Browser** for users and this property is set to `false` by default. Group names in human tasks must be identical to what is seeded in the user directory. However, if you also want group names in human tasks to be case agnostic, you must set the `caseSensitiveGroups` property to `false`. To enable case agnostic behavior for group names in human tasks, perform the following steps:

1. Log in to Oracle Enterprise Manager Fusion Middleware Control.
2. Right-click on **soa-infra** and navigate to **Administration | System MBean Browser**.
3. Expand **Application Defined MBeans | oracle.as.soainfra.config | [server_name] | WorkflowIdentityConfig | human-workflow | WorkflowIdentityConfig.PropertyType | caseSensitiveGroups**.
4. Click on the **Operations** tab.
5. Click on the **setValue** property.
6. Enter a value of false in the form field, and click on **Invoke**.

Mapping users and groups to application roles

The next thing would be to assign users or groups available from the directory server to application roles. For example, you might want to give certain users in the organization the right to access and edit human task configurations from the SOA Composer at runtime. Most of the time, process participants and users assigned to manual tasks in a business process would like to get this access to be able to work on task instances assigned to them. Access to users and groups with predefined application roles is granted by following these steps:

1. Log in to Oracle Enterprise Manager Fusion Middleware Control.
2. Under the navigator, select **WebLogic Domain | Farm_[Domain_Name] | Security | Application Roles**.
3. To search for a specific role, select the radio button beside **Select Application Stripe to Search**.
4. The dropdown is now enabled. Select **soa-infra** from it and press the ⊚ icon.

5. All default application roles for **soa-infra** are listed down. Clicking on the **SOADesigner** screen provides an option to add or assign available individual users or groups to a specified application role.

The following screenshot visually depicts how clicking on **Add User** opens a pop up where a user wildcard search returns a set of organizational users from which one user from the **Available Users** column is moved to the **Selected Users** column.

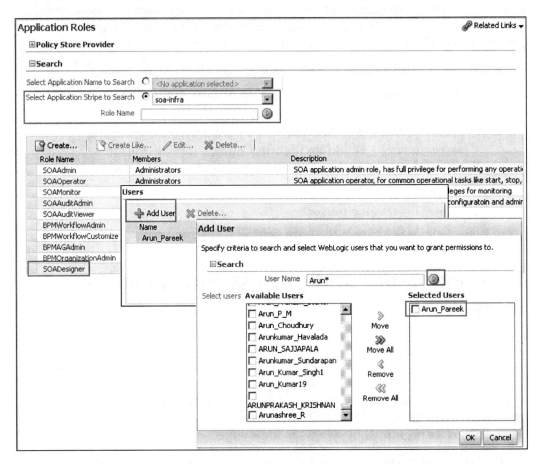

Migrating Human Workflow data from test to production environment

When process participants work on tasks assigned to them in the worklist application, they may not find the default inbox view very helpful. For instance, process participants may need to view additional columns required to prioritize tasks in the inbox. These additional columns may be added from the default available column list or you can use a mapped attribute (flex fields) to store and display important values from the task payload. Mapped attributes in Human Workflow store and query use case-specific custom attributes that typically come from the task payload values.

However, the problem it poses for you as an administrator, in the long run, is migrating worklist customizations across different environments. Assume that a bunch of participants create custom views, vacation rules, and add mapped attributes in the test environment which will then have to be promoted to a production environment. Oracle SOA Suite 11*g* provides a Human Workflow User Config Data Migrator that is available as an ant target and can be executed at the command line.

The Human Workflow User Config Data Migrator provides you with the following two operations:

- **Export**: This operation extracts all the human workflow user-configurable data from the source SOA server and saves it to an XML file on the disk.

- **Import**: This operation recreates all human workflow custom configurations and imports data in the target SOA server by reading them from the source XML file.

The Human Workflow User Config Data Migrator utility has two key files:

`migration.properties`: This file contains all required input properties in terms of key-value pairs for migration operations. It also determines what type user configuration has to be imported or exported.

`ant-worklist-t2p.xml`: This is an ant build file containing default ant target `runHwfMigrator` responsible for exporting customizations from one environment and importing them to another depending upon the operation.

The following screenshot shows a custom view configured by the weblogic user in the worklist application for task approvals. The **Priority Approvals** view is configured to accommodate and show the **orderDiscount** field (mapped attribute) on the worklist screen. We will now learn to set up and execute the Data Migrator wizard to extract these customizations in an XML file and then import them into another server.

To move human workflow data from test to production environments, perform the following steps:

1. Ensure that JAVA_HOME ($MW_HOME/jdk160_21) and ANT_HOME ($MW_HOME/modules/org.apache.ant_1.7.1) exist as environment variables. Also ensure that the PATH environment variable contains bin directories of both the JDK and ANT home (for example, $JAVA_HOME/binandANT_HOME/bin).

2. Open a command prompt or terminal and change the prompt to the $MW_HOME/ORACLE_SOA1/bin directory.

3. Create a migration.properties file in the bin directory to export user metadata for the worklist application (for example, group rules, views, mapped attribute mappings, and vacation rules) from the test environment. The following code snippet is one such example of migration.properties that contains properties to export custom worklist views. The connection and file location properties highlighted in the following snippet need to be replaced with values corresponding to your environment:

```
# Connection Properties
soa.hostname=localhost
soa.rmi.port=8001
soa.admin.user=weblogic
soa.admin.password=welcome1
realm=jazn.com
```

```
# Migration File Location
migration.file=/home/oracle/worklist_data/export_all_migration.xml
map.file=/home/oracle/worklist_data/export_all_map_mapper.xml

# hwfMigrator Properties
operationType = EXPORT
objectType = VIEW
name = ALL
user = weblogic
group =
grantPermission = true
migrateAttributeLabel = true
override = true
skip = true
migrateToActiveVersion = true
```

4. The following table explains each of the properties from the preceding snippet in detail:

Property	Definition
`migration.file`	This property specifies the directory location where task definition mapping data is exported to or imported from.
`map.file`	This property specifies the directory location where user configuration data is exported to or imported from.
`operationType`	Flag to specify whether to EXPORT data from the server or IMPORT into it.
`objectType`	This property specifies the type of custom object to migrate. Possible values are either VIEW, RULE, or TASK_PAYLOAD_FLEX_FIELD_MAPPING.
`Name`	This property specifies the object name if you have specified VIEW or TASK_PAYLOAD_FLEX_FIELD_MAPPING values for `objectType`. You can specify an individual `viewName` or `taskDefinitionId`. Specify ALL to identify all objects of this type.
`User`	This property specifies the user name for VIEW or RULE `objectType` properties. If a user is not specified for VIEW, it implies STANDARD_VIEW.
`Group`	This property specifies the group for only RULE `objectType` property to identify the group name. Leave it blank if user name property is specified.

Property	Definition
grantPermission	A `true` flag migrates view definitions and grants, whereas a `false` value migrates only view definitions. This is applicable only for `VIEW` `objectType`.
migrateAttributeLabel	A `true` value migrates only attribute labels whereas the `false` flag doesn't migrate attribute labels.
Override	While using the `IMPORT operationType`, this property specifies whether or not to override the data on the target SOA server if the flag is set to `true`.
Skip	If an error happens while migrating a `true` value of this flag, it specifies that errors are skipped and the migration utility continues processing. If this property is set to `false`, the migration is halted if an error occurs.
migrateToActiveVersion	A `true` value maps task definition IDs to the active version in the target SOA server instance.

5. The directory has an ant build file containing the `runHwfMigrator` default target. Execute the ant command by passing `ant-t2p-worklist.xml` as the file argument to export user configuration data:

```
ant -f ant-t2p-worklist.xml -Dbea.home=$MW_HOME -Dsoa.home=$MW_
HOME/Oracle_SOA1
```

If all properties are correctly specified, you'll get a successful build output.

6. The following screenshot shows how to verify whether the export was successful by locating the migration and map file in the directory specified in the `migration.properties` file. The `export_all_migration.xml` contains exported data for the **Priority Approval View** along with its view columns.

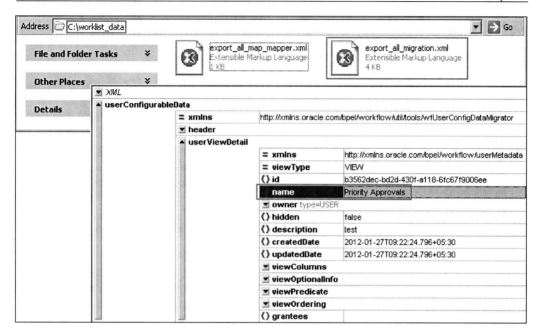

However, keep the following things in mind when using the migration utility:

- Only one type of data (`objectType`) can be exported or imported at a time.
- Each particular user's or group's data must be exported or imported in separate operations.
- Attribute labels must be exported or imported before mapped attribute mappings.
- Human Workflow artifacts such as task mapped attribute mappings, rules, views, and approval groups are defined based on namespace. The worklist data migration utility migrates Human Workflow artifacts based on namespace. Therefore, it is not possible to migrate Human Workflow artifacts based on a partition.

The test to production scripts, properties, and build output is available in the chapter code. Refer to `Readme.txt` to find out more about this.

Administering and configuring Oracle Business Activity Monitoring

Oracle Business Activity Monitoring (BAM) provides the tools for monitoring key business and performance indicators for business services in an enterprise. It allows correlating market indicators to actual business processes allowing business processes to change quickly or take corrective actions in the ever changing and dynamic business environment. Oracle BAM provides the necessary tools and runtime services to create enterprise dashboards that display real-time data inflow and metrics, and defines rules to send alerts under specified conditions.

Oracle BAM components and architecture

BAM Server is a Java EE application deployed to a standard application server and its architecture leverages the push-based mechanism (using AJAX) to deliver high a volume of data changes in business processes to the frontend web browser in real time. This is also a key differentiator from other reporting solutions that instead use the pulling approach for fetching data and report rendering. The architecture of Oracle BAM, with various components involved and message flow from data gathering applications to reporting service applications, is shown in the next screenshot.

Business data can be pushed to the BAM **Active Data Cache** (**ADC**) by a variety of ways such as having sensors in a business process, using an asynchronous messaging framework, sending data through a BAM JCA adapter, or even using a web service interface in its most simplified way. The ADC is a high-performance, persistent, and memory-based storage system designed to receive continuous data streams from various data sources.

A **Report Cache** is used to off-load the burden of maintaining changes to active data snapshot in memory from active data cache. Report Cache opens view sets and caches the snapshot and data changes before sending them over to the **Report Server**, which then renders static and active reports by applying report definitions to the retrieved dataset for presentation in a browser. The Report Server also manages persistent connections between web browser clients and BAM server.

The **Event Engine** does the task of continuously monitoring complex data conditions and implementing user-defined rules and takes corresponding action in response to those changes, including notifying appropriate user(s) with an alert and/or report(s). Lastly, **Oracle BAM Web Applications** are a set of web-based applications that are responsible for building and managing data models, creating views and reports, viewing reports, and performing administrative tasks through an access-controlled user interface. User management in Oracle BAM is delegated to the WebLogic Server console and role management to the Oracle Enterprise Manager Fusion Middleware Control.

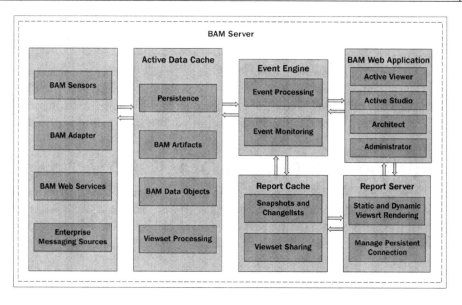

Configuring the Oracle BAM Adapter

The most convenient mechanism used to push data to the BAM Active Data Cache is by either using sensors in business processes or using the BAM Adapter. However, a BAM sensor action in turn invokes BAM Adapter APIs to send data to the active data cache. BAM Adapter configuration, such as the JNDI name for the connection factory, ADC server connection parameters, batching properties, and so on, can be done from the Weblogic Server Administration Console by executing the following steps:

1. Log in to the Oracle WebLogic Server Administration Console.
2. Click on **Deployments** under the **Domain Structure** pane and then select **OracleBamAdapter** from the list of deployments.
3. Navigate to **Configuration | Outbound Connection Pools | oracle.bam. adapter.adc.RMIConnectionFactory | eis/bam/rmi**, which is the JNDI location for the RMI connection factory.
4. Enter the values to connect to the BAM server in the **Outbound Connection Properties** table such as **HostName**, **PortName**, **InstanceName** (default is **ADCServer1**), and BAM server connection credentials.
5. Press the *Enter* key after setting each value and click on **Save**.
6. Update the `OracleBamAdapter` deployment to persist these changes to the deployment plan (`Plan.xml`) file in a new directory.
7. Click on **Finish** to finish updating the deployment for the Oracle BAM Adapter.

The Oracle BAM Adapter uses either RMI or SOAP communication protocols to connect to an Oracle BAM Server. You need to either configure the `eis/bam/rmi` instance under the `oracle.bam.adapter.adc.RMIConnectionFactory` group for using RMI protocol or configure `eis/bam/soap` under `oracle.bam.adapter.adc.soap.SOAPConnectionFactory` for SOAP communication. Using the RMI connection protocol provides better performance as the Oracle BAM Adapter internally invokes the active data cache Session Bean interface via remote EJB call.

Configuring batching in Oracle BAM Adapter

By default, the Oracle BAM Adapter operates in a synchronous mode, or in other words, the client thread blocks and waits for a response from the BAM Adapter operations. If the Active Data Cache Server is down or unreachable, operations are blocked until a JTA transaction timeout occurs.

To overcome this, it is recommended to enable Batching while using the BAM Adapter. If Batching is enabled, the BAM Adapter operations are invoked asynchronously, so that the client can continue processing in parallel while the BAM Adapter continues to perform its operations. It becomes the adapter's responsibility to handle batching operations, such as maintaining batch sizes, batch queuing, implementing retries, and so on.

Consider a case where a business process attempts to insert N records, using an Oracle BAM Adapter into the Active Data Cache. If Batching is not enabled, the BAM Adapter invokes the Active Data Cache API by sending one record at a time, and the client of the BAM Adapter will be blocked until all records have been processed by the BAM Server. With Batching enabled, the situation can be optimized by sending a batch of all records in one API call to gain significant performance improvement by reducing the remote method invocations and network round trips. Needless to say that since the invocation is asynchronous, the client can continue processing without waiting for a response from the BAM Adapter.

You can enable Batching through the Oracle BAM Adapter configuration wizard, or simply editing the BAM Adapter `.jca` file by setting the `InBatch` property to `true` and redeploying the SOA composite, as shown here:

```
<property name="InBatch" value="true"/>
```

A batch being sent to a BAM Server is controlled by the elapsed time configured for the `Batch_Timeout` property or when the number of records in the batch reaches the `Batch_Lower_Limit` threshold. All these and many more properties that determine batching behaviors, such as how many records can be included in a batch, how many batches can be queued up in the Oracle BAM Adapter, and so on, can be configured by performing the following steps (a description of these properties is provided in the next table):

1. Log in to the Oracle WebLogic Server Administration Console.

2. Click on **Deployments** under the **Domain Structure** pane and then select **OracleBamAdapter** from the list of deployments.

3. Navigate to **Configuration | Properties**.

4. Set the specific Batching properties and click on **Save**.

5. Go to the **Deployments** page again, select the checkbox for **OracleBamAdapter**, and click on **Update**.

6. Click on **Finish** to finish updating the deployment for the Oracle BAM Adapter.

7. Restart the SOA server at which `OracleBamAdapter` is targeted.

Property Name	Property Definition
`Batch_Lower_Limit`	This property determines the threshold representing the minimum number of records in a batch when a batch is to be sent to a BAM Server. The default value of `Batch_Lower_Limit` is `1000`.
`Batch_Timeout`	This property represents the threshold time after the Oracle BAM Adapter operations are invoked. The default value is `5000` milliseconds.
`Batch_Upper_Limit`	This property represents the maximum number of records to be sent in one batch and is set to a default value of `5000`.
`Block_On_Batch_Full`	The property represents a Boolean flag to indicate whether or not the client will block if the last batch is full. The default value is `false`.
`Number_Batches`	This property represents the number of batches that are allowed to be queued up before sending to a BAM Server. The default value is `10`.

Configuring Oracle BAM Web and ADC Server properties

Oracle BAM provides many advanced properties to control the behavior of the Active Data Cache and web server, available in configuration files that are located in the following directory on the host machine where Oracle BAM components are installed:

```
$MW_HOME/user_projects/domains/[domain_name]/servers/bam_server1/tmp/_
WL_user/oracle-bam-11.1.1/[tmpdir]/APP-INF/classes/config
```

The directory contains `BAMServerConfig.xml`, `BAMWebConfig.xml`, and `BAMCommonConfig.xml` files that are used to store properties for the Active Data Cache Server, BAM web server, and common properties across all BAM components. You can manually edit these configuration files and override their default values. These advanced properties can also be configured from Oracle Enterprise Manager Fusion Middleware Control by navigating to **Application Defined MBeans | oracle. bam.common | [bam_server] | Application: oracle-bam | Config** under the **System MBean Browser** in the **OracleBAMWeb** or **OracleBAMServer** menu. These property changes in the configuration files or MBeans require a reboot of the BAM managed server. For more information on these properties refer the documentation at `http://docs.oracle.com/cd/E15523_01/integration.1111/e10226/bam_config.htm#CEGHHFDG`.

The default host and port number of the Oracle BAM managed server are configured as `localhost` and `9001` respectively. It is very likely that your environment may have to point to a different URL of the BAM server. In this case, you will have to override the following properties in the configuration files mentioned earlier in this chapter:

- The `ApplicationURL` parameter in `BAMCommonConfig.xml` should contain the new URL of the BAM server (for example, `http://localhost:9011`)
- Change the `ADCServerName` and `ADCServerPort` properties in the `BAMServerConfig.xml` to the correct values of the Active Data Cache Server
- In `BAMWebConfig.xml`, the `ServerName` and `ServerPort` need to be changed to point to the actual BAM web server host and port (or the load balancer)

Using ICommand to import/export BAM data objects

Oracle BAM comes with a command-line utility to manage BAM artifacts and data models by interacting with the BAM Active Data Cache. In this section, you will learn how to use ICommand to export BAM data objects and their contents, which can then be imported into another environment. This is very handy in scenarios where you want to migrate data objects from one BAM instance to another (for example, test environment to production). Before running the ICommand utility, ensure that the `JAVA\HOME` environment variable is pointing to a valid JDK home directory.

Configuring ICommand properties

BAM ICommand uses BAM server configuration details in `BAMICommandConfig.xml` located in the `$MW_HOME/Oracle_SOA1/bam/config` directory for executing the export/import tasks. To configure ICommand, you need to modify the following two properties in `BAMICommandConfig.xml`:

- `ADCServerName`: This is the BAM server hostname. You can use localhost as the server name if ICommand is executed on the same host as the BAM server.

- `ADCServerPort`: This is the BAM server listening port. By default, it is `9001`. If you have changed the listening port of the BAM server, this property needs to be updated accordingly.

Optionally, you can configure default security credentials used by ICommand so that it will not prompt you to enter a username and password when executed. To configure the default username and password, you need to set the `ICommand_Default_User_Name` and `ICommand_Default_Password` properties in `BAMICommandConfig.xml`. Your ICommand properties should be set to something like what is shown here:

```
<ADCServerName>localhost</ADCServerName>
<ADCServerPort>9001</ADCServerPort>
<ICommand_Default_User_Name>user</ICommand_Default_User_Name>
<ICommand_Default_Password>password</ICommand_Default_Password>
```

Running ICommand

To run ICommand, enter the following command in a terminal or command prompt. You need to enter the full file name path for the export file, unless the file is not located in the current directory where ICommand is being run:

- **On Windows**: `%MW_HOME%\Oracle_SOA1\bam\bin\icommand.bat -cmd export -file <FILE_NAME>`

- **On Unix/Linux**: `%MW_HOME/Oracle_SOA1/bam/bin/icommand -cmd export -file <FILE_NAME>`

You should now be able to import the same data objects and their contents by using the ICommand import utility. This time make sure that the `BAMICommandConfig.xml` file has the ADC server host and port values of the server where data needs to be imported:

- **On Windows**: `%MW_HOME%\Oracle_SOA1\bam\bin\icommand.bat -cmd import -file <FILE_NAME>`

- **On Unix/Linux**: `$MW_HOME/Oracle_SOA1/bam/bin/icommand -cmd import -file <FILE_NAME>`

The preceding commands export and import the entire data from the Active Data Cache Server. You may need to migrate a particular type or subset of data. See the chapter sample code for more ways to use the ICommand utility.

Administering and configuring event engine and business events

The **Event Delivery Network (EDN)** in Oracle SOA Suite 11g provides a declarative way to generate and consume business events that are managed by the event engine. When a business event is published, other service components or database agents can subscribe to it. The event engine in Oracle SOA Suite 11g is a typical publisher-subscriber model that has two different implementations:

- **EDN-DB**: This implementation uses an underlying database as a backend store and depends on event delivery queue tables and stored procedures to manage events. You can find these packages in the [PREFIX]_SOAINFRA schema with the EDN suffix.

- **EDN-JMS**: This implementation uses backbone JMS queues. Event messages are published to and subscribed from the EDNQueue (jms/fabric/EDNQueue) under SOAJMSModule in Oracle WebLogic Server.

Administering and testing business events

Oracle Enterprise Manager Fusion Middleware Control provides the ability to configure, test, and manage business events used by various service components in a composite. Switching between database and JMS-based EDN is quite simple. Simply right-click on **soa-infra**, navigate to **SOA Infrastructure | SOA Administration | Common Properties | More SOA-Infra Advanced Configuration Properties**, and change the EdnJmsMode MBean to either true or false. By default it is set to false meaning that the infrastructure uses EDN-DB for managing events. To change the mode to EDN-JMS, set this property to true and initiate a server restart for the change to take effect. All other aspects of the EDN framework can be administered from the **SOA Infrastructure | Business Events** dashboard:

1. The **Business Events** dashboard provides the ability to search for a specific business event by specifying a full or partial event name and clicking on the **Search** icon.

2. Click on **Show Event Definition** to see the schema used to build an event definition.

3. The following screenshot shows various events that are published and subscribed to, along with their total **Subscriptions** and **Failed Deliveries** count. The **Business Events** dashboard also allows testing the EDN framework as a standalone application by selecting a particular event, clicking on the **Test** button, and invoking the framework with a sample payload based on the event type in the pop-up window.

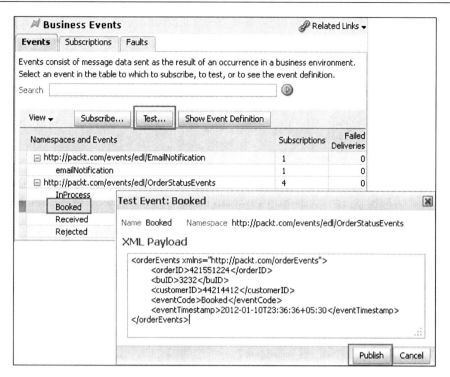

4. The message **The Event published successfully** would confirm that an event message is published to the backend framework used by the EDN.

5. You may also configure database agents to subscribe to events at runtime from the **Subscribe** button by either selecting an existing agent or creating a new one.

The **Subscriptions** tab in the dashboard is used to create, edit, and delete existing database subscriptions. When a business event is published, service components or database agents can subscribe to it. However, the **Subscriptions** page allows you to manage event subscriptions by database agents only. Service component subscriptions are created during design time and cannot be modified from the **Business Events** dashboard.

 If an SOA composite application includes a business event subscription and different revisions of the composite are deployed, event subscriptions from all revisions of the composite are active and receive messages. To receive an event with the latest revision of the composite only, it is recommended that previous revisions of the composite be retired or undeployed.

Business events that have faulted and been identified as recoverable can be retried or aborted by clicking on the **Faults** tab in the **Business Events** dashboard. The faults page enlists errors occurring in business events including the error message, if a recovery can be attempted for the fault, fault occurrence timestamp, event namespace, event name, subscriber, and the subscription type (database or service component). Recoverable faults for which recovery actions can be performed are made available by selecting the **Show only recoverable faults** checkbox and performing the **Retry** operation.

Even though the EDN framework is designed to pretty much be a black box, it provides the ability to view event payloads. You can do this in two ways. If the mode is set to **EDN-JMS**, pause consumption from the EDNQueue queue to be able to see what payload is being sent to the event engine. Follow these steps to do this:

1. Log in to the Oracle WebLogic Server Administration Console.
2. Click on **JMS Modules** under the **Messaging** panel.
3. Click on **SOAJMSModule**.
4. Click on **EDNQueue**.
5. Click on the **Control** tab.
6. Select **SOAJMSModule!EDNQueue** under **Destinations**, click on the **Consumption** button, and click on **Pause**.
7. Next time an event is published, you can view its details by going to the **Monitoring** tab, selecting **SOAJMSModule!EDNQueue**, and clicking on the **Show Messages** button.

Alternatively, if the mode is set to **EDN-DB**, event messages are intermittently stored in the **EDN_EVENT_QUEUE advanced queue (AQ)** table. To pause consumption on this AQ, connect to the [PREFIX]_SOAINFRA schema and execute the following query. The query will let the queue receive messages, but will not transmit them to subscribers.

```
BEGIN
  SYS.DBMS_AQADM.START_QUEUE (
    QUEUE_NAME => 'DEV_SOAINFRA.EDN_EVENT_QUEUE',
    ENQUEUE    => TRUE,
    DEQUEUE    => FALSE
  );
END;
```

If an event is raised now, it will be available in `EDN_EVENT_QUEUE_TABLE` and can be queried from the `USER_DATA` column, using the code below. The code queries for the business event payload for a particular composite instance. If you wish to access all the event messages, remove the `WHERE` clause from the query.

```
SELECT XMLTYPE.EXTRACT(XMLTYPE(T.USER_DATA.EVENT), '/EDN_BUSINESS_
EVENT/PAYLOAD/*/*/*[LOCAL-NAME()="EVENTDATA"]', NULL).GETSTRINGVAL()
EVENT_MESSAGE
FROM DEV_SOAINFRA.EDN_EVENT_QUEUE_TABLE T
WHERE XMLTYPE.EXTRACT(XMLTYPE(T.USER_DATA.EVENT), '/*/*/*/*/*[LOCAL-
NAME()="COMPOSITEINSTANCEID"]/TEXT()', NULL).GETSTRINGVAL() =
'990004';
```

You should, however, maintain extreme caution when you pause consumption on these queues for debugging purposes. Ensure that the consumption is resumed after you are done troubleshooting.

Administering Domain Value Maps and Cross References

Domain Value Maps (DVMs) are simply mapping objects. They are used in composites to map data that may be stored in one application in one format, to that of the target application in another format. For example, the contents of the `CountryCodes.dvm` file can have the following:

```
<?xml version = '1.0'?>
<dvm name="CountryCodes" xmlns="http://xmlns.oracle.com/dvm">
  <description>DVM description</description>
  <columns>
    <column name="CountryCode"/>
    <column name="CountryName"/>
  </columns>
  <rows>
    <row>
      <cell>US</cell>
      <cell>United States</cell>
    </row>
    <row>
      <cell>UK</cell>
      <cell>United Kingdom</cell>
    </row>
    <row>
      <cell>ZA</cell>
      <cell>South Africa</cell>
    </row>
  </rows>
</dvm>
```

In this example, the country code may be stored as US in one application and United States in another, and by using transformation functions within the SOA code, developers can look up and map values as needed.

Though database tables can be used as a substitute for DVMs, DVMs are static in nature and are optimized for speed and performance. DVMs are typically created by developers at design time, or they can be created manually and the .dvm files can be imported directly into the MDS via ant. See *Chapter 2, Management of SOA Composite Applications* for more details on how to import DVMs into the MDS.

Cross References are slightly different in that they are used to dynamically map values from one application to another. For example, you may have two applications, each maintaining its own Customer table wherein customer-specific information, such as customer ID, customer name, customer address, and other customer metadata, is stored. However, each application may have a different format for the unique identifier called **customer ID**. For example, SAP may create customer IDs in a format different than Oracle E-Business Suite, as shown in the following table:

SAP	EBS
SAP_001	EBS_1001
SAP_002	EBS_1002

Thus, Cross References are used to map these dynamic customer IDs across applications. Cross References, or XREFs, consist of two parts:

Metadata: It is created as .xref files and stored in the MDS.

Data: It consists of actual values that are stored in the XREF_DATA table in the database.

Similar to DVMs, Cross References can be created by the developer at design time, or they can be created manually and the .xref files can be imported directly into the MDS via ant. The good news is that from an administrative standpoint, aside from using ant to import .dvm and .xref files to the MDS, there is not much to do. In general, it is valuable to understand both DVMs and XREFs.

Administering DVMs

The SOA Composer, which provides access to modify the contents of DVMs at runtime, is a web-based application installed with Oracle SOA Suite 11g. This eliminates the need to use ant to reimport DVMs, if a single value changes. Furthermore, non-administrators can be provided access to the SOA Composer console by assigning the SOADesigner role to their WebLogic user account.

The expected administrative tasks related to DVMs include:

- Using ant to import DVMs into the MDS
- Using SOA Composer to add or edit values in a DVM at runtime

Perform the following steps to modify DVM values at runtime:

1. Log in to SOA Composer at `http://<host>:<soaport>/soa/composer`
2. Click on **Open**
3. Click on **Open DVM**
4. In the pop-up window, select a DVM and click on **Open**
5. Click on the **Edit** button
6. Click on one of the add (⊕), edit (✎), or delete (✖) icons, to modify a DVM row

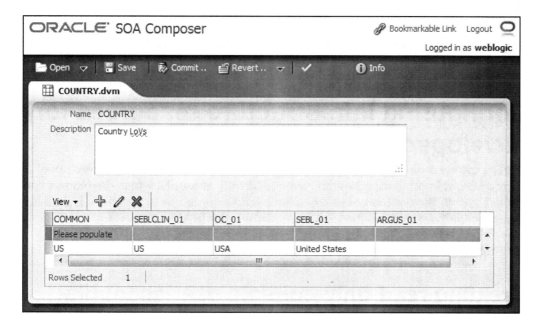

7. When done, click on the **Save** button

Administering XREFs

The expected administrative tasks related to XREFs include:

- Using ant to import XREF metadata into the MDS.

- Monitoring the growth of the XREF_DATA table.

- Monitoring the performance of composites that use XREF lookups. If performance is poor, consider creating custom XREF database tables.

Although Oracle SOA Suite 10g provided tools to export and import XREF data, Oracle SOA Suite 11g does not. Be careful when manually exporting XREF data from one environment (for example, test) and importing it to another (for example, production). Dynamic data and/or IDs may not be identical across applications in different environments, thus rendering the migrated XREF data invalid.

More information on how to create custom XREF tables can be found at http://docs.oracle.com/cd/E25054_01/dev.1111/e10224/med_xrefs.htm.

Configuring infrastructure resources for developers

Developers are a demanding bunch, always wanting access! In this final section of the chapter, we will discuss how to create read-only accounts, which developers can use to log in to the various consoles, to have read-only access to the MDS. It is always recommended not to share the weblogic password with developers.

In this section, we will also describe how to configure custom XPath functions.

Creating read-only console user accounts

We previously discussed how to give process participants access to SOA Composer. We may also need to provide developers with read-only access to the Oracle WebLogic Server Administration Console, Oracle Fusion Middleware Enterprise Manager Control, and SOA Composer consoles for them to be able to deploy and monitor business processes.

Follow the next steps to assign a developer the appropriate permissions for deployment and monitoring:

1. Log in to Oracle WebLogic Server Administration Console.

2. Navigate to **Security Realms | myrealm | Users and Groups**.

3. If an LDAP directory server is integrated with the WebLogic domain, a list of all users is available. Select a user by clicking on it (for example, john.doe).

4. Click on the **Groups** tab.

5. Add one of the available groups, and click on **Save**.

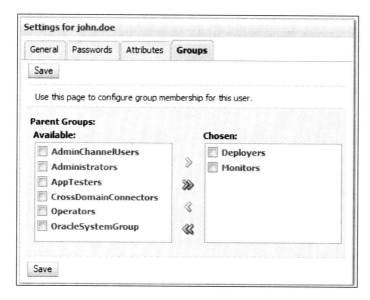

The **Monitors** group provides read-only access to Oracle Fusion Middleware Enterprise Manager Control, while the **Deployers** group grants an ability to deploy applications to the SOA server.

Creating read-only MDS database accounts

Developers will require a database account to access the MDS during their development, as it is necessary for them to create a database connection to the [PREFIX]_MDS schema in JDeveloper 11*g* in order to access MDS artifacts. Shared objects that are maintained in the MDS such as DVMs, schemas, and WSDLs need to be accessible to the developers during the development cycle. The last thing you want is to share the [PREFIX]_MDS schema password.

Follow these instructions to create a generic database role that can be granted to developer accounts. The following instructions assume that the schema name for the MDS is DEV_MDS:

1. Log in to the database with a user account with the SYSDBA privileges:

   ```
   sqlplus "/ AS SYSDBA"
   ```

2. Create a role called SOA_READONLY:

   ```
   CREATE ROLE soa_readonly;
   ```

3. Capture the output of the following commands and execute each of them:

   ```
   SELECT 'GRANT select ON ' || ' dev_mds.' || table_name || ' TO
   soa_readonly;' FROM dba_tables WHERE OWNER = 'DEV_MDS';
   SELECT 'GRANT select ON ' || ' dev_mds.' || table_name || ' TO
   soa_readonly;' FROM dba_tables WHERE OWNER = 'DEV_SOAINFRA';
   SELECT 'CREATE PUBLIC SYNONYM ' || table_name || ' for ' || owner
   || '.' || table_name || ';' FROM dba_tables WHERE OWNER = 'DEV_
   MDS';
   ```

4. Grant execute permissions to SOA_READONLY for specific packages:

   ```
   GRANT execute ON dev_mds.mds_internal_common TO soa_readonly;
   GRANT execute ON dev_mds.mds_internal_shredded TO soa_readonly;
   GRANT execute ON dev_mds.mds_internal_utils TO soa_readonly;
   ```

5. Create public synonyms for these packages:

   ```
   CREATE PUBLIC SYNONYM mds_internal_common for dev_mds.mds_
   internal_common;
   CREATE PUBLIC SYNONYM mds_internal_shredded for dev_mds.mds_
   internal_shredded;
   CREATE PUBLIC SYNONYM mds_internal_utils for dev_mds.mds_internal_
   utils;
   ```

6. Create your developer account:

   ```
   CREATE USER developer IDENTIFIED BY welcome1;
   GRANT resource, connect, soa_readonly TO developer;
   ```

Setting up custom XPath

Developers use a multitude of XPath functions as they are developing their SOA code. These functions are mostly used within transformation files (that is, xsl files) or assignment activities.

There may be cases where developers create their own custom XPath functions in Java, but they must be deployed to the server to be available to the composite during runtime. Custom XPath functions are available under the **User Defined Extension Function** palette. The `validateSchematron()` function, as depicted in the following screenshot, is a user created custom function that validates the input XML for business content. Though describing how to create custom XPath functions is beyond the scope of this book, the deployment of them is not.

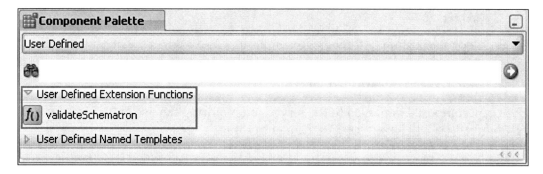

To deploy a custom XPath function to Oracle SOA Suite 11g:

1. Get a copy of the JAR file with the custom XPath function(s) (for example, `customXPathFunctions.jar`).

2. Get the following information from the developer of the custom XPath function:

    ◦ Namespace of the class (for example, `http://www.mycompany.com/XSL/Transform/java/mycompany.functions.xpath.myFunctions`)

    ◦ Namespace prefix (for example, `utl`)

    ◦ Fully qualified name of the Java class (for example, `com.mycompany.functions.xpath.myFunctions`)

    ◦ Name of the XPath function (for example, `validateSchematron`)

    ◦ Details on the parameters

3. Edit the file `$MW_HOME/Oracle_SOA1/soa/modules/oracle.soa.ext_11.1.1/classes/META-INF/ext-soa-xpath-functions-config.xml`.

4. Add the namespace and prefix as highlighted here:

```
<soa-xpath-functions xmlns="http://xmlns.oracle.com/soa/config/
xpath" xmlns:<prefix>="<namespace>">
```

5. Add the following snippet to the bottom of the file, using values from step 1:

```
<function name="utl:validateSchematron">
  <className>com.mycompany.functions.xpath.myFunction
  </className>
  <return type="string"/>
  <params>
    <param name="formatString" type="string" minOccurs="0"/>
  </params>
</function>
```

6. Copy the custom JAR file (for example, `customXPathFunctions.jar`) to `$MW_HOME/user_projects/domains/[soa_domain]/lib`.

7. Restart the SOA managed server.

Now, any composite deployed to the server and requiring the use of these custom XPath functions will have access to them at runtime.

Summary

This was quite a long chapter and a lot of diverse topics were presented. The goal was to provide you with different subject areas that can be referenced at any time on an as-needed basis. Oracle Fusion Middleware Enterprise Manager Control provides end-to-end administration capabilities and navigating it can be overwhelming at first. BPEL, Mediator, UMS, BAM, and Human Workflow components were covered in varying detail. Numerous administrative areas of Oracle SOA Suite 11*g* have also been detailed including areas of administration and configuration of the service engines, a scripted mechanism to starting up and shutting down the infrastructure, administering DVMs and XREFs, performing log rotation, and creating read-only MDS accounts for developers.

In the next chapter, you will learn the art of troubleshooting issues, exceptions, and common problems associated with the Oracle SOA Suite 11*g* platform.

6

Troubleshooting the Oracle SOA Suite 11*g* Infrastructure

It is almost a guarantee that administrators of Oracle SOA Suite 11*g* will have a need to continuously address issues within the infrastructure. Sometimes developers may report deployment issues in the non-production environments. Other times, the administrator may get an automated alert regarding an infrastructure failure. In many cases, the root causes of these issues are clear. For example, if a composite instance that inserts a record to a database fails with an ORA-12541, that is quite straightforward, as the error indicates that the database listener is unreachable. Simply starting up the listener should resolve this problem.

However, there are many cases where the error thrown requires a deeper level of troubleshooting to resolve. For example, if an SOA managed server crashes or crashes frequently, this is obviously not normal behavior and a root cause needs to be identified. Is it because the JVM ran out of memory? Or is it due to corruption in the persistent stores? Even if it is confirmed that an OutOfMemoryError exception is found in the logs, why did this happen?

[The four core problem areas an Oracle SOA Suite 11*g* administrator will often troubleshoot revolve around infrastructure, code deployment, performance, and composite instances.]

There is no step-by-step guide that walks through exactly what to do in every scenario, as the types of errors you may encounter are endless. However, this chapter will address the four core troubleshooting areas to provide a guideline on what you should consider for your troubleshooting strategies. These are infrastructure, code deployment, performance, and composite instance errors.

Most troubleshooting guides, including the one included in the *Oracle Fusion Middleware Administrator's Guide for Oracle SOA Suite and Oracle Business Process Management Suite 11g Release 1*, simply list out solutions to common errors. In this chapter, we focus more on introducing a troubleshooting methodology, which, when coupled with the foundational knowledge that you have learned in the previous chapters, will better equip you with the ability to solve most problems.

We begin the chapter with describing the art of troubleshooting, which includes:

- Troubleshooting infrastructure problems
- Troubleshooting performance issues
- Troubleshooting composite instances
- Troubleshooting deployment issues

The art of troubleshooting—where do you start?

Troubleshooting is part art, part science. Without the proper understanding of Oracle SOA Suite 11g, it becomes very difficult to know what tools, features, and capabilities are available to help you in your troubleshooting effort. Furthermore, it helps to understand certain fundamentals on how both the infrastructure and transactions behave.

Fortunately, the previous chapters covered numerous areas to prepare you for this:

- *Chapter 1, SOA Infrastructure Management – What you Need to Know* introduced the various consoles, and more importantly the Oracle WebLogic Server Administration Console and Oracle Enterprise Manager Fusion Middleware Control. These two are the core consoles for all administration, configuration, monitoring, and management that you will need to perform.

- *Chapter 3, Monitoring SOA Oracle Suite 11g* described various areas of monitoring. You should now know how to monitor the Oracle WebLogic Server and the JVM, leverage SQL queries to obtain instance specific information, use the DMS Spy Servlet to get various runtime values, and have a thorough understanding of the various server log files.

- *Chapter 4, Tuning SOA Oracle Suite 11g for Optimum Performance* though focused primarily on performance tuning, described areas such as when, how, and why to modify JVM settings, connection pool properties, timeout values, and other service engine properties.

- *Chapter 5, Configuring and Administering Oracle SOA Suite 11g* talked about further configuration and administration of the infrastructure—everything from JCA binding properties, fault management, configuring timeouts, and overriding resource adapter properties.

With this, you are now armed with the tools and knowledge to troubleshoot any number of issues. However, before embarking on troubleshooting any issue, you must at least have some starting point:

- Is this an infrastructure issue?
- Is this a performance issue?
- Is this an issue specific to a single composite or instance?
- Is this a deployment issue?

Based on the type of problem, you can somewhat narrow down the troubleshooting activity. The goal in this chapter is not to walk through all actual errors and their resolution. You will encounter many examples of errors throughout this chapter, each and every one of them requiring further investigation. It is not often the case that you will stumble upon an error and immediately identify its resolution. Therefore, some of the other approaches you should consider utilizing are:

- Perform web searches for your error.
- Search within **My Oracle Support and the Oracle Technology Network** forums.
- Review the multiple log files (for example, `soa_server1.out`, `soa_server1.log`, and `soa_server1-diagnostic.log`).
- Increase logging to get more information about the error.
- Engage Oracle Support.

Troubleshooting infrastructure problems

Infrastructure issues can be related to problems starting up the server. Or the server being unavailable or unresponsive. Or transactions failing. It might even be due to errors in backbone resources that your infrastructure is dependent on, such as data sources and persistent stores. These are all examples of infrastructure problems, and in most of these cases it's the logs that will guide you to what the real issue is. In other cases, however, the log information may not be sufficient, at which point you may have to consider increasing the logger levels to obtain more information.

Extending logging

Chapter 3, *Monitoring Oracle SOA Suite 11g* includes a section titled *Identifying and viewing log file entries*, wherein we describe how to configure logger levels. For example, you can easily increase a logger from NOTIFICATION:1 (INFO) to TRACE:32 (FINEST) to dump more information into the logs. Regardless of the type of problem (including composite issues), increasing the logger level may temporarily help in obtaining more information.

Logger Name	Oracle Diagnostic Logging Level (Java Level)	
⊞ oracle.bpm	NOTIFICATION:1 (INFO) [Inherited from parent]	▼
⊞ oracle.integration	NOTIFICATION:1 (INFO) [Inherited from parent]	▼
⊞ oracle.sdp	NOTIFICATION:1 (INFO) [Inherited from parent]	▼
oracle.sdpinternal	NOTIFICATION:1 (INFO) [Inherited from parent]	▼
⊞ oracle.soa	NOTIFICATION:1 (INFO) [Inherited from parent]	▼
oracle.sysman	NOTIFICATION:32	▼
⊞ oracle.wsm	NOTIFICATION:1 (INFO) [Inherited from parent]	▼

Logger levels can help in providing more information on pretty much everything. The top-level logger names are shown in the preceding screenshot. For example, some of the loggers that can be modified include DVMs (oracle.soa.dvm), BPEL engine (oracle.soa.bpel.engine.*), Mediator filters (oracle.soa.mediator. filter), human workflow (oracle.soa.services.workflow.*), Enterprise Manager console (oracle.sysman), and Oracle Web Services Manager (oracle. wsm.*). There are too many loggers to mention and there is no comprehensive list that describes each one of them. However, many are self-descriptive, and often Oracle Support can guide you as to what you may need to increase during your troubleshooting efforts. The logs themselves can point you to a logger. Observe the logger highlighted in the following snippet:

```
<Aug 5, 2011 12:00:02 AM EDT> <Error> <oracle.soa.bpel.engine.
dispatch> <BEA-000000> <failed to handle message
javax.ejb.EJBException: EJB Exception: : java.lang.StackOverflowError
```

Here, the oracle.soa.bpel.engine.dispatch logger threw the StackOverflowError exception. Increasing this specific logger may (or may not) yield additional useful information.

An important thing to keep in mind is that loggers contain hierarchies. Exercise caution when setting root level loggers to FINE, FINER, or FINEST. Consider the preceding case where you have encountered an EJB exception in the BPEL engine. If the root logger (that is, `oracle.soa.bpel.engine`) is set to FINEST, all the descendants that inherit from it will have the same logging level. As a result, a large amount of unused log entries are produced, which might actually make troubleshooting the issue much more difficult. Therefore, if possible, you should set only the corresponding child logger (`oracle.soa.bpel.engine.dispatch`) to a higher level without enabling the root logger.

Using logs

You will likely notice a lot of errors in the `soa_server1.out` log file. The key is to be able to differentiate between infrastructure errors and composite instance errors. In most cases it is obvious, though some cases may require further troubleshooting. Here, we describe eight such examples of various error categories and how they are differentiated.

Infrastructure error—StackOverflowError

`StackOverflowError` is usually an indication of an infrastructure error, as the error does not appear tied to any specific composite. Based on the logger `oracle.soa.bpel.engine.dispatch`, it is thrown by the BPEL dispatch engine:

```
<Aug 5, 2011 12:00:02 AM EDT> <Error> <oracle.soa.bpel.engine.
dispatch> <BEA-000000> <failed to handle message
javax.ejb.EJBException: EJB Exception: java.lang.StackOverflowError
```

For errors like this, when you have little or no information even after you throttle all your loggers to full, it is wise to search My Oracle Support (`http://support.oracle.com`) or engage Oracle Support. In this particular error, it was actually related to a bug in the **Oracle Platform Security Services** (**OPSS**) module in Oracle WebLogic Server 11*g* (10.3.5), specifically in the `jps-api.jar` library. A patch was later released to address this issue.

Composite instance error—SOAPFaultException

There may be a large number of instances in the infrastructure that receive processing faults from external systems they are interacting with. Here, the Mediator Service Engine (as shown by the `oracle.soa.mediator.serviceEngine` logger) appears to have thrown a `SOAPFaultException`, which in itself is not very useful. However, the details of the error are quite clear. This is a business exception thrown by some external service or resource. Though there is no information here to tie it back to a specific composite or instance, the same error, in more detail, can be found in the `soa_server1.log` file, which will provide you with that information. Rest assured, this exception will also appear in the composite instance fault on the console:

```
<Aug 6, 2011 10:10:33 AM EDT> <Error> <oracle.soa.mediator.
serviceEngine> <BEA-000000> <Got an exception: oracle.fabric.common.
FabricInvocationException: javax.xml.ws.soap.SOAPFaultException:
CreateOrder failed with Message: Cannot insert the value NULL into
column 'OrderID', table '@Orders'; column does not allow nulls. INSERT
fails.
```

The error is obvious; a table column does not allow `NULL` and, therefore, insertion is rejected by the database.

Infrastructure error—DeploymentException

Some infrastructure exceptions are related to the backend components not being available or configured properly. Some of them may be categorized by a warning and not an error, but this is still a problem. Note the following error that appears to be related to a WebLogic JMS Server. In this case, the JMS Server named `CustomJMSServer` is referencing a persistent file store `CustomFileStore` that does not exist:

```
<Dec 25, 2011 7:30:41 PM EST> <Warning> <Management> <BEA-141197> <The
deployment of CustomJMSServer failed.
weblogic.management.DeploymentException: Internalerror activating the
JMS Server CustomJMSServer: weblogic.management.DeploymentException:
The persistent store "CustomFileStore" does not exist
```

Such exceptions can be resolved by making sure the backbone infrastructure required is in place. This can be resolved by creating the required filestore and restarting the servers.

Composite instance error—FabricInvocationException

FabricInvocationException is the most generic error reported by the Oracle SOA Suite 11*g* SOA Infrastructure. This could be caused by invalid SOAP requests, WS-Addressing issues, or even due to non-accessible endpoints. The following FabricInvocationException error provides a little information about its probable cause. Furthermore the Unable to access the following endpoint(s) explanation is also inadequate and in most cases could be misleading, as it may be related to any number of exceptions.

```
<Dec 29, 2011 11:45:06 AM EST> <Error> <oracle.soa.mediator.
serviceEngine> <BEA-000000> <Got an exception: oracle.fabric.common.
FabricInvocationException: Unable to access the following endpoint(s):
http://payment-processing-server-dev:7777/proc/servlet/createCustomer
```

By reviewing the nested exception later on (not shown here), you will find that this particular error was due to a timeout of the external service. Though technically this is not a coding error since it is something that occurred only at runtime, it is not an SOA Infrastructure error either, as it is related to an external service over which you may have no control. From a development standpoint, the developer should be able to handle these cases by enabling some type of retry and/or error logging. You can also enable more detailed logging for these issues by enabling debugging while starting the server as follows:

```
-Djavax.net.debug=all
```

You can also consider increasing the timeout for external service if these errors happen frequently. Refer to *Chapter 5, Configuring and Administering Oracle SOA Suite 11g* to see how you can do this.

Infrastructure error—Unable to allocate additional threads

This Unable to allocate additional threads error appears to be quite serious, but it really is not. This is clearly an infrastructure related issue though:

```
<Sep 30, 2011 11:30:04 PM EDT> <Warning> <oracle.integration.platform.
instance.store.async> <BEA-000000> <Unable to allocate additional
threads, as all the threads [10] are in use. Threads distribution :
Fabric Instance Activity = 1, Fabric-Instance-Manager = 9, >
```

This error is apparently due to a failed transaction that continues to retry, but there are no issues with ignoring this warning. The Oracle WebLogic Server is unable to process more messages in parallel, but has run out of threads which would eventually clear themselves up. It is possible to increase the number of threads, if this becomes a persistent problem. See *Chapter 4, Tuning Oracle SOA Suite 11g for Optimum Performance* for more details regarding tuning of threads.

Infrastructure or composite instance error— MDSException

The following exception is due to the fact that at runtime an XSD that was being referred from the MDS was not available:

```
java.io.IOException: oracle.mds.exception.MDSException: MDS-00054: The
file to be loaded oramds:/apps/Fault/Common/XSD/SalesOrderHeader.xsd
does not exist.
```

This actually could either be a coding error or an infrastructure error. Therefore, further investigation is required. If the soa-mds data source is unavailable, this error would be attributed to an infrastructure problem. If the data source is available though, it is likely due to the code referring to a resource that does not exist in the MDS.

Infrastructure error—BeanInstantiationException

By now you must know that the engine that is responsible to execute composite instances in your infrastructure is soa-infra, which in itself is a J2EE application. The soa-infra application, in some cases, may fail to load in all the managed servers across a cluster and is partially available due to the following exception:

```
Instantiation of bean failed; nested exception is org.
springframework.beans.BeanInstantiationException: Could not
instantiate bean class [oracle.integration.platform.blocks.cluster.
CoherenceClusterInterfaceImpl]: Constructor threw exception; nested
exception is com.tangosol.net.RequestTimeoutException: Timeout during
service start: ServiceInfo(Id=0, Name=Cluster, Type=Cluster
```

The above issue is due to the fact that the coherence multicast channel in use by the domain in a clustered mode, is overloaded. The coherence cluster address for the domains is set to a unique multicast address and port in the setDomainEnv.sh file. To confirm if the multicast channel in use is not overloaded, use a simple multicast test by following the next set of steps:

```
export PATH=$MW_HOME/jrockit/jrockit_160_17/bin/
export CLASSPATH=$WL_SERVER/server/lib/weblogic.jar
java utils.MulticastTest -N [managedServerName] -A [multicastHost] -P
[multicastPort] -T 10 S 2
```

The issue can be resolved by untargeting the soa-infra application from all servers in the cluster, bouncing back all managed servers, and retargeting it back to the cluster. This is clearly an infrastructure problem.

Infrastructure error—Unable to extend LOB segment

Not all errors are directly due to issues within your SOA infrastructure. All running and completed instances in Oracle SOA Suite 11*g* are saved in a backend datastore. Lack of free space in the database may prevent the composite instances from completing their processing. For instance, you are most likely to see the following exception if your database runs out of disk space:

```
oracle.toplink.exceptions.DatabaseException
Internal Exception: java.sql.BatchUpdateException: ORA-01691: unable
to extend lob segment DEV_SOAINFRA.SYS_LOB$$ by 128 in tablespace DEV_
SOAINFRA
```

These messages typically indicate space issues in the database that will likely require adding more data files or more space to the existing data files. Additionally, completed instances can be purged and disk space can be reclaimed by executing the purge scripts. You will learn more about this in *Chapter 8, Managing the Metadata Services Repository and Dehydration Store*.

We have covered several brands of exceptions that can be encountered to give you an idea of the types of errors that you might expect. It is impossible to provide a comprehensive list of errors, and our intent is to show you why we have classified some errors as infrastructure while others are composite instance ones. Most of the time it is obvious, but other times it is not. Differentiating between both helps limit your troubleshooting efforts to a particular area.

Using thread dumps

The following screenshot shows a warning on `AdminServer`. Warnings do not necessarily mean that a server is unresponsive, but are clearly an indication that you should look into the cause.

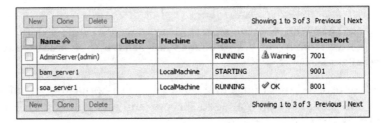

Without understanding that the health of managed server in the **Warning** state is usually related to stuck threads, you won't know that you need to click on **AdminServer** and navigate to **Monitoring | Threads** to get more information.

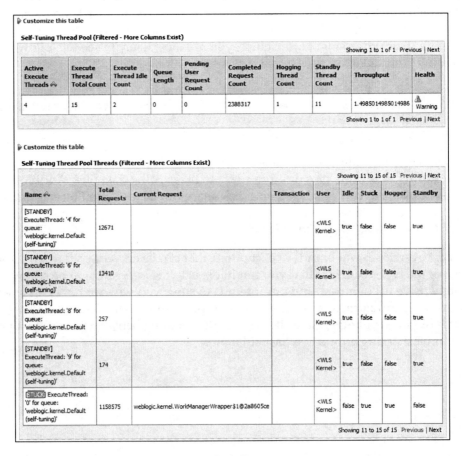

Under **Self-Turning Thread Pool** in the preceding screenshot, we see a warning which is likely due to the fact that **Hogging Thread Count** is greater than 0. In the **Self-Tuning Thread Pool Threads** table immediately below it, you can see the stuck thread, indicated by **[STUCK] ExecuteThread: '0' for queue: 'weblogic.kernel. Default (self-tuning)'**. All we can ascertain from this error is that ExecuteThread '0' is the stuck thread, yet this is still not enough information.

So we take a look at the $MW_HOME/user_projects/domains/soa_domain/ servers/AdminServer/logs/AdminServer.log log file. Here, we see the stuck thread, which apparently had kept on working for over 10 minutes:

```
####<Dec 23, 2011 6:03:49 PM EST> <Error> <WebLogicServer> <soahost1>
<AdminServer> <[ACTIVE] ExecuteThread: '8' for queue: 'weblogic.
kernel.Default (self-tuning)'> <<WLS Kernel>> <> <cb680017c6a0acfe:-
606797c4:134357968da:-8000-0000000000001062> <1324681429443> <BEA-
000337> <[STUCK] ExecuteThread: '0' for queue: 'weblogic.kernel.
Default (self-tuning)' has been busy for "658" seconds working on the
request "weblogic.kernel.WorkManagerWrapper$1@2a8605ce", which is more
than the configured time (StuckThreadMaxTime) of "600" seconds.
```

It turns out that we had just tried to unsuccessfully start the BAM managed server 10 minutes earlier. By observing $MW_HOME/user_projects/domains/soa_domain/ servers/bam_server1/logs/bam_server1.log, we find the same ExecuteThread '0' unable to register an MBean due to a java.lang.OutOfMemoryError exception:

```
####<Dec 23, 2011 5:53:36 PM EST> <Error> <JMX> <soahost1> <bam_
server1> <[ACTIVE] ExecuteThread: '0' for queue: 'weblogic.kernel.
Default (self-tuning)'> <<WLS Kernel>> <> <> <1324680816405> <BEA-
149500> <An exception occurred while registering the MBean com.bea:Nam
e=AdminServer,Type=WebServiceRequestBufferingQueue,
WebServiceBuffering=AdminServer,Server=AdminServer,
WebService=AdminServer.
java.lang.OutOfMemoryError: PermGen space
```

Fortunately, looking back at AdminServer.log a few hours later, we see that ExecuteThread '0' has become "unstuck":

```
####<Dec 23, 2011 10:42:42 PM EST> <Info> <WebLogicServer> <soahost1>
<AdminServer> <[STUCK] ExecuteThread: '0' for queue: 'weblogic.kernel.
Default (self-tuning)'> <<WLS Kernel>> <> <cb680017c6a0acfe:-606797c4
:134357968da:-8000-0000000000001070> <1324698162702> <BEA-000339>
<[STUCK] ExecuteThread: '0' for queue: 'weblogic.kernel.Default (self-
tuning)' has become "unstuck".>
```

In this example, we navigated multiple areas starting from the stuck thread to get to the root cause of the warning on the health state of AdminServer. To recap:

- We found AdminServer to be in the **Warning** state, which is usually due to a stuck thread.

- We confirmed that there was indeed a stuck ExecuteThread as shown on both the Oracle WebLogic Administration Console and the AdminServer. log file.

- By reviewing the soa_server.log and bam_server1.log files, we found startup errors in the BAM server log.

- The BAM server was unable to register an AdminServer MBean due to the java.lang.OutOfMemoryError exception that was thrown.

- Eventually the stuck thread was able to self-tune and eventually unstuck itself.

No action was needed in this scenario, but the root cause was identified by utilizing the thread dump and log files.

Troubleshooting performance issues

Troubleshooting performance issues is a rather vast and complicated area, which we will only be able to touch upon lightly. In general, performance becomes a concern when a transaction is unable to execute within a reasonable or expected time, or when the system is unavailable to process expected volumes. Sometimes this may be specific to a single transaction, other times it is something that is affecting every composite instance running on the server. The ultimate aim is to speed up the execution time of transactions by minimizing any undue delays and waits at the infrastructure level.

Server wide performance issues

When server wide performance problems occur, this should impact most or all of the transactions currently executing on your infrastructure. For example, if the dehydration store database is down or performing poorly, this will undoubtedly have an impact on all running instances.

Consider asking yourself a few questions to determine if there is an overarching infrastructure problem:

- Is logging in to Oracle Enterprise Manager Fusion Middleware Control extremely slow?

- Are all composite instances completing in an unusually longer period of time?

- Are the logs or your dehydration database growing unusually quickly?

- Are you seeing an exceptionally high number of errors in the logs?

These are usually indications that there may be a server wide performance problem. Performance issues impacting the entire server are usually related to either one or a few specific issues. In this case, take a look at the following.

Checking available disk space

Lack of available disk space is known to have an adverse effect on instance execution. Sometimes this is due to excessive logging filling up the disk or logs not being rotated periodically.

Following is an example of how to view the available disk space. Here, the /u01 mount point on which Oracle SOA Suite 11*g* is installed has 74.5 GB available, so space is not an issue:

```
root@soahost1:/root> df -m
Filesystem    1M-blocks    Used    Available    Use%    Mounted on
/dev/sda8          996      451          494     48%    /
/dev/sda9       815881   697454        76314     91%    /u01
/dev/sda7          996       36          909      4%    /home
/dev/sda5         1984      138         1744      8%    /tmp
/dev/sda3         1984      283         1598     16%    /var
/dev/sda2         5950     3842         1802     69%    /usr
/dev/sda1           99       12           83     13%    /boot
tmpfs             8023        0         8023      0%    /dev/shm
```

Checking CPU, memory, and I/O utilization

Some processes can hog the CPU, be it a backup job, a bug in AdminServer, unauthorized code deployments, or your monitoring tool agent. For example, some intelligent monitoring agents, such as the Oracle Enterprise Manager Grid Control Agent, perform constant queries against the database to retrieve metrics and statistics that may result in undue burden on your environment. Ensure that there is sufficient memory available and that SWAP space (Unix) or virtual memory (Windows) is not actively being used.

By reviewing the output of the Linux command vmstat as shown in the following snippet, we see that SWAP utilization is 0 MB (good!), the amount of free memory is 59 MB (keep an eye on it!), the numbers of bytes in and bytes out at this point in time (to measure I/O) are 2 and 16, respectively (extremely low!), and the CPU is 96 percent idle (no problem here!):

```
root@soahost1:/root> vmstat -S m
procs -----------memory---------- ---swap-- -----io---- --system-- ---
--cpu------
 r  b   swpd   free   buff  cache   si   so   bi    bo   in   cs us
sy id wa st
 0  0      0     59    402  15055    0    0    2    16    0    0  2
2 96  1  0
```

Checking operating system resources and logs

For example, in Linux, the /var/log/messages log reveals critical events at the operating system level. This log file can reveal errors that may have a direct impact on the stability, behavior, and/or performance of the SOA Infrastructure. In the following example, it appears that we have exceeded certain ulimit resources.

```
root@soahost1:/root> cat /var/log/messages
Aug 31 20:53:22 uslx286 sshd[22480]: fatal: setresuid 10000: Resource
temporarily unavailable
```

The lsof command in Linux can list the number of open files. Too many may exhaust operating system resources:

```
root@soahost1:/root> lsof | wc -l
6064
```

The ps command in Linux can list the number of running processes. Ultimately, too many of them may also exhaust operating system resources:

```
root@soahost1:/root> ps -A | wc -l
297
```

Checking JVM available memory and frequency of full garbage collection

Not enough available heap may result in excessive garbage collection, or depending on the garbage collection algorithm being used, increased pause times may occur which could also result in higher CPU utilization. Revisit *Chapter 4, Tuning Oracle SOA Suite 11g for Optimum Performance* for information on monitoring and running the JVM. Note that JRockit and Sun JDK have different tuning approaches and we recommend reviewing the *Oracle Fusion Middleware Performance and Tuning for Oracle WebLogic Server 11g Release 1* documentation for details regarding additional JVM tuning.

Checking connection pools

When connection pools are exhausted, this may lead to transactional failures. The errors though are quite obvious in both the logs and in the Flow Trace of the composite instances. Connections pools may be subject to constant dimensioning depending upon the throughput and interaction with the database.

Checking database performance

Often under heavy load, a larger number of writes to the database may have a direct impact on I/O on the database server. Tools such as Oracle Enterprise Manager Database Control or Oracle Enterprise Manager Grid Control can give you an insight into the performance of your database. Other times, data growth can also contribute to slow console performance. Oracle Database tuning is a huge topic in itself, but we provided a few recommendations in *Chapter 4, Tuning Oracle SOA Suite 11g for Optimum Performance*. Run a few queries to determine if your database has adequate free space to process instance requests, such as the following:

```
SELECT A.TABLESPACE_NAME TABLESPACE, B.AUTOEXTENSIBLE, B.INCREMENT_BY,
SUM (A.BYTES)/1024/1024 FREE_SPACE_MB, SUM (A.BLOCKS) FREE_BLOCKS, SUM
(B.BYTES)/1024/1024 ALLOCATED_SPACE_MB
FROM SYS.DBA_FREE_SPACE A SYS.DBA_DATA_FILES B
WHERE A.TABLESPACE_NAME=B.TABLESPACE_NAME AND A.TABLESPACE_NAME ='DEV_
SOAINFRA' GROUP BY A.TABLESPACE_NAME, B.AUTOEXTENSIBLE, B.INCREMENT_BY;
```

The output of this query is shown in the following screenshot. It shows that the AUTOEXTENSIBLE column of SOAINFRA data space is TRUE (good!), the amount of free space is approximately 835 MB (worrisome) of a total allocated space of 1050 MB:

TABLESPACE_NAME	ALLOCATED_SPACE_MB	FREE_SPACE_MB	AUTOEXTENSIBLE	INCREMENT_BY
DEV_SOAINFRA	1050	835.5625	YES	6400

Of course, you may just have too many transactions at which point your hardware can't keep up. But by monitoring the various hardware, operating system, and infrastructure metrics, over time you should be able to determine whether you have maxed out your current hardware capacity or not.

Is your environment always slow? Or does it demonstrate poor performance under heavy loads only? Monitoring the performance of your environment is not a one-time activity. You should have monitoring tools in place to help you pinpoint unusual or high utilization, and compare them to average usage times. In *Chapter 3, Monitoring Oracle SOA Suite 11g* we proposed using Oracle Enterprise Manager Grid Control, which provides end-to-end monitoring and alerting (and even some administration) capabilities for both your SOA Infrastructure and operating system.

By adding the SOA Management Pack, you would also be able to get composite specific information of all your environments through a single console. Otherwise you may have to rely on the scripts provided here and in *Chapter 3, Monitoring Oracle SOA Suite 11g* for to getting instance performance statistics.

Composite instance performance

When we refer to the inadequate composite instance performance, we mean to say that a particular composite is behaving poorly. In these cases, performance issues are often isolated to one (or a few) composites, but not all. For example, this could be due to the response times from external systems, a badly designed process, or due to a suddenly poor performing database or queue that the SOA composite is using to read or write data to.

Consider a scenario where your composite begins processing an instance by consuming messages from a JMS queue. During peak load, if sufficient threads are not available to the polling adapter, the overall performance of the composite is degraded. There may be no problem with your infrastructure and it may be capable of handling extra load by allocating more threads. The easiest way to overcome this bottleneck is to increase the value of the adapter.jms.receive.threads property that controls the number of threads from its default value of 1. This is a binding property that can be set in an individual composite as shown:

```
<property name="adapter.jms.receive.threads" type="xs:string"
many="false">4</property>
```

We cannot address all scenarios that may cause a specific composite to behave poorly, as they are unlimited. However, we can provide the means and direction to identify poorly behaving composites and help retrieve the specific composite instance ID of the offending instance, so that we may navigate to its details and find out more of what's going on.

Refer to the ReadMe.txt file of this chapter to get a copy of all SQL scripts listed here.

Average, minimum, and maximum duration of components

These queries look complex, but they actually are not. The reason they look complicated is because of the way they organize the data into a more easy to read format.

This first query, when run against the `[PREFIX]_SOAINFRA` schema, returns the name of the BPEL or BPMN component name, the partition it is deployed to, its state, as well as average, minimum, and maximum execution times along with the total count. The following query is filtered to retrieve statistics for the last 24 hours, via the `sysdate-1` clause. If you choose to, you can further limit the query to a specific composite (`COMPOSITE_NAME LIKE '%<composite_name>%'`) or component (`COMPONENT_NAME LIKE '%<component_name>%'`):

```
-------------------------------------------------
-- BPEL/BPMN AVG/MIN/MAX                      --
-------------------------------------------------
SELECT DOMAIN_NAME,
    COMPONENT_NAME,
    DECODE(STATE,'5','COMPLETE','9','STALE','10','FAULTED') STATE,
    TO_CHAR(AVG((TO_NUMBER(SUBSTR(TO_CHAR(MODIFY_DATE-
    CREATION_DATE),12,2))*60*60) +
    (TO_NUMBER(SUBSTR(TO_CHAR(MODIFY_DATE-CREATION_DATE),15,2))*60) +
    TO_NUMBER(SUBSTR(TO_CHAR(MODIFY_DATE-
    CREATION_DATE),18,4))),'999990.000') AVG,
    TO_CHAR(MIN((TO_NUMBER(SUBSTR(TO_CHAR(MODIFY_DATE-
    CREATION_DATE),12,2))*60*60) +
    (TO_NUMBER(SUBSTR(TO_CHAR(MODIFY_DATE- CREATION_DATE),15,2))*60) +
    TO_NUMBER(SUBSTR(TO_CHAR(MODIFY_DATE-
    CREATION_DATE),18,4))),'999990.000') MIN,
    TO_CHAR(MAX((TO_NUMBER(SUBSTR(TO_CHAR(MODIFY_DATE-
    CREATION_DATE),12,2))*60*60) +
    (TO_NUMBER(SUBSTR(TO_CHAR(MODIFY_DATE- CREATION_DATE),15,2))*60) +
    TO_NUMBER(SUBSTR(TO_CHAR(MODIFY_DATE-
    CREATION_DATE),18,4))),'999990.000') MAX,
    COUNT(1) COUNT
FROM    CUBE_INSTANCE
WHERE   CREATION_DATE >= SYSDATE-1
--AND      COMPONENT_NAME LIKE '%%'
--AND      COMPOSITE_NAME LIKE '%%'
GROUP BY DOMAIN_NAME, COMPONENT_NAME, STATE
ORDER BY COMPONENT_NAME, STATE
```

The output of the preceding query is shown in the following screenshot. Here, we can see that the **ChangeAddress** BPEL component had **112** executions within the last 24 hours with an average execution time of **0.279** seconds and a maximum of **7.300** seconds.

DOMAIN_NAME	COMPONENT_NAME	STATE	AVG	MIN	MAX	COUNT
default	ChangeAccount	Complete	0.144	0.000	1.300	36
default	ChangeAddress	Complete	0.279	0.100	7.300	112
default	DeleteAccount	Complete	0.547	0.100	2.200	62
default	DeleteAddress	Complete	0.620	0.300	0.900	5
default	UpdateAccount	Complete	0.486	0.100	1.400	85
default	UpdateAddress	Complete	0.550	0.300	0.800	2

This next query is specific to Mediator instances and provides exactly the same output:

```
-----------------------------------------------------
-- MEDIATOR AVG/MIN/MAX                          --
-----------------------------------------------------
SELECT SUBSTR(COMPONENT_NAME, 1, INSTR(COMPONENT_NAME,'/')-1)
PARTITION,
       SUBSTR(COMPONENT_NAME, INSTR(COMPONENT_NAME,'/')+1,
INSTR(COMPONENT_NAME,'!')-INSTR(COMPONENT_NAME,'/')-1) COMPONENT,
       DECODE(COMPONENT_STATE, '0', 'COMPLETED', '16', 'STALE', '2',
'FAULTED', '4', 'RECOVERY NEEDED', '8', 'RUNNING') STATE,
       TO_CHAR(AVG((TO_NUMBER(SUBSTR(TO_CHAR(UPDATED_TIME-CREATED_
TIME),12,2))*60*60) + (TO_NUMBER(SUBSTR(TO_CHAR(UPDATED_TIME-CREATED_
TIME),15,2))*60) + TO_NUMBER(SUBSTR(TO_CHAR(UPDATED_TIME-CREATED_
TIME),18,4))),'999990.000') AVG,
       TO_CHAR(MIN((TO_NUMBER(SUBSTR(TO_CHAR(UPDATED_TIME-CREATED_
TIME),12,2))*60*60) + (TO_NUMBER(SUBSTR(TO_CHAR(UPDATED_TIME-CREATED_
TIME),15,2))*60) + TO_NUMBER(SUBSTR(TO_CHAR(UPDATED_TIME-CREATED_
TIME),18,4))),'999990.000') MIN,
       TO_CHAR(MAX((TO_NUMBER(SUBSTR(TO_CHAR(UPDATED_TIME-CREATED_
TIME),12,2))*60*60) + (TO_NUMBER(SUBSTR(TO_CHAR(UPDATED_TIME-CREATED_
TIME),15,2))*60) + TO_NUMBER(SUBSTR(TO_CHAR(UPDATED_TIME-CREATED_
TIME),18,4))),'999990.000') MAX,
       COUNT(1) COUNT
FROM   MEDIATOR_INSTANCE
WHERE  CREATED_TIME >= SYSDATE-1
--AND    COMPONENT_NAME LIKE '%%'
GROUP BY COMPONENT_NAME, COMPONENT_STATE
ORDER BY COMPONENT_NAME, COMPONENT_STATE
```

Although the average execution time, as shown in the following screenshot, of the **DeleteAddress** Mediator component is **0.055** seconds, which is exceptionally low, the maximum time is **20.200** seconds. This may require some investigation if needed. You can further limit the query to a specific Mediator component, but it must be within the LIKE clause.

PARTITION	COMPONENT	STATE	AVG	MIN	MAX	COUNT
default	CreateAccount	Completed	0.678	0.000	23.600	181
default	CreateAddress	Completed	0.667	0.100	2.300	30
default	CreateCustomer	Completed	0.398	0.100	6.300	327
default	CreateOrder	Completed	0.822	0.100	13.000	894
default	DeleteAccount	Completed	0.586	0.200	1.300	14
default	DeleteAddress	Completed	0.055	0.000	20.200	1832

Poor execution times of BPEL, BPMN, and Mediator components may not be due to slowness of the infrastructure or code, but could be due to poor response times from the invocation of external services or resources.

These queries come in very handy, as they are simple to use and quickly retrieve good, aggregated information on your overall component instance performance.

Duration of single component instances

In other cases, the performance may be isolated to a single transaction, which could be related to one or more composite and/or component. Regardless, you will have to start somewhere and have some general idea of the composite that is reportedly responding poorly.

The following SQL query lists all BPEL and BPMN instances within the last 24 hours (see sysdate-1 in the WHERE clause) that have completed in over 10 seconds (see 10 in the WHERE clause):

```
--------------------------------------------------
-- BPEL/BPMN COMPONENT INSTANCE DURATION TIMES  --
--------------------------------------------------
SELECT CMPST_ID,
  TO_CHAR(CREATION_DATE, 'YYYY-MM-DD HH24:MI') CREATION_DATE,
  COMPONENT_NAME,
COMPONENTTYPE,
  DECODE(STATE,'5','COMPLETE','9','STALE','10','FAULTED') STATE,
```

```
      TO_CHAR((TO_NUMBER(SUBSTR(TO_CHAR(MODIFY_DATE-
      CREATION_DATE),12,2))*60*60) +
      (TO_NUMBER(SUBSTR(TO_CHAR(MODIFY_DATE-CREATION_DATE),15,2))*60) +
      TO_NUMBER(SUBSTR(TO_CHAR(MODIFY_DATE-
      CREATION_DATE),18,4)),'999990.000') DURATION
FROM    CUBE_INSTANCE
WHERE   TO_CHAR(CREATION_DATE, 'YYYY-MM-DD HH24:MI') >= TO_
CHAR(SYSDATE-1,'YYYY-MM-DD HH24:MI')
AND     (TO_NUMBER(SUBSTR(TO_CHAR(MODIFY_DATE-CREATION_
DATE),12,2))*60*60) + (TO_NUMBER(SUBSTR(TO_CHAR(MODIFY_DATE-CREATION_
DATE),15,2))*60) + TO_NUMBER(SUBSTR(TO_CHAR(MODIFY_DATE-CREATION_
DATE),18,4)) > 10
--AND     COMPONENT_NAME LIKE '%%'
--AND     COMPOSITE_NAME LIKE '%%'
ORDER BY COMPONENT_NAME, CREATION_DATE
```

You can further limit the query to a specific composite or component as needed.

From the output of the query shown in the following screenshot, we can see that there are seven instances that have taken longer than 10 seconds, and one in particular took **26.700** seconds. The good thing is that the query outputs the composite instance ID! Now, we can log in to the console and navigate to the Flow Trace of that particular instance to find out exactly what activity was taking so long.

CMPST_ID	CREATION_DATE	COMPONENT_NAME	COMPONENTTYPE	STATE	DURATION
85436814	2012-02-03 19:02	SimpleApprovalBPEL	bpel	Faulted	14.100
85436815	2012-02-03 19:02	SimpleApprovalBPEL	bpel	Faulted	14.100
85497427	2012-02-03 22:07	SimpleApprovalBPEL	bpel	Faulted	14.100
85497428	2012-02-03 22:07	SimpleApprovalBPEL	bpel	Faulted	14.000
85498409	2012-02-03 22:12	SimpleApprovalBPEL	bpel	Faulted	14.200
85498410	2012-02-03 22:12	SimpleApprovalBPEL	bpel	Faulted	14.000
85506489	2012-02-03 22:09	SimpleApprovalBPEL	bpel	Complete	26.700

The equivalent query for Mediator is identical in concept:

```
----------------------------------------------------
-- MEDIATOR COMPONENT INSTANCE DURATION TIMES    --
----------------------------------------------------
SELECT COMPOSITE_INSTANCE_ID,
  TO_CHAR(COMPOSITE_CREATION_DATE, 'YYYY-MM-DD HH24:MI')
  CREATION_DATE,
  SUBSTR(COMPONENT_NAME, INSTR(COMPONENT_NAME,'/')+1,
  INSTR(COMPONENT_NAME,'!')-INSTR(COMPONENT_NAME,'/')-1) COMPONENT,
  DECODE(COMPONENT_STATE, '0', 'COMPLETED', '16', 'STALE', '2',
  'FAULTED', '4', 'RECOVERY NEEDED', '8', 'RUNNING') STATE,
```

```
TO_CHAR((TO_NUMBER(SUBSTR(TO_CHAR(UPDATED_TIME-
CREATED_TIME),12,2))*60*60) +
(TO_NUMBER(SUBSTR(TO_CHAR(UPDATED_TIME-CREATED_TIME),15,2))*60) +
TO_NUMBER(SUBSTR(TO_CHAR(UPDATED_TIME-
CREATED_TIME),18,4)),'999990.000') DURATION
FROM    MEDIATOR_INSTANCE
WHERE   TO_CHAR(COMPOSITE_CREATION_DATE, 'YYYY-MM-DD HH24:MI') >= TO_
CHAR(SYSDATE-1,'YYYY-MM-DD HH24:MI')
AND     (TO_NUMBER(SUBSTR(TO_CHAR(UPDATED_TIME-CREATED_
TIME),12,2))*60*60) + (TO_NUMBER(SUBSTR(TO_CHAR(UPDATED_TIME-CREATED_
TIME),15,2))*60) + TO_NUMBER(SUBSTR(TO_CHAR(UPDATED_TIME-CREATED_
TIME),18,4)) > 10
-- AND    COMPONENT_NAME LIKE '%%'
ORDER BY COMPONENT_NAME, CREATION_DATE
```

You can further limit the query to a specific component, but it must be within the LIKE clause. The following screenshot shows the output of the preceding query. Once again, we can now navigate to the particular composite instance ID for further investigation.

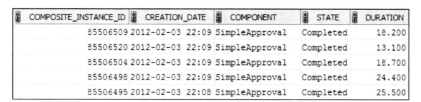

COMPOSITE_INSTANCE_ID	CREATION_DATE	COMPONENT	STATE	DURATION
85506509	2012-02-03 22:09	SimpleApproval	Completed	18.200
85506520	2012-02-03 22:09	SimpleApproval	Completed	13.100
85506504	2012-02-03 22:09	SimpleApproval	Completed	18.700
85506498	2012-02-03 22:09	SimpleApproval	Completed	24.400
85506495	2012-02-03 22:08	SimpleApproval	Completed	25.500

Troubleshooting composite instances

This section is not about troubleshooting composite instance failures, but rather troubleshooting composite instances in general. Just because a composite is not reported as failed does not mean it does not warrant investigation. Take, for example, a scenario where there are asynchronous processes that are deployed to the service infrastructure. By their nature, whenever there is a dehydration point in the process, the threads running the process instances try to access the underlying database schemas for reading, retrieving, and writing instance information. In these cases, it is entirely possible that there might be synchronization issues between concurrent threads trying to access the database schema and, as such, the default server level thread locking mechanism could lead to a deadlock. This would leave the transaction in a pending state and not faulted. This behavior, though intermittent, may require further investigation.

Chapter 5, Configuring and Administering Oracle SOA Suite 11g describes in detail how to administer and manage faults. Faulted instances, in a way, are easier to deal with than non-faulted instances as at least you have some error to begin with. Refer to *Chapter 5, Configuring and Administering Oracle SOA Suite 11g* to understand how to recover faults manually, automatically, and in bulk.

In the section titled *Identifying and viewing log file entries* in *Chapter 3, Monitoring Oracle SOA Suite 11g* we described how to search through logs for a particular ECID and how to enable Selective Tracing. This will help you trace the lifecycle of an ECID from beginning to end. You may have to increase logger levels if you would like more logging specific to a certain behavior (for example, if you only need to increase logging for adapter invocations).

How do you obtain the ECID anyway? There are a few approaches.

If you are troubleshooting a particular instance in the console, the ECID is on the top-right of the **Flow Trace** header (as shown in the following screenshot).

Another approach is by obtaining the payload from any of the applications within the integration. For example, if the message is still in an Oracle **Advanced Queue (AQ)**, it is possible to perform some SQL queries to retrieve the payload. The ECID is included in the `<instra:tracking.ecid>` header element of the payload as highlighted in the following code snippet:

```
<env:Envelope xmlns:env="http://www.w3.org/2003/05/soap-envelope"
xmlns:wsa="http://www.w3.org/2005/08/addressing">
  <env:Header>
    <wsa:ReplyTo>
      <wsa:Address>http://www.w3.org/2005/08/addressing/
      anonymous</wsa:Address>
      <wsa:ReferenceParameters>
        <instra:tracking.ecid
        xmlns:instra="http://xmlns.oracle.com/sca/tracking/1.0
        ">004hedvDpwsCOty6w7jc6G0001E000EUCV</instra:tracking.ecid>
        <instra:tracking.parentComponentInstanceId
        xmlns:instra="http://xmlns.oracle.com/sca/tracking/1.0">
        reference:9216307</instra:tracking.parentComponentInstanceId>
        <instra:tracking.compositeInstanceCreatedTime
        xmlns:instra="http://xmlns.oracle.com/sca/tracking/1.0">
        2012-01-16T14:47:14.802-
        05:00</instra:tracking.compositeInstanceCreatedTime>
```

```
      </wsa:ReferenceParameters>
    </wsa:ReplyTo>
  </env:Header>
  <env:Body>
    .
    .
    .
  </env:Body>
</env:Envelope>
```

Now that you have the ECID, you can use it to search the logs.

We now move to an example where perhaps no action would be necessary on the part of the administrator. For example, the console reported a failure of a specific instance as shown in the following screenshot. Upon navigating to the faulted instance in the console, we see how the instance retried itself and processed successfully.

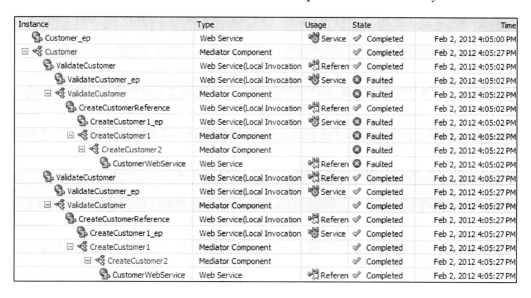

By clicking on **CreateCustomer2** to drill down in that component's flow, the output is as shown in the following screenshot. Here, we can see that there was an invocation to an external service, which apparently took 20 seconds (compare **4:05:02** to **4:05:22**). It turns out that we have a 20 second timeout configured on this reference. Excellent! This is the behavior we prefer. However, referring back to the preceding screenshot, we see that the instance was retried. This turns out to be a function of the fault policy attached to this particular composite. A job well done by the developer! The composite has retried and the subsequent invocation went through just fine. Note that the retried instances are actually new instances.

The reason why we see both the original transaction and the retried one in the same flow trace is because the same ECID is maintained when the instance retries.

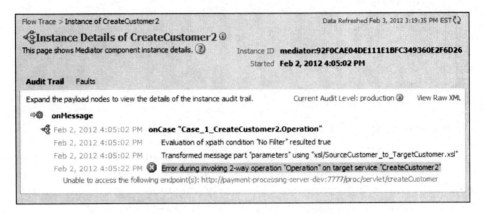

In this example, aside from trying to find out why the external service timed out the first time, there may not be much that is needed to do at this point.

Troubleshooting generic composite instance errors

More often than not, it is most likely that you will encounter a generic ORABPEL-05002 type error in your infrastructure. The error may be thrown for a host of common issues like transaction errors, adapter errors, coding, configuration, and even transformation errors. The ORABPEL-05002 message is a wrapper-type generic error message and is always associated with an embedded error message that causes the actual issue. It is, therefore, necessary for this reason to investigate an ORABPEL-05002 error in your log files and its entire trail to find out additional information associated with it. In case there is no additional message logged, set the BPEL Engine loggers to FINEST as discussed earlier. This will narrow down the subsystem or component causing the actual issue. Observe the following error snippet where an ORA-01432 error, which occurs due to an invalid database insert, is wrapped inside ORABPEL-05002 message:

```
Failed to handle dispatch message ... Exception ORABPEL-05002
Error while attempting to process the message "com.collaxa.cube.
engine.dispatch.message.invoke.InvokeInstanceMessage"; the reported
exception is: Exception not handled by the Collaxa Cube system. An
unhandled exception has been thrown in the Collaxa Cube system;
exception reported is "java.sql.SQLDataException: ORA-01438: value
larger than specified precision allowed for this column
```

Troubleshooting deployment issues

It is important to understand that deploying composites, in fact, consumes server resources. If you deploy tens or hundreds of composites to the server, you will see a direct impact on the size of the JVM heap (that is, the available heap size will continue to go down as more and more composites are deployed within a short period of time). We therefore recommend not deploying during expected heavy or peak times.

Chapter 2, Management of SOA Composite Applications describes how to use ant to deploy composite projects, but here we will take a closer look at the entire deployment process.

Knowing where to look

Let's observe the output of the ant deployment of the HelloWorld composite as shown in the following snippet. As you can see, the deployment failed due to a java.lang.OutOfMemoryError: PermGen space error.

```
deploy:
   [input] skipping input as property serverURL has already been
   set.
   [input] skipping input as property sarLocation has already been
   set.
   [deployComposite] setting user/password..., user=weblogic
   [deployComposite] Processing
   sar=/u01/svn/HelloWorld/deploy/sca_HelloWorld_rev1.0.jar
   [deployComposite] Adding sar file -
   /u01/svn/HelloWorld/deploy/sca_HelloWorld_rev1.0.jar
   [deployComposite] INFO: Creating HTTP connection to
   host:soahost1, port:8001
   [echo]
   [echo] ERROR IN TRYCATCH BLOCK:
   [echo] /u01/scripts/build.soa.xml:112: The following error
   occurred while executing this line:
   [echo] /u01/scripts/build.soa.xml:138: The following error
   occurred while executing this line:
   [echo] /u01/app/oracle/middleware/Oracle_SOA1/bin/ant-sca-
   deploy.xml:188: java.lang.OutOfMemoryError: PermGen space
```

Here, it is assumed that the SOA server has somehow run out of memory. This is, however, not the case. In fact, this OutOfMemoryError exception is on the machine executing the ant command, not the SOA server itself. Confusing, isn't it?

It is, thus, important to understand a few points regarding ant deployments:

- Deploying SOA composites is really a two-step process — the compilation of the code followed by the actual deployment itself.

- The compilation of the composite takes place on the machine executing ant, not the SOA server.

- The compilation process will validate external references. For example, if there is a schema imported in the composite that resides on some external web server, it is validated at compilation time. If, for example, that web server is down during the compilation, the compilation will fail.

- Although deployment failures are usually a result of some issue on the SOA server, that is not always the case.

In regards to the earlier error, as it is clearly thrown by the `ant-sca-deploy.xml` script, we understand it to be something on the machine executing ant. The solution in this case is quite simple, which is to increase the `PermSize` and `MaxPermSize` values in the `ANT_OPTS` environment variable prior to running ant. To do so in Linux is simple (if running JRockit):

```
export ANT_OPTS="-Xmx1536M -Xms1536M -XX:MaxNewSize=800M
-XX:NewSize=800M -XX:SurvivorRatio=12 -XX:+UseConcMarkSweepGC
-XX:+UseParNewGC"
```

Compilation issues

The compilation of a composite takes place via the package target in the `ant-sca-package.xml` build script. This target calls several other targets to complete the compilation process.

It first calls the `clean` target, which removes any existing SAR files:

```
clean:
    [echo] deleting /u01/svn/HelloWorld/deploy/sca_HelloWorld_rev1.0.jar
```

It then recreates the deploy subdirectory via the `init` target:

```
init:
    [mkdir] Created dir: /u01/svn/HelloWorld/deploy
```

The `scac-validate` target, which sets certain environment variables, is subsequently called to validate all resources within the code.

```
scac-validate:
    [echo] Running scac-validate in
    /u01/svn/HelloWorld/composite.xml
```

```
[echo] oracle.home =
/101/apps/oracle/middleware/Oracle_SOA1/bin/..
[input] skipping input as property compositeDir has already been
set.
[input] skipping input as property compositeName has already
been set.
[input] skipping input as property revision has already been
set.
```

Finally, the `scac` target, which performs the actual compilation itself, is called:

```
scac:
[scac] Validating composite "/u01/svn/HelloWorld/composite.xml"
[scac] error: location
{/ns:composite/ns:import[@location='file:/
u01/svn/HelloWorld/HelloWorld.wsdl']}: Load of wsdl
"HelloWorldWebService.wsdl with Message part element undefined in
wsdl [file:/u01/svn/HelloWorld/HelloWorld.wsdl] part name =
parameters type = {http://soahost1/SOA/HelloWorldWebService}
GetHelloWorldResponse" failed
[scac] error: location {/ns:composite/ns:import[@location=
'file:/u01/svn/HelloWorld/HelloWorldWebService.wsdl']}:
 Load of wsdl "HelloWorldWebService.wsdl with Message part element
undefined in wsdl [file:/u01/svn/HelloWorld/
HelloWorldWebService.wsdl] part name = parameters  type =
{http://soahost1/SOA/HelloWorldWebService}GetHelloWorldResponse"
failed
[echo]
[echo] ERROR IN TRYCATCH BLOCK:
[echo] /opt/subversion/deploy/build.soa.xml:112: The following
error occurred while executing this line:
[echo] /opt/subversion/deploy/build.soa.xml:127: The following
error occurred while executing this line:
[echo] /101/apps/oracle/middleware/Oracle_SOA1/bin/ant-sca-
package.xml:46: The following error occurred while executing this
line:
[echo] /101/apps/oracle/middleware/Oracle_SOA1/bin/ant-sca-
compile.xml:269: Java returned: 1 Check log file : /tmp/out.err for
errors
```

A lot of times when compiling composites, the error returned on the prompt is not descriptive enough. Additional information can be found in the automatically created out.err file. This is located in /tmp/out.err in Linux/Unix based operating systems and C:\Users\[user]\AppData\Local\Temp\out.err in Windows. If the error on the standard output is not clear, we always recommend reviewing the out.err file for additional information.

Most compilation errors are actually due to coding issues. In the preceding example, one of the schemas in the project was importing a non-existent schema. `HelloWorldWebService.wsdl` had the following import statement:

```
<xs:import schemaLocation="http://externalserver/schema.xsd"
namespace="http://soahost1/SOA/HelloWorldWebService"/>
```

Trying to access `http://externalserver/schema.xsd` returned an `HTTP Error 503. The service is unavailable` error. Because this imported schema was not available and could not be validated at compilation time, the compilation subsequently failed, as expected.

Another common issue at compilation time is when you use the `oramds://` protocol to refer to external resources that are available in the metadata store. Here, you can see that the composite build failed when `HelloWorld.xsd`, which was being referenced from the MDS, was not loaded during compilation:

```
oracle.fabric.common.wsdl.SchemaBuilder.loadEmbeddedSchemas
(SchemaBuilder.java:492) Caused by: java.io.IOException: oracle.mds.
exception.MDSException: MDS-00054: The file to be loaded oramds:/apps/
Common/HelloWorld.xsd does not exist.
```

It is important to understand that at compilation time, ant would refer to an MDS location that is configured in an `adf-config.xml` file. This file contains information to connect either a file or database based MDS. This file is available at one of the following two locations:

- Under the `[Composite_Home]\SCA-INF\classes\META-INF` project folder where the MDS configuration is specific to a particular composite.

- In the `[Application_Home]\.adf\adf-config.xml` file under the application folder.

The following snippet is an example of the database based `adf-config.xml`. This configuration file essentially tells your composite where your MDS is located at, so that `oramds://` lookups know where to look. As you can see, the highlighted text refers to the MDS database instance:

```
<?xml version="1.0" encoding="windows-1252" ?>
  <adf-config xmlns="http://xmlns.oracle.com/adf/config"
  xmlns:adf="http://xmlns.oracle.com/adf/config/properties">
  <adf:adf-properties-child
  xmlns="http://xmlns.oracle.com/adf/config/properties">
  <adf-property name="adfAppUID" value="TemporaryMDS-2296"/>
  </adf:adf-properties-child>
  <adf-mds-config xmlns="http://xmlns.oracle.com/adf/mds/config">
    <mds-config xmlns="http://xmlns.oracle.com/mds/config">
```

```
<persistence-config>
  <metadata-namespaces>
    <namespace metadata-store-usage="mstore-usage_1"
    path="/apps"/>
  </metadata-namespaces>
  <metadata-store-usages>
    <metadata-store-usage id="mstore-usage_1">
      <metadata-store class-
      name="oracle.mds.persistence.stores.db.DBMetadataStore">
        <property value="DEV_MDS" name="jdbc-userid"/>
        <property value="welcome1" name="jdbc-password"/>
        <property value="jdbc:oracle:thin:
        @//dbhost:1521/orcl" name="jdbc-url"/>
        <property value="soa-infra" name="partition-name"/>
      </metadata-store>
    </metadata-store-usage>
  </metadata-store-usages>
</persistence-config>
  </mds-config>
  </adf-mds-config>
</adf-config>
```

It is recommended for developers to set the MDS configuration at the application folder level since it is not deleted after compilation and applies globally to all composite projects.

Common deployment issues

Deployment issues have their own set of challenges. In some cases, the error is quite obvious:

```
deploy:
  [input] skipping input as property serverURL has already been
  set.
  [input] skipping input as property sarLocation has already been
  set.
[deployComposite] setting user/password..., user=welcome1
[deployComposite] Processing sar=/u01/svn/HelloWorld/deploy/sca_
HelloWorld_rev1.0.jar
[deployComposite] Adding sar file - /u01/svn/HelloWorld/deploy/sca_
HelloWorld_rev1.0.jar
[deployComposite] INFO: Creating HTTP connection to host:soahost1,
port:8001
[deployComposite] java.net.UnknownHostException: soahost1
```

In other cases, it is more difficult. Consider the common error shown in the following snippet that you may face during composite deployment:

```
<Error> <oracle.integration.platform> <SOA-20003> <Unable to register
service. oracle.fabric.common.FabricException: Error in getting XML
input stream:
 http://soahost1:8001/soa-infra/services/default/QueryOrder?WSDL:
Response: '503: Service Unavailable' for url:
```

This is a common deployment error that you are almost certain to encounter either when you are deploying a composite or when the composite is trying to register external references during server startup. However, you might find yourself in a fix when the same error keeps recurring, even when the reference service is available. What can you make of errors like these? Firstly, let's understand what happens here. When you start an SOA server or deploy a composite, the engine tries to activate the composite by trying to register with all its endpoints. If unsuccessful, the composite is marked as **inactive**.

As the cause of a composite becoming inactive when a target service is down, the errors in this case can be prevented in the following two ways:

- From Oracle Enterprise Manager Fusion Middleware Control, navigate to the composite dashboard and reactivate the composite. The composite will now once again try to establish a communication with all its endpoints and attempt to start gracefully. This is often the first attempt done by the administrator.

- You can also altogether avoid the composite going into a retired state in the first place by using abstract WSDLs of all external services. When you use an abstract WSDL, the engine treats it as local and keeps the composite active. The concrete WSDL can be copied to a shared MDS location and in turn be referred from the abstract WSDL. This must be done at design time by the developer.

To briefly understand the difference between concrete and abstract WSDLs, click on the ⊕ icon on the composite dashboard of the referenced composite service. This opens a popup showing the concrete WSDL.

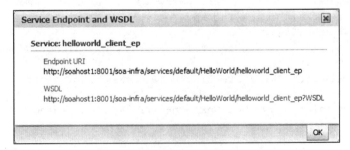

If you click on the concrete WSDL, a new browser window opens displaying its contents. In it, you can obtain the abstract WSDL as shown in the following screenshot:

```
<?xml version="1.0" encoding="UTF-8"?>
<wsdl:definitions xmlns:soap="http://schemas.xmlsoap.org/wsdl/soap/" xmlns:wsdl="http://schemas.xmlsoap.org/wsdl/"
xmlns:client="http://xmlns.oracle.com/SOA11g/HelloWorld/HelloWorld"
xmlns:pink="http://schemas.xmlsoap.org/ws/2003/05/partner-link/"
targetNamespace="http://xmlns.oracle.com/SOA11g/HelloWorld/HelloWorld" name="HelloWorld">
  - <wsdl:documentation>
      <abstractWSDL>http://soahost1:8001/soa-infra/services/default/HelloWorld!1.0/HelloWorld.wsdl</abstractWSDL>
   </wsdl:documentation>
```

The preceding screenshot shows a version specific abstract WSDL, which is:

```
http://soahost1:8001/soa-infra/services/default/HelloWorld!1.0/
HelloWorld.wsdl.
```

The default version can be referenced as follows:

```
http://soahost1:8001/soa-infra/services/default/HelloWorld/
HelloWorld.wsdl
```

Here, it is the responsibility of the developer to make this change and ensure that references are made to abstract versus concrete WSDLs.

Consider another scenario where you have multiple composites deployed to your infrastructure and they refer to each other to achieve a business function. During server startup, if one composite A calls another composite B with a concrete WSDL file, and composite A starts up before composite B, you will get the same error as shown earlier. This is because composite A is unable to load composite B's WSDL file, which is not yet available. Unfortunately, in Oracle SOA Suite 11*g*, it is not possible to control the order in which composites are loaded. In this case too, the same solutions that were discussed earlier apply. The second approach is preferred so as to save repetitive activation of composites every time.

Summary

Without the appropriate understanding of how the SOA Infrastructure and underlying composites behave, it would be very difficult to know where to begin when troubleshooting a particular issue. Fortunately, the previous chapters have covered a lot of ground in this regard.

The approaches covered in this chapter are intended to provide you with more of a troubleshooting methodology instead of a typical approach of listing out common errors and their resolutions. This includes:

- Understanding how and when to increase logger levels
- Understanding how to use logs and thread dumps to troubleshoot infrastructure problems
- Troubleshooting service wide infrastructure performance problems
- Leveraging SQL queries to obtain various composite durations to help identify composite instance performance bottlenecks
- Troubleshooting common composite instance issues
- Understanding the composite compilation and deployment process, and how to address common problems

This chapter is reliant on information learned in previous chapters, but hopefully introduces you to a different approach that will guide you in your troubleshooting efforts. There may be cases where you have exhausted your knowledge and skills in troubleshooting particular errors, and you should remember that Oracle SOA Suite 11g is still a relatively new technology and it is not uncommon to run into bugs or product related issues. Don't hesitate to contact Oracle Support for assistance.

The next chapter introduces yet another critical administration activity related to the configuration and management of security within your SOA Infrastructure. Businesses are relying more and more on establishing a central security management framework for service oriented applications. We will cover in detail how to set up, use, and administer the out-of-the-box declarative policy based framework in Oracle SOA Suite 11g.

7
Configuring Security Policies for SOA Composites

Securing composite applications is a critical and pressing requirement especially in a service oriented environment where business processes need to interact with numerous external service providers, vendors, and trading partners. Setting up security at the infrastructure as well as the application level is of primary importance while dealing with both on premise (departmental or internal) and external web services such as cloud based, across DMZs (Demilitarized Zones), and so on.

Whether it's choosing when to use SSL for encrypted HTTP transport, authenticating and authorizing users across different systems, or preserving message integrity, significant effort is put into protecting information that is critical and privileged to businesses. A security exposure can be disastrous and, therefore, protecting data in business transactions is critical to reducing security related risks. Add to this the fact that security requirements keep changing due to regulatory and integration needs and you can see why security is of utmost importance. As an administrator delegated to maintain control over security aspects of your SOA infrastructure in an ever changing and dynamic environment, it can be very confusing and cumbersome to implement a holistic security landscape. Owing to its loosely coupled and open nature, SOA implemented via web services requires deliberations over several security considerations.

Of the numerous what-ifs and how-tos, some of the main questions you will encounter while planning to put in place a protected infrastructure are:

- How do you authenticate that a service access requestor is who he claims to be?

- In what ways can access control grants be authorized to specific requestors based on their entitlements?

- Is there a way to ensure confidentiality and privacy to keep information secret when it is transmitted to external systems?

- How do you preserve integrity of messages to be sure that they remain unaltered during transit and also have non-repudiation to prevent replaying the same messages more than once?

These are a selected few of the issues you will need to consider. Rest assured you will come across many more! Security in general can be implemented at either the transport level by implementing SSL to protect communication channels between the provider and consumer of services, at the application level by using several message level security management techniques, or a combination thereof. For instance, an identification token can be generated and sent along with a message to authorize and authenticate service requestors, and/or message privacy and confidentiality can be achieved by encrypting the content of a message and obfuscating the sending and receiving parties' identities, while a timestamp in the signature prevents anyone from replaying this message after its expiry and, thus, providing non-repudiation. However, an important point to consider before building security into the application layer is that it makes the security framework inhibitive if security requirements change. It is, therefore, wise and smart to build and enforce security through the middleware layer instead, external to any individual application. Not only will this allow building a security framework that is flexible to changes and not requiring any change in the deployed applications, but having this strategy also allows for a centralized administration of security policies. If security requirements happen to change, a change in the declarative policy components and some supported configuration in the infrastructure is all that is required to cater to the change. The challenge, however, lies with the infrastructure administrator, like you, to manage and configure security across different integration points and components. Although security can be implemented in many ways, the preferred approach to implementing common security patterns in Oracle SOA Suite 11*g* is by leveraging **Oracle Web Services Manager (OWSM)** policies and this will be the primary focus of this chapter.

This chapter introduces you to the OWSM-based policy framework, how it provides security as a service, and how to implement it in your infrastructure in a step-by-step fashion. You will also learn to transpire the theories into real life use cases showcasing security implementations using OWSM.

Understanding the OWSM-based policy framework in Oracle SOA Suite 11*g*

OWSM lays the foundation to implement security through runtime enforcement and declarative policy attachment for different types of use case scenarios. For instance, OWSM has policies supporting **Security Assertion Markup Language (SAML)** token profiles, Kerberos, **Web Service Security (WSS)** 1.0/1.1, and **Secure Socket Layer (SSL)**, allowing you to easily attach policies for security, auditing, and management of components, services, and references in a composite as well as any standalone web services deployed to the infrastructure. It also provides consistency and ease of use in such a way that developers can attach a particular security policy at design time and system administrators can prepare the infrastructure for the policies to work. Security policies can be attached to any web service-based client apart from all the artifacts in the service composite assembly.

The policy framework is built using the **Web Services Policy (WS-Policy)** standard wherein each policy describes the capabilities and requirements of a service such as whether and how a message must be secured, whether and how a message must be delivered reliably, and so on. You can read about WS-Policy Framework in more detail at `http://www.w3.org/Submission/WS-Policy/`.

Oracle SOA Suite 11*g* has support for the following types of security policies:

- **WS-Reliable Messaging**: These policies implement the WS-RM standard over a wire-level protocol that allows guaranteed delivery of SOAP messages and can maintain the order of sequence in which a set of messages are delivered.

- **Management**: Management policies log request, response, and fault messages to a message log. Management policies may include custom policies and are useful to audit security implementations.

- **WS-Addressing**: These policies verify that SOAP messages include addressing headers to propagate conversation tokens. Transport level data is included in the SOAP header rather than relying on the network level transport to convey this information.

- **Security**: Security policies implement WS-Security 1.0 and 1.1 standards by enforcing message protection (message integrity and confidentiality), authentication, and authorization of service requesters and providers. They also support a range of token profiles including but not limited to username tokens, X.509 certificates, Kerberos tickets, and SAML-based assertions.

- **Message Transmission Optimization Mechanism (MTOM)**: These policies enable binary and streamed content, such as an image in JPEG format to be passed between clients and services.

Policy interceptor

OWSM uses a pipeline interceptor to execute different categories of policies in a predefined order for the request and response messages. The order of execution depends on whether the policy is being implemented at the client side or the service side. The screenshot under the *Putting it all together* section, discussed later in this chapter, describes a typical web service client making a request to a web service provider through an intermediate interception by an OWSM agent that executes the pipeline policies. There is a central **Policy Manager** application embedded in an application server to distribute policy enforcement tasks to OWSM agents. If the policy assertions are successful, the web service client and the invoked service are allowed to communicate.

Policy assertions

OWSM policies are made up of one or multiple policy assertions. For example, a security policy can be made up of a Log assertion and a WS-Security assertion. Policy assertions are executed in the order they are listed within a policy. An existing OWSM policy with **oracle/wss11_username_token_with_message_protection_service_policy** is shown in the following screenshot. Here, the Log assertion is executed first (logging the request message to a log file), followed by the WS-Security assertion (authenticating the requester based on the username token).

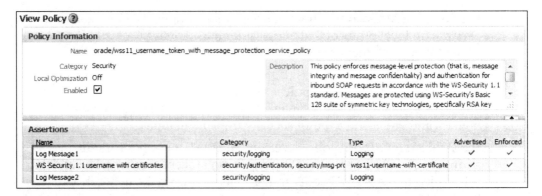

Policies and logging will be discussed in further detail in later sections of this chapter.

Policy assertion templates

OWSM policy assertions are instances of policy assertion templates that are added to a policy store at policy creation time. OWSM ships with a predefined set of policy assertion templates. Additional templates, to meet an organization's specific policy needs, can be created through Oracle Enterprise Manager Fusion Middleware Control, using built-in functionality or through custom implementations. Access the protected URL `http://[host]:[soaport]/wsm-pm/validator` with your administrator credentials to get a list of all policies and assertion templates available for your infrastructure. The following screenshot shows the output of the **Policy Manager Validator** page. On this particular SOA Infrastructure, a total of 88 policies are available.

Policy Manager Status: Operational

Policies (88)

Name	Latest Version	Description
oracle/wss11_kerberos_token_with_message_protection_client_policy	1	This policy includes a Kerberos token in the WS-Security header, and uses Kerberos keys to guarantee message integrity and confidentiality, in accordance with the WS-Security Kerberos Token Profile v1.1 standard. The Kerberos token is provided automatically by the operating system or manually using the JRE's kinit tool. This policy can be applied to any SOAP-based client. This policy is compatible with MIT KDC only.
oracle/wss_http_token_over_ssl_service_policy	1	This policy extracts the credentials in the HTTP header and authenticates users against the configured identity store. It also verifies that the transport protocol is HTTPS. Requests over a non-HTTPS transport protocol are refused. This policy can be applied to any HTTP-based endpoint. Note: Currently only HTTP basic authentication is supported.

Putting it all together

Typically in OWSM, a service policy is attached to a **Policy Subject** to enforce a set of predefined security rules. A Policy Subject is either a web service or a web service client. Both end services and their clients must be able to communicate with each other properly, often requiring a policy to be attached to both of them. If an end service is protected with a certain policy, a corresponding client policy is attached to the client in order to transform the outgoing SOAP message to a format expected by the server side policy. OWSM performs the following functions — many of them are discussed shortly in this chapter — to implement security between a client and a service:

- Intercepts the SOAP message request for the end service at the client side.
- Creates and injects a relevant token, depending on the policy defined, if the end service is protected by a security authentication or authorization token.

- Encrypts and digitally signs a message, if message protection and confidentiality has to be enforced.

- At the server side, OWSM extracts the relevant tokens in the message to verify the client's credentials against the configured identity store, checks the message timestamp, and also decrypts it, if it is encrypted.

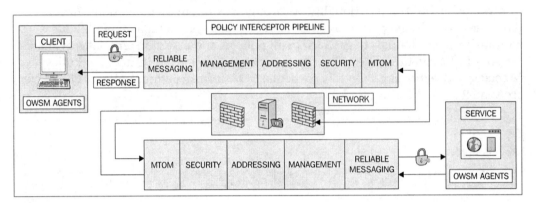

Configuring OWSM policies for Oracle SOA components

Since the 11g release, OWSM has been integrated with SOA Suite. This means you now have a greater ease of managing web service policies for security and administration of your SOA components. OWSM defines security through externally defined policies that are applied to the web service components at invocation time rather than applying security during implementation. At the server side, a security policy attached to the consumer adds the required security token to the SOAP header and performs assertions specified in the policy. At the provider side, an equivalent policy pair validates all the security tokens and delegates the assertion to the **Oracle Platform Security Services (OPSS)** layer, discussed shortly, which then verifies its validity against the configured identity store. Most of the security related configuration and administration can be done through Oracle Enterprise Manager Fusion Middleware Control.

A set of predefined security policies are persisted in the MDS, enabling them to be available at both design time and runtime. Policies in OWSM are defined generically without any context, that is, in general they are not application specific. There are a number of ways in which you can attach or detach OWSM policies to composite artifacts, which is discussed in detail later, but before that you should know that most policies require additional configuration on the infrastructure first. Consider a few examples:

- Policy endpoints that are password protected need to have an OPSS credential store setup.

- Policies requiring message protection through encryption require keystore setup with a self-signed certificate or one issued by a **certificate authority (CA)**.

- Authentication and authorization policies require an identity store to be set up, which can either be LDAP, OID, OAM, and so on.

- WS-Trust-based policies require Secure Token Service (STS).

By now, you must have realized that security policies don't work all by themselves. Defining security mechanisms through policies provides ease and flexibility to use them as reusable services that can be plugged on and off at will. As discussed above, they need the infrastructure to be set up first to provide the required implementation support. In the coming sections, you will learn in detail various methods to configure the necessary changes to your infrastructure so as to set up a backbone for the OWSM-based security framework to work.

Oracle Platform Security Services

Oracle Platform Security Services (OPSS) is the default out-of-the-box security configuration that OWSM relies on for most password protected and identity related services. The OPSS architecture externalizes security to let application developers focus on business logic and system administrators to manage security.

The following diagram shows the OPSS layered architecture that allows it to support different security and identity systems without needing to change anything at the application level:

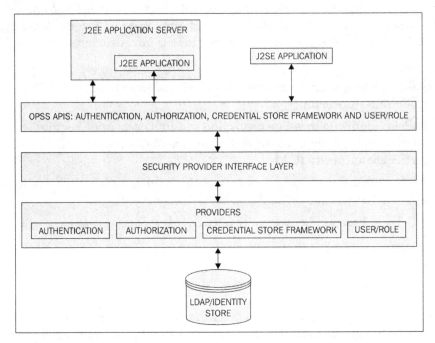

At runtime, OWSM hooks to OPSS via the `jps-config.xml` file (located at `$DOMAIN_HOME/config/fmwconfig`) from the `jpsContext` element with an attribute named `default`. An extract of `default jpsContext` in the standard `jps-config.xml` looks like this:

```
<jpsContexts default="default">
<!-- This is the default JPS context. All the mandatory services and
Login Modules must be configured in this default context -->
  <jpsContext name="default">
  <serviceInstanceRef ref="credstore"/>
  <serviceInstanceRef ref="keystore"/>
  <serviceInstanceRef ref="policystore.xml"/>
  <serviceInstanceRef ref="audit"/>
  <serviceInstanceRef ref="idstore.ldap"/>
</jpsContext>
```

A careful inspection of the preceding XML snippet gives a fair idea as to how OWSM looks up service instance references that are registered for OPSS. Among these services are login modules, authentication providers, authorization policy providers, credential stores, and auditing services. A detailed read about OPSS can be accessed at `http://www.oracle.com/technetwork/middleware/id-mgmt/index-100381.html`.

Understanding keystores and credential stores

A **keystore** contains keys used to sign, encrypt, and/or decrypt messages, and configuring a keystore to be used by the application server is mandatory while working with message protection policies in OWSM. A keystore can have multiple keys and each key in the keystore is referred to by an **alias**. These aliases and their corresponding passwords are stored in a credential store called a `cwallet.sso` file in an encrypted format. The keystore itself is protected with a password that is in the same file. When access to the keystore is required, the credential store is first queried for the necessary aliases and passwords. It is confusing to visualize what keys and certificates are exchanged in scenarios like message signing and encryption. But without a proper understanding of them, it will be impossible for you to configure security using OWSM.

Both the default keystore and credential store are domain wide artifacts that an application server expects under the `$DOMAIN_HOME/config/fmwconfig` folder. The keystore configuration is available in `jps-config.xml` under the `serviceInstance` element with an attribute titled `keystore`:

```
<!-- KeyStore Service Instance -->
<serviceInstance name="keystore" provider="keystore.provider"
location="./default-keystore.jks">
  <description>Default JPS Keystore Service</description>
  <property name="keystore.type" value="JKS"/>
  <property name="keystore.csf.map" value="oracle.wsm.security"/>
  <property name="keystore.pass.csf.key" value="keystore-csf-
  key"/>
  <property name="keystore.sig.csf.key" value="sign-csf-key"/>
  <property name="keystore.enc.csf.key" value="enc-csf-key"/>
</serviceInstance>
```

The preceding configuration in property name value pairs indicates that `./default-keystore.jks` is the keystore file of **JKS (Java Keystore)** type, and it is in the current directory containing the certificate keys responsible for message level security such as message signing and encryption. However, as stated earlier, the credentials required to access a keystore as well as the aliases defined within it are stored separately in a credential store. The credential store is a file-based store materialized as an encrypted `cwallet.sso` file and configured in `jps-config.xml` as shown:

```
<!-- JPS Credential Store Service Instance -->
<serviceInstance name="credstore" provider="credstoressp"
location="./">
  <description>File Based Credential Store Service Instance
  </description>
</serviceInstance>
```

The following diagram shows a logical depiction of the relationship between a keystore and a credential store. For the ease of explanation, the diagram depicts a single alias storekey that is used for all the keys in the credential store. The credential store is split into maps containing a set of keys that points to the actual credential. The aliases created in the keystore must have a corresponding credential in the credential store. The predefined credential map used in OWSM is `oracle.wsm.security`. For example, if you name an alias as `storekey` in the keystore, there must be a credential defined as `storekey` in the credential store. Such a credential is mapped by a predefined key name. The out-of-the-box keys defined in the credential store are `sign-csf-key` and `enc-csf-key`, used to sign and encrypt/decrypt messages. Custom `csf` keys can also be added to the credential store to map to different aliases in the keystore. Another important key is `keystore-csf-key` that holds the keystore alias and password used to open the keystore. When a policy is executed, it uses the username and password belonging to either `sign-csf-key` or `enc-csf-key` to retrieve the actual private key from the keystore to create a signature or encrypt a message by using the username as an alias.

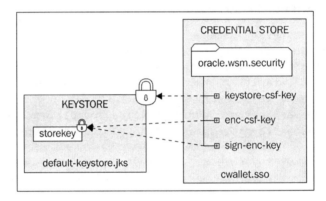

To establish a secured connection between the client and the server at runtime, it is necessary to export a client's key from the client keystore and import to the keystore of the server, and vice versa.

A credential store must not be confused with an identity store. A subtle and fundamental distinction is important to be made here—credentials and identities are not the same thing. Simply put, in OPSS, identities are what authentication requests are done against, while credentials are securely kept objects that are somehow presented to authentication providers to be matched against identities.

 Identity is what is authenticated, while a credential is the key information to authenticate identity.

Understanding authorization policies

Oracle SOA Suite 11*g* has a policy-based authorization mechanism in place to determine what permission a user can have when accessing infrastructure resources. Users or groups are mapped to an **application role**, which is a virtual group defined in a centralized policy store to access protected application server resources. Application roles provide authorization by decoupling your application level permissions with principles defined in identity stores, as any changes to users or groups in the backend store will automatically reflect their permissions when accessing protected resources. Oracle SOA Suite 11*g* defines a set of predefined application roles in its default policy store, which is file-based and available in the `$DOMAIN_HOME/config/fmwconfig/system-jazn-data.xml` file. A definition of an application role such as that of the `SOADesigner` role is shown in the following code snippet:

```
<app-role>
  <name>SOADesigner</name>
  <display-name>SOA Designer</display-name>
  <description>SOA Designer</description>
  <guid>81F7F169651A11E0AF6A79660AB4F93C</guid>
  <class>oracle.security.jps.service.policystore.ApplicationRole
  </class>
  <members>
    <member>
      <class>weblogic.security.principal.WLSGroupImpl</class>
      <name>Administrators</name>
    </member>
    <member>
      <class>oracle.security.jps.service.policystore.
      ApplicationRole</class>
      <name>SOAAdmin</name>
      <guid>81F7F160651A11E0AF6A79660AB4F93C</guid>
    </member>
    <member>
      <class>oracle.security.jps.service.policystore.
      ApplicationRole</class>
      <name>BPMWorkflowAdmin</name>
      <guid>81F7F165651A11E0AF6A79660AB4F93C</guid>
    </member>
  </members>
</app-role>
```

Notice that the SOADesigner role contains preconfigured groups, defined in the server by default, such as Administrators, SOAAdmin, and BPMWorkflowAdmin, and implements the oracle.security.jps.service.policystore.ApplicationRole class. Principles available in an identity or a directory server, such as existing organizational users and groups, can be added to either the logical groups associated with an application role or explicitly to the application role itself. *Chapter 5, Configuring and Administering Oracle SOA Suite 11g* described how to configure an external LDAP server and map real users to application roles.

Apart from application roles the system-jazn-data.xml file also contains application policies, which are **Java Authentication and Authorization Service (JAAS)** based policies, to define mapping rules between principals (users, groups, or application roles) and permissions for accessing protected resources. Policies registered in the policy store determine the permissions granted to application roles. Observe the following snippet from system-jazn-data.xml, illustrating how a default application role, that is, SOAOperator is granted the soadeploy permission to deploy composites to the infrastructure:

```
<grant>
  <grantee>
    <principals>
      <principal>
        <class>oracle.security.jps.service.policystore.
        ApplicationRole</class>
        <name>SOAOperator</name>
        <guid>81F7F161651A11E0AF6A79660AB4F93C</guid>
      </principal>
    </principals>
  </grantee>
  <permissions>
    <permission>
      <class>oracle.security.jps.JpsPermission</class>
      <name>soadeploy</name>
    </permission>
  </permissions>
</grant>
```

Should you need custom authorization policies, we recommend adding your own by granting proper permissions to your application roles and not modifying the default ones. You can even create a policy by granting permissions to specific users or groups, instead of application roles, but this tight association between physical principles and permissions is not recommended.

Configuring keystores and credential stores for OWSM

Ensure that you have JDK 6 in CLASSPATH to generate a keystore compatible with OWSM. You can then create a keystore with a key pair (self-signed certificate or one issued by a trusted CA) in it with the help of the Java keytool utility. Before you proceed with any configurations to set up OWSM-based security on the infrastructure, we recommend taking a backup of the jps-config.xml and cwallet.sso files in the $DOMAIN_HOME/config/fmwconfig directory. The following steps describe how to configure the keystore:

1. Open a prompt or terminal and go to the $DOMAIN_HOME/config/fmwconfig directory.

2. A keystore with a key-pair can be created by executing the following command. For example:

   ```
   keytool -genkeypair -keyalg RSA -alias storekey -keypass
   welcome123 -keystore default-keystore.jks -storepass welcome123
   -validity 3600
   ```

3. You will need to enter several subparts, which will form the distinguished name of your keystore, as shown in the following screenshot:

4. This will generate the default-keystore.jks keystore, which is protected with a store password valid for 3600 days, in the fmwconfig directory.

5. If you have received a security certificate from a trusted CA, import it to your keystore. An example is demonstrated with the following command:

   ```
   keytool -importcert -alias trustcer -file trusted.cer -keystore
   default-keystore.jks -storepass welcome123
   ```

6. Alternatively you can generate your own self-signed certificate and then import it to the keystore. For example:

```
keytool -exportcert -v -alias selfcer -keystore default-keystore.
jks -storepass welcome123 -rfc -file selfsign.cer
```

7. Next, you will need to configure the application server to use this keystore by logging in to Oracle Enterprise Manager Fusion Middleware Control and navigating to **WebLogic Domain | Farm_[Domain_Name] | Security | Security Provider Configuration**.

8. Select **Configure** in the **Keystore** section and provide a password to access the keystore and the key alias (`storekey` as alias and `welcome123` as password). As stated earlier, for the sake of this chapter the same alias is used for both these keys. However, they can be different.

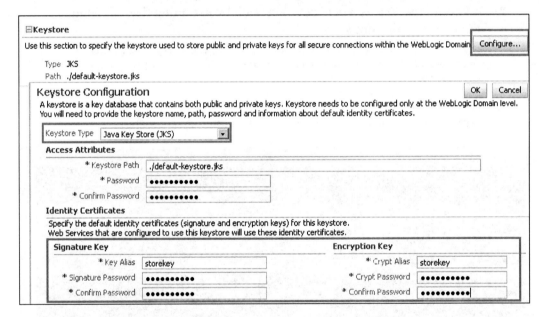

9. You would now have to configure the credential store from the same Enterprise Manager console.

10. Navigate to **Weblogic Domain Farm_[Domain_Name] | Security | Credentials**.

11. Highlight **oracle.wsm.security** and click on the **Edit...** button to edit the keys in the wallet. It will prompt a dialog box to edit the default key information. The following screenshot shows how an alias for the signature key is updated:

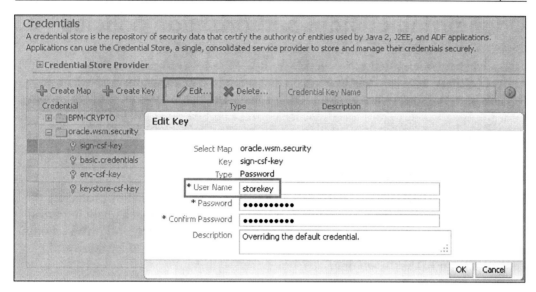

Instead of editing the already existing keys, you may also create your own custom keys from the **Create Key** button.

Changes to the keystore require a server restart as these configurations are read when the administration server is booting up.

Populating credential stores with WLST

The credential store can also be populated through WLST. To do so, start a WLST offline prompt by running `$MW_HOME/oracle_common/common/bin/wlst.sh` in a terminal. The following commands, when run, connect to a running server, create a basic credential key to an existing map `oracle.wsm.security` with a username and password, and thereafter update its password. The `listCred()` command displays the updated key in the console:

```
Wls:offline>connect('<userName>','<password>', '<host>:<adminPort>')
wls:/[Domain]/serverConfig>createCred(map="oracle.wsm.
security",key="basic-credential",user="owsm",password="welcome1",desc=
"Keystore key")
wls:/[Domain]/serverConfig>updateCred(map="oracle.wsm.
security",key="basic-credentials",user="owsm",password="welcome123",de
sc="Update Password")
wls:/[Domain]/serverConfig>listCred(map="oracle.wsm.
security",key="basic-credential")
```

Configuring custom authorization policies

Oracle SOA Suite 11*g* ships a set of preconfigured application role based authorization policies that are available in the `system-jazn-data.xml` file. However, there may be cases where you just want to create custom authorization policies and map principles to them. Or, for instance, you may even think of moving your file-based policy store to a database or an LDAP-based store. In this section, you will see how we can perform both.

Changing default policy store

You may want to do away with a file-based policy store, which is less protected and more prone to corruption, and have a more sophisticated mechanism to persist application and system security policies in a database (with a preconfigured schema) or an active directory. Follow the next steps to view the default policy store and change it to an LDAP-based one:

1. Log in to Oracle Enterprise Manager Fusion Middleware Control.

2. Right-click on **soa-infra** and navigate to **SOA Infrastructure | Security | Application Policies**.

3. Under **Application Policies | Policy Store Provider**, you will notice that the default policy store is an XML-based `system-jazn-data.xml` file.

Application Policies

Application policies are the authorization policies that an application relies upon for controlling access to its resources. These are typically JAAS policies.

To manage users and groups in the WebLogic Domain, use the Oracle WebLogic Server Security Provider.

Policy Store Provider

Scope	WebLogic Domain
Provider	XML
Location	./system-jazn-data.xml

4. In order to change the default policy store, navigate to **WebLogic Domain | Farm_[Domain_Name] | Security | Security Provider Configuration**.

5. Under **Security Stores**, click on the **Change Store Type** button.

6. The following screenshot shows how an **Oracle Identity Directory** (which is an LDAP-based store) is selected and configured from the **Store Type** drop-down list. You can even test the connection to the store from here by clicking on **Test LDAP Authentication** button:

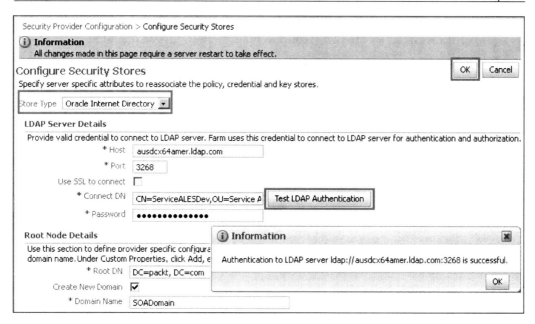

7. Clicking on **OK** will take a while and reconfigure your policy store from the default file-based directory to what is configured now.

Creating custom authorization policies

While we have already mentioned earlier that you can create a custom policy and add principles to it, in the next sequence of steps you will see how to actually do this. The next screenshot shows how a custom policy is created to grant access to the business rules editor from SOA composer to principles that include both a single user and an application-based role. The related steps are as follows:

1. Right-click on **soa-infra** and navigate to **SOA Infrastructure | Security | Application Policies**.

2. Click on **Create**.

3. In the **Grant Details** page, click on **Add** to add custom permissions.

4. Select **oracle.rules.adf.permission.RulesEditorPermission** from the **Permission Class** dropdown in the pop-up screen.

5. Click on the ◉ icon adjacent to the **Resource Name** field and select the default resource name from the search result. This automatically populates the **Customize** section in the screen.

6. From the **Grantee** section, you can now click on either **Add User**, **Add Application Role**, or **Add Group** to map them to this application policy.

7. Click on **OK** and the new policy will be successfully defined. You can search and view it either under the **Application Policies** page in the console, or in the policy store.

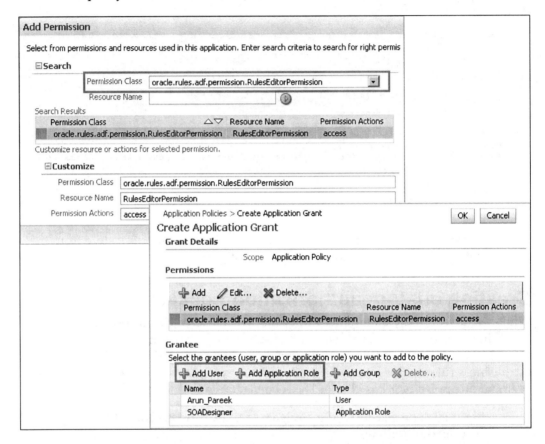

Managing OWSM policies at runtime

In this section, we will discuss how to manage OWSM policies at runtime.

Attaching and removing policies

As an administrator, you have a number of options available to attach/remove OWSM-based security policies to web service components deployed in your infrastructure. If you have a standard web service available inside a WAR application, policies can be attached to it from even the Oracle WebLogic Server Administration Console. For SOA composites, from Oracle Enterprise Manager Fusion Middleware Control, you can navigate to the particular service, component, or reference and attach a predefined or custom policy to them. Then, you have your reliable friend, that is, WLST, which offers handy and convenient ways to list, attach, detach, enable, and/or disable security policies for your service artifacts.

Having said this, the question on which you can deliberate is when to use which approach. If you like scripting things out once and then applying them whenever and wherever you like, WLST would be the ideal choice for you. If you prefer using web-based configuration screens, you have the WebLogic Server and Fusion Middleware consoles at your disposal. In this section, you will learn to exercise all the available options.

Attaching/removing OWSM policies to composite artifacts

Policies can be attached to services or references at runtime through Oracle Enterprise Management Fusion Middleware Control. Even after attaching them, they can be enabled and/or disabled, giving you complete flexibility, at runtime, on whether you want the policies to take effect or not. The following steps demonstrate how to attach a client policy to a reference of an already deployed composite:

1. Log in to Oracle Enterprise Manager Fusion Middleware Control and navigate to your deployed composite that you want to secure with OWSM.

2. Click on the **Policies** tab.

3. Select the down arrow next to the **Attach To/Detach From** box. Here you will have all services, references, and components for the selected composite listed. You can select the one to which you want to attach a policy. The one selected in the following screenshot is a reference called **GetOrderLines**.

4. This action will fetch all the predefined OWSM policies from the MDS. Locate **oracle/wss11_username_token_with_message_protection_client_policy**, highlight the policy by clicking on it, and then click on the **Attach** button.

5. You have to follow the same sequence of steps to remove a policy from a certain artifact of a composite, only this time click on the **Detach** button instead.

 Note that policies ending in `*_service_policy` are attached to an actual service endpoint, while those with `*_client_policy` are attached to the client (reference).

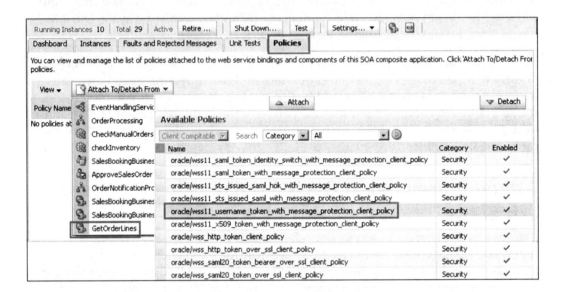

Attaching Policies from WebLogic Server Administration Console

In the previous section, you learnt how easy it is to add or remove security policies to composite artifacts. But that is not all! What if you have a packaged Java archive containing an implementation of a JAX-based web service? While you saw how a client policy was applied to a composite reference in the previous example, you will now learn how to apply an equivalent service policy to an actual service endpoint. This is done by following the next steps:

1. On the Oracle WebLogic Server Administration Console home page, click on **Deployments**.

2. From the list of deployed resources, click on the ⊞ sign next to the archive containing the implemented web service (in this example, **OrderDetailsApp**).

3. Click on the link for **GetOrderLines** link under the **Web Services** branch.

4. Click on the **Configuration | WS-Policy** tab.

5. Click on **GetOrderLinesPort**, make sure the OWSM radio button is selected, then click on **Next**.

6. Select **oracle/wss11_username_token_with_message_protection_service_ policy** under the **Available Endpoint Policies** box on the left and click on the ≫ arrow to shuttle to the **Chosen Endpoint Policies** box.

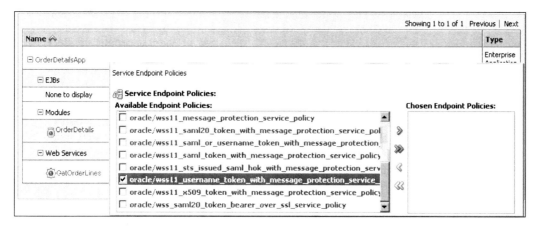

7. Go back to **Deployments** and select the checkbox next to your archive.

8. Click on the **Update** button to update its deployment plan to have the policy take effect.

This example illustrates how to attach and remove OWSM policies for JAX-WS or JAX-RPC style web services for a standard WebLogic domain that is not extended with an Enterprise Manager console. You can perform the same activity from Oracle Enterprise Manager Fusion Middleware Control. Simply log on to the console and navigate to **[Farm_Domain]** | **Application Deployments** | **[Deployed WAR]** | **Web Services**. Afterwards, click on the **Attach/Detach** button under the **OWSM Policies** tab.

Using WLST to Attach/Remove Policies

You have already read earlier in this chapter that WLST can be leveraged for runtime policy administration. In this section, you will see how it offers a more convenient way to manage policies across endpoints of both standard J2EE applications as well as components of a composite. While the commands to add or remove policies are quite descriptive, it is important to know the correct set of arguments required by them. Have a look at the signature of the command to add a particular policy to a service endpoint using WLST:

```
attachWebServicePolicy(application, moduleOrCompName, moduleType,
serviceName, subjectName, policyURI, subjectType)
```

These and other such WLST commands for OWSM policy administration share a common set of input arguments. The following table discusses each of these arguments and a mechanism to derive them to make your job easier:

Parameter name	Parameter description	Remarks
Application	This is the relative name of the deployed J2EE application in the format domain-name/server-name/application-name. For example, /soa_domain/AdminServer/OrderDetailsApp	Application name for standard J2EE components can be viewed from the **Deployments** tab in WebLogic Server Administration Console. For composite application, the value is static and can be entered as None.
moduleName	This is either the module name in case of a J2EE archive or the Composite DN for a composite application. A typical Composite DN has the following pattern: `<partition-name>/<composite-name>[revision-id]` For example, default/OrderBookingComposite[1.0] You can look up this value from the URL of the service from Oracle Enterprise Manager Fusion Middleware Control.	Locate the module name for a J2EE component from the **Deployments | [Application] | Overview | Modules** section in WebLogic Server Administration Console. For example, the module name for OrderDetailsApp is OrderDetails. For a composite, connect to the [PREFIX]_SOAINFRA schema and execute the following query below: `SELECT DISTINCT REPLACE (REPLACE(SUBSTR(composite_dn,0,INSTR(composite_dn,'*')),'!','[') ,'*',']') FROM composite_instance;`
moduleType	Module type is a static value describing the type of a particular module depending on whether it is a standard J2EE archive or an SOA composite.	The default static value for a J2EE web application is web and for an SOA composite is soa.
serviceName	This attribute is the name of the service.	This is the value of the name attribute in the wsdl:service tag of the WSDL file. For example, <wsdl:service name="OrderDetailsService">.
subjectName	This attribute represents the policy subject, port, or service operation name.	This is the value of the name attribute for the wsdl:port tag in the WSDL file. For example, <port name="OrderDetailsPort "binding="tns:OrderDetailSOAPBinding">.

Parameter name	Parameter description	Remarks
`policyURI`	This is the name of the OWSM security client and service policy URI. For example, `oracle/ wss_username_token_service_ policy`.	You can get a list of all OWSM-based policies from the Policy Manager at `http://<host>:<adminPort>/ wsm-pm/validator`.
`subjectType`	The policy subject type flag is set depending upon the value specified in the `subjectName` attribute.	The default value is P for port and the value O is used when `subjectName` is for an operation.

Listing attached policies

You may want to list the policies that are already available for a service endpoint. The syntax to view those policies and command usage is as follows:

```
listWebServicePolicies(application, moduleName, moduleType,
serviceName, subjectName)
```

Notice how the following script is used to show all available policies for a composite reference:

```
wls:/soa_domain/serverConfig>listWebServicePolicies('None',
'default/OrderBookingComposite[1.0]', 'soa','OrderDetailsService',
'GetOrderLines')
```

Attaching/removing a policy

In a dynamically changing security environment, managing policy administration tasks is quite essential. Take an example where a remote service was protected, using a username/password token. It is consciously decided to immediately switch over to SAML-based authentication and the task is assigned to you. In this case and ones similar to it, you can accomplish the task by running a few WSLT-based scripts to attach and remove OWSM security policies.

The following script shows the signature and usage patterns for attaching a message protection policy to a web service endpoint:

```
attachWebServicePolicy(application, moduleOrCompName, moduleType,
serviceName, subjectName, policyURI, [subjectType=None])
```

An example of this is shown here:

```
attachWebServicePolicy('/soa_domain/adminServer/OrderDetailsApp',
'OrderDetails', 'web', 'GetOrderLines', 'OrderDetailsPort', 'oracle/
wss11_username_token_with_message_protection_service_policy', 'P')
```

This can be used to detach a security policy applied to the service:

```
detachWebServicePolicy(application, moduleOrCompName, moduleType,
serviceName, subjectName, policyURI, [subjectType=None])
```

An example of this is shown here:

```
detachWebServicePolicy('None', 'default/OrderBookingComposite[1.0]',
'soa', 'OrderDetailsService', 'GetOrderLines', 'oracle/wss11_username_
token_with_message_protection_client_policy')
```

Enabling/disabling a policy

Policies that are attached to an endpoint are either in an enabled or disabled state. Policy enforcement will take place only when the policy state is enabled. This is useful as you are spared from attaching and detaching policies to endpoints every time there is a change in security requirements. When a policy is still attached, but is in a disabled state, it has no effect at all. The syntax and a brief usage scenario for this command is as follows:

```
enableWebServicePolicy(application, moduleOrCompName, moduleType,
serviceName, subjectName, policyURI, [enable], [subjectType=None]
```

Here, setting the `enable` property value to `true` enables the attached security policy and a Boolean value of `false` disables it.

An example of this is shown here:

```
enableWebServicePolicy('/soa_domain_dev/AdminServer/
EmpDeptService', 'empDeptService', 'web', 'EmpDeptBCService',
'EmpDeptBCServiceSoapHttpPort', 'oracle/wss_saml_or_username_token_
service_policy', false)
```

> A restart of the application to which the policies are attached is required in order to activate the configuration changes. This can be verified by either viewing the output from the `listWebServicePolicies()` command or locating the new attached policy from Oracle Enterprise Manager Fusion Middleware Control.

Customizing OWSM policies

Security management in most organizations is increasingly being tasked off from developers and handed over to platform administrators. Up until now you have learned how you can accomplish various facets of security policy administration using Oracle Enterprise Manager Fusion Middleware Control.

You navigate to the attachment point and simply pick the policy you want and the enforcement starts immediately. However, a policy is made up of multiple assertions and is able to provide a more fine-grained level of control. For example, all predefined security policies contain an instance of the logging assertion template, `oracle/security_log_template`, to log the entire message before and after the primary security assertion is executed. By default, the log assertion is not enforced. You may need to modify a policy and enable this assertion in cases where the logging assertion has to be asserted for debugging. It is recommended not to change the original policy for your customizations, but to create a similar one and then add, change, or remove specific assertions as needed. Policy properties can be overridden by clicking on the **Create Like** button under **WebLogic Domain | Farm_[Domain_ Name] | Web Services | Policies** dashboard page from Oracle Enterprise Manager Fusion Middleware Control in order to create a new policy template. Once a similar policy is created, you can define your own name and validate it in the console itself. Clicking on the **Save** button will persist the policy into the policy repository.

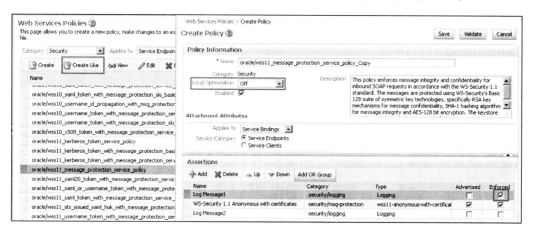

Generating a client or service policy

If you create a custom policy applicable to service endpoints from any of the default policy templates, you will also need to generate an equivalent client policy and vice versa. Oracle Enterprise Manager Fusion Middleware Control provides you with an important and useful feature through which you can generate the equivalent policy pair. From the **Web Services Policies** dashboard under **WebLogic Domain | Farm_ [Domain_Name] | Web Services | Policies**, you can select a particular policy, and click on the **Generate Client Policies** button to create its equivalent pair.

Versioning OWSM policies

Apart from creating and saving custom changes to standard policies' templates as different policies altogether, you can also choose to maintain a single policy that has multiple versions, where each version includes the changes specific to it. It provides easy to maintain security policies, as having multiple similar policies can prove to be cumbersome if there are too many changes being made. Whenever default policy assertions are modified with Oracle Enterprise Manager Fusion Middleware Control, the changes are maintained in a version history. To view the version history for any policy follow the next steps:

1. Log in to Oracle Enterprise Manager Fusion Middleware Control and navigate to **WebLogic Domain | Farm_[Domain_Name] | Web Services | Policies**.

2. Highlight the policy that has been changed and click on the **View** button.

3. This opens a pop-up window, as shown in the following screenshot, displaying additional policy details and versioning information:

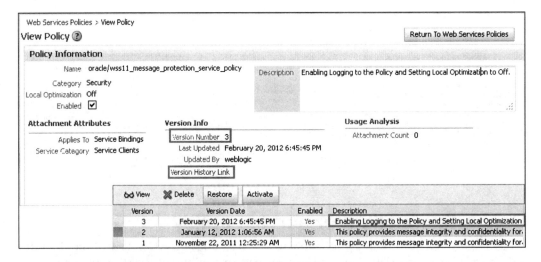

4. Clicking on **Version History Link** will show all the versions along with the description that was entered when changes were made and the policy was saved.

You can click on a particular revision and either select **Delete** to delete the selected version or **Activate** to make it the default version. Though you may have multiple versions available for a policy, enforcement is always based on the latest version. You may, however, revert back to, or activate an older version, if the latest changes which were made were not satisfactory for some reason. Also, since there is no way available to view the difference between different versions of the same policy, it is recommended that the changes be captured in the description field while saving the updated policy.

Administering policy exceptions

In this section, you will learn how to manage and administer policy exceptions.

Monitoring policy exceptions

Critical statistics such as total number of failed requests and number of failures due to authentication, authorization, or integrity violations for OWSM-based policies are, fortunately, available. To view a count of these violations to policies attached to composite artifacts, click on the **Policies** tab from the composite dashboard. For JAX-RPC or JAX-WS type services bundled inside a Java deployment archive, security violations are available in the **Web Service** dashboard under **Farm_[Domain_Name] | Application Deployments | [App] | Web Services**. While there is no additional error log available for the violations, these statistics are important and should be looked at in the first place, as they give you an idea that something is wrong with either your security configurations or with the way the secured services are being invoked. In the next few sections, you will learn about the various options that allow you to configure OWSM logging coarsely at the infrastructure level, to the most granular level of an individual policy.

Configuring logging for OWSM policies

By default, OWSM policies do not generate any logs in the servers. Though this should be optimal for a production environment, it is certain that additional logging is needed to debug and troubleshoot security related issues in the infrastructure. There are several ways to capture this information.

Changing OWSM log configuration

In *Chapter 3, Monitoring Oracle SOA Suite 11g,* you learned how overriding the default log configuration from Oracle Enterprise Manager Fusion Middleware Control instructs the infrastructure to capture and dump additional logs in the server log files. The easiest way to enforce logging at the entire infrastructure level, applicable to all OWSM-based policy components, is to set the `oracle.wsm` logger to the FINEST level, that is, TRACE:32.

Logger Name	Oracle Diagnostic Logging Level (Java Level)	Log File	Persistent Log Level State
⊞ oracle.wsm	TRACE:32 (FINEST) ▾	odl-handler	TRACE:32

With this logger level increased, the log file dumps additional information, which gives you insight into what the actual values used in the policy and assertions are. Observe the following snippet from the `soa_server1.out` log after the logger levels have been increased:

```
INFO: SSLSocketFactoryManagerImpl.getKeystoreLocation Expected SOA
Keystore location: /u01/app/oracle/middleware/user_projects/domains/
soa_domain/config/fmwconfig/default-keystore.jks
FINE: LocalOptimizationManagerImpl.checkPolicySet Using policy set
from cache to determine local optimization status.
[policySetStatus=SUCCESS, timestamp=Fri Jan 13 09:37:38 EST 2012, ...
  [{Policy
    [status:enabled]
    [Name:
    oracle/wss10_x509_token_with_message_protection_client_policy]
    [{Wss10MutualAuthWithCertsScenario
      [Enforced:true]
      [{AssertionBindings
        [{Config
          [{PropertySet
            [{Property[name:keystore.recipient.alias]
            [Value:myalias]}]
            [{Property[name:keystore.sig.csf.key]
            [Value:sign-csf-key]}]
            [{Property[name:keystore.enc.csf.key]
            [Value:enc-csf-key]}]
          }]
        }]
      }]
    }]
  }], cause=[]
]
FINE: AbstractWebServiceBindingComponent.dispatchRequest Invoking
external request: https://services.oracle.com/Services.wsdl
```

Though the actual output is not formatted as cleanly as shown in the preceding snippet, from this log fragment, we can extract some great information that would have otherwise been unavailable had the logger levels not been increased. In this example, we were able to confirm the following:

- The location of the SOA keystore file `default-keystore.jks` that was previously configured.
- The status of the policy which is enabled.
- The actual policy `oracle/wss10_x509_token_with_message_protection_client_policy` is used and in effect.
- The assertion `Wss10MutualAuthWithCertsScenario` is enforced.
- The values of the `keystore.recipient.alias`, `keystore.sig.csf.key`, and `keystore.enc.csf.key` properties.

Often when configuring OWSM, you will run into many difficulties, and verifying the actual values being used at runtime as shown proves incredibly valuable during the set up and troubleshooting efforts.

Modifying the platform audit policy

It is easy to blankly set the log configuration to a higher level without much thought and thereby have everything being written to the server log files. However, this has its own implications as far as performance and active troubleshooting are concerned. To save yourself from these perils, you can do a couple of things like navigating the hierarchy of the `oracle.wsm` logger and only increasing a selected few loggers within it. On the other hand, sometimes you may be faced with unique scenarios that require conditional logging. Consider a scenario where you need to log requests that are being successfully authorized to access services on your platform and are not coming from a trusted client (or only a registered IP). See the following screenshot, which explains how this particular use case is catered for, by overriding the default audit policy settings. To apply custom audit policy configurations, follow the next steps:

1. Log in to Oracle Enterprise Manager Fusion Middleware Control and navigate to **WebLogic Domain | Farm_[Domain_Name] | Security | Audit Policy**. In the **Audit Policy configuration** page, select **Custom** from the **Audit Level** dropdown.

2. Expand **Oracle Web Services Manager | Agent | Authorization** by clicking on the ⊞ icon.

3. Click on the pencil icon under the **Edit Filter** column corresponding to the **Success** row.

4. This will open an **Edit Filter** pop up wherein you can specify any kind of a filter by choosing and combining one or more conditions.

5. Create an audit filter for when a client IP address doesn't match a preconfigured one.

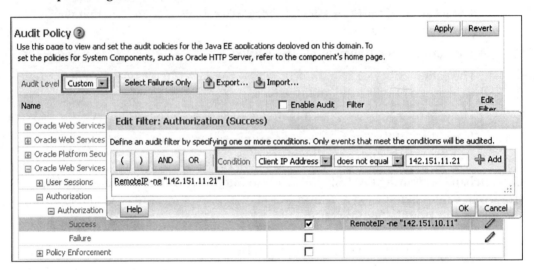

6. Click on the ✦ icon and then **OK**.

Adding a logging assertion to a policy

That's not all. Selective logging can also be enabled at the most granular single policy level by adding or enabling a log assertion to a policy. The logging assertion also allows you to specify whether to log either or both the input and output requests (here, again, you can choose to log the payload, header, or the entire SOAP message) when a certain policy is enforced. To enable and override the default logging assertion for an OWSM policy, follow these steps:

1. Browse to **WebLogic Domain | Farm_[Domain_Name] | Web Services | Policies** from the navigator pane.

2. Highlight any policy from the available list for which a logging assertion needs to be enabled and click on **Edit**.

3. Highlight the **Log Message1** assertion and change the **Request** and **Response** options under **Settings** to **soap_envelope**. Refer to the following screenshot:.

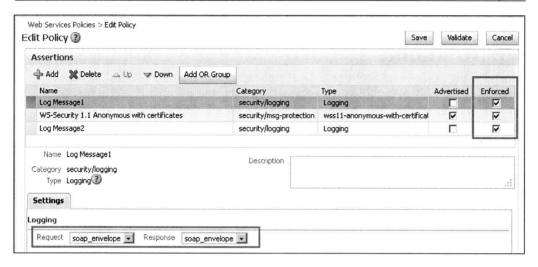

4. Select the checkboxes for **Enforced** column corresponding to both **Log Message1** and **Log Message2**.

Enter a reasonable description and click on **Save** to persist the changes. No prizes for guessing that this will create a new version of this policy. To view the logs generated by enforcing security/logging assertion to a policy, go to the `$DOMAIN_HOME/servers/ [owsm_server]/logs/owsm/msglogging` directory and view the `diagnostic.log` file. Carefully examine the entries in this file as depicted in the following screenshot and you will notice that the first entry showing the SOAP envelope request prior to the policy being applied contains no security header and nothing is encrypted. The second line shows the policy that is being applied to this message and the third entry shows the protected request message after the policy is applied and prior to sending it to the destination service. The subsequent entries will show the handshake in reverse.

Migrating custom policies across environments

Customizing and overriding the default policies or creating new ones based on existing templates serves an excellent purpose by giving your infrastructure a great deal of flexibility. All changes made from Oracle Enterprise Manager Fusion Middleware Control to the security policy components at runtime are persisted in the mds-owsm partition of the MDS store. Changes to these policies can be migrated with ease across different environments at different stages, such as from development to production. There are two ways in which security policies can be migrated from one domain to another and each has its own practical uses.

Migrating policies from Oracle Enterprise Manager Fusion Middleware Control

The most convenient mechanism to migrate customized and newly created policies is to export them from the source domain and then import them into the target domain by using Oracle Enterprise Manager Fusion Middleware Control. Navigating to the **Web Services Policies** dashboard and clicking on **WebLogic Domain | Farm_ [Domain_Name] | Web Services | Policies** lists all the policies that are available for that environment. The **Export to File** and **Import from File** buttons, available when selecting a policy, allow you to export and import policies to your filesystem one at a time. If there are only a handful of customizations in the environment that you are managing, this approach is suitable.

Policy import works only for unique policy names. You should ensure that while importing a policy into a domain, the policy name should not be already present in the repository. A policy name is different from the name of the exported file and is specified by the name attribute in the policy content.

Migrating policies by using WLST

It will not be convenient to individually export and import policy files if there are a large number of customizations or when you are unsure about the changes made to the base policy templates. To facilitate bulk exports and imports from and to the policy repository, you can leverage the importRepository and exportRepository WLST commands. Again, to execute these commands, go to the $MW_HOME/oracle_ common/common/bin directory and run the wlst.sh script from there.

Exporting a repository

Policy documents such as assertion templates, policies, and policy sets can be exported all at once from the policy repository to a supported archive by using the following export command. In the archive argument, you need to specify the name and path of the archive where all policy documents are exported to:

```
exportRepository(archive, [documents=None],
[expandReferences='false'])
```

For example, to export everything from the policy repository to the `Policies.zip` archive, the command is:

```
exportRepository('Policies.zip')
```

The `documents` argument is optional and is used to specify the kind of documents that are to be exported into the archive. If no argument is specified, everything gets exported, as is the case with the preceding command. The `documents` argument can take a policy file name just to export that particular policy, or use a search expression to find and export specific documents in the repository. For example, to export all message protection policies from the domain, enter the following command:

```
exportRepository('MessageProtectionPolicies.zip', ['policies:oracle/
wss10_message_protection_%', 'policies:oracle/wss11_message_
protection_%'])
```

Importing a repository

Importing documents into a policy repository uses the following command:

```
importRepository(archive, [map=none], [generateMapFile='false'])
```

Similar to the `export` command, the `archive` argument in the `importRepository` command reads a valid policy archive and its location. The optional `map` argument saves mapping information in a policy set, from the source environment to the target environment, in a target file. For example, a map file ensures if the resource scope expression in a policy set is updated to match the target environment, such as `Domain("dev")=Domain("prod")`.

For example, to import a valid exported policy archive into a new domain, the command is as follows:

```
importRepository('Policies.zip')
```

To generate the `policyMap.txt` map file for the `Policies.zip` archive, enter the following command. Note that no documents are imported when the `generateMapFile` argument is set to `true`.

```
importRepository('Policies.zip', 'policyMap.txt', true)
```

Now, you can manually open the map file and update the map definitions, if there are any. The command used to import the policies along with the updated map file is as follows:

```
importRepository('Policies.zip', 'policyMap.txt')
```

Summary

OWSM is the policy framework used by Oracle SOA Suite 11*g* to implement service level security. This chapter covered a huge amount of information surrounding the ability to secure your Oracle SOA Suite 11*g* services. Not only that, but numerous topics including logging, exporting, importing, and versioning by using a combination of WLST and console approaches were introduced. Web services security is a vast topic in itself, and this chapter focused on certain core concepts followed by explanations on how to administer, monitor, and promote these policies.

To understand how the OWSM framework works as well as cover various areas of administration surrounding it, this chapter covered the following points:

- An overview of the OWSM policy framework
- Policy interceptors, assertions, and templates
- Concepts surrounding the credentials and keystores, and how to configure them
- Managing OWSM policies at runtime, such as attaching/removing policies from services as well as enabling/disabling policies
- Other areas such as versioning, monitoring, logging, and migrating policies

In the next chapter, you will learn about managing the metadata services repository and the database dehydration store. The chapter will discuss the operational aspects of the metadata services layer including deploying applications to use an MDS repository, exporting and importing metadata across environments, and database growth management activities, such as tuning, purging, and partitioning, surrounding the dehydration store.

8

Managing the Metadata Services Repository and Dehydration Store

Oracle Metadata Services (MDS) is a declarative metadata repository used with Oracle SOA Suite 11*g* to store metadata of composites and web-based applications that are deployed to the service infrastructure. While a composite is being deployed, its associated metadata, including component configurations, web service definitions, business rule dictionaries, and security policy definitions are seeded first into the MDS repository and are then made available to the service infrastructure at runtime. In this way the MDS framework facilitates dynamic runtime configurations to be applied to already deployed composites to cater to ad hoc customizations with ease and flexibility. A customized composite application consists of an original metadata snapshot of the composite and a layer containing all customizations. The MDS stores the customizations in a metadata repository that are retrieved at runtime and merged with the base metadata to reveal the customized application. Having an MDS in place allows the Oracle SOA Suite 11*g* infrastructure to enable runtime modifications to business rules, domain value maps, human workflow, and certain aspects of business processes. As an administrator it is of great use to know the basics of MDS, the underlying database it resides on, activities involved in creating MDS partitions, migrating customizations, and so on.

Another important and widely adopted development practice is the use of MDS as a repository for all common components that are shared across multiple composites and applications. Reusable integration artifacts such as XML schemas defining your canonical data model, WSDLs defining enterprise business services, common fault policies, event definitions, and business rules can all be seeded to the MDS as a **Metadata Archive (MAR)**—a compressed archive of selected metadata, and can then be used and looked up from across multiple projects.

MDS assets can be maintained in either the database or in a file-based store. For reasons of scalability, reliability, and usability, we recommend the use of a database-based repository for all production purposes. This provides a range of features such as versioning metadata, querying, and change detection that are typically not supported by a file-based MDS repository. An added advantage of using an MDS backed with a database is that it allows updates from multiple hosts to the metadata information. This is ideal in a multiserver installation, where each of the servers can access the same repository and save concurrent changes that become available immediately for the remaining servers in a domain. On the contrary, a file-based MDS can only update from one host at a time.

For most production-enabled systems, Oracle SOA Suite 11*g* utilizes a set of database schemas to store metadata and instance information during the lifecycle of a composite's execution. In a standard installation, the repository schemas are created prior to creating the WebLogic domain by executing the **Repository Creation Utility (RCU)**. Typically, these schemas are appended to a user defined prefix at the time of installation. The two schemas of prime importance are `[PREFIX]_SOAINFRA`, used to manage composite instance information, and the `[PREFIX]_MDS` schema, which stores shared artifacts, metadata, and runtime customizations of composites. In the sections that follow, you will learn in detail about all the aspects of administration which are related to these schemas, as they impact the performance of your infrastructure at runtime in a big way.

The product database schemas include a user defined prefix so that multiple installations can share the same database instance, for example, DEV_SOAINFRA, TEST_SOAINFRA, and so on.

These respective schemas are loaded during the startup of the managed server after the database connections are established via WebLogic JDBC connection pools. SOA composites are then checked out from the database repository and loaded on the platform when the server successfully establishes a connection with the underlying database. The Oracle SOA Suite 11*g* infrastructure registers a database-backed MDS repository with the domain where composites can commit their customizations. This is usually done when the domain is extended with SOA Suite. However, there may be situations where you will need to register a new repository with the domain. Consider an example where there is a need for separate metadata repositories to store data of two different composites, catering to different business functions, but deployed to a common domain. Achieving this is possible using the Oracle Enterprise Manager Fusion Middleware Control console or WebLogic Scripting Tool (WLST) scripts that allow registering new repositories post domain creation. The following figure shows the various components of the MDS runtime engine and how they interact to provide the implementation of metadata storage:

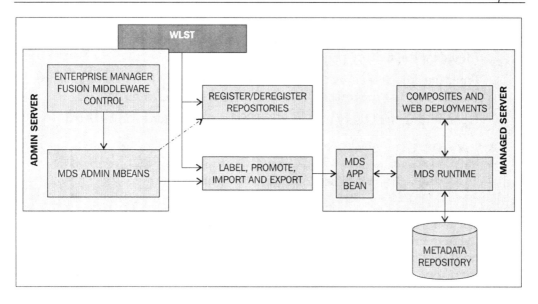

In this chapter, we cover various areas related to MDS management that include:

- Registering a database-based MDS repository
- Managing metadata repository partitions
- Purging metadata version history
- Managing the Dehydration Store

Registering a database-based MDS repository

Upon installing Oracle SOA Suite 11*g*, the MDS is typically registered with your SOA domain, but there are cases when it may not have been registered or cases where you have to create a new one, as explained earlier. There are multiple ways of registering an MDS repository; one method is to use Oracle Enterprise Manager Fusion Middleware Control. If you prefer, or if you have not installed Oracle Enterprise Manager Fusion Middleware Control in your Oracle WebLogic Server domain, you can instead use the WLST command-line utility to perform the registration. This chapter will demonstrate both the available options, starting with the first one.

An MDS repository can be registered by following the steps outlined:

1. Log in to Oracle Enterprise Manager Fusion Middleware Control.

2. Click on **Farm_[Domain_Name] | WebLogic Domain | Metadata Repositories**.

3. On the **Metadata Repositories** page, click on the **Register** button under the **Database-Based Repositories** section. Now, the **Register Database-Based Metadata Repository** page is displayed.

4. Enter the database connection information to connect to a service instance that already has the unused [PREFIX]_MDS schema created.

5. Upon hitting the **Query** button, all MDS-based schemas will be listed.

 Only those schemas that are currently not registered with any other domain can be registered.

6. The following figure shows how a metadata repository is registered with the domain using an existing but non-registered database schema. You will need to supply a repository name and password in this page to be able to create one.

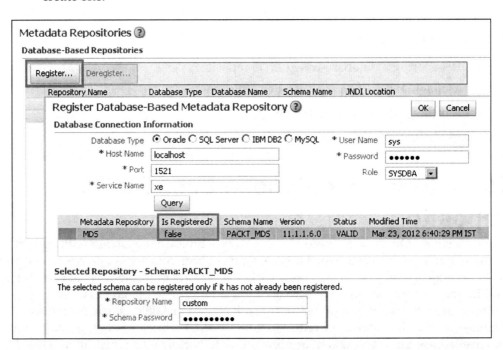

When the repository is registered with the Oracle WebLogic Server domain, a system level global nontransactional data source named mds-[Repository_Name] is also created along with it. Should a repository no longer be required, deregistering it is also straightforward and can be done from the same dashboard. However, it has to be ensured that there is no application referencing the repository while it is being deregistered.

Another approach to registering a database-based metadata repository is to execute the `registerMetadataDBRepository` command from the WLST command line. The following script shows the syntax of a command to register an MDS Repository named `mds-custom` using database connection parameters, where the highlighted text may be replaced with values specific to your environment:

```
registerMetadataDBRepository(name='mds-custom', dbVendor='ORACLE',
host='localhost', port='1521', dbName='orcl',
user='sys', password='password', targetServers='soa_server1')
```

> The WLST scripts that allow executing commands specific to administration of MDS related components have to be executed from the `$ORACLE_HOME/common/bin` directory rather than the conventional `$ORACLE_HOME/wlserver_10.3/common/bin` directory. To be able to execute all WLST scripts covered in this chapter, execute the `wlst.sh` file provided in the code bundle of this chapter from the `$ORACLE_HOME/common/bin` directory of your middleware installation.

Managing metadata repository partitions

In an MDS repository, each application (that is, Oracle SOA Suite, Oracle Web Services Manager, and Oracle Business Process Management) is deployed to its own partition so that they can be logically separated. This is not to be confused with partitions as described in *Chapter 2, Management of SOA Composite Applications*. A **metadata repository partition** is an independent logical directory within a physical MDS repository that is used to manage metadata of these different Oracle Fusion Middleware components and applications. You can create, clone, delete, import, and export metadata from a specified partition. Either Oracle Enterprise Manager Fusion Middleware Control or WLST command line scripting can be leveraged for all partition management activities which will be covered in detail in this section. To view the existing metadata repository partitions available for the domain, simply log in to Oracle Enterprise Manager Fusion Middleware Control, navigate to **Farm_[Domain_Name] | Metadata Repositories** and click on one of the repositories. Alternatively, you may execute the **listPartitions** MBean operation (discussed shortly).

Creating a new metadata partition

Partitions in a metadata repository can be created by accessing the MDS domain runtime MBean and invoking the `createMetadataPartition` operation from the Oracle Enterprise Manager Fusion Middleware Control console. The following sequence of steps listed describes the order to browse to the **MDSDomainRuntime** MBean and then invoke specific operations that it exposes:

1. Log in to Oracle Enterprise Manager Fusion Middleware Control.
2. Expand **Farm_[Domain_Name] | WebLogic Domain**, right-click on your SOA domain and click on **System MBean Browser**.
3. Navigate to the **MDSDomainRuntime** MBean located under **Application Defined MBeans | oracle.mds.lcm | Domain : [Domain_Name] | MDSDomainRuntime** and click on the **Operations** tab.
4. Click on the **createMetadataPartition** operation and in the parameter list enter a valid name of an existing MDS repository and a suitable partition name to create a new partition.

Alternatively, you can also create a new partition using the `createMetadataPartition` command from the WLST command line. It is important to note that a partition name must be unique within a repository. The following script creates a partition named `soacustom` in the `mds-custom` repository:

```
createMetadataPartition(repository='mds-custom',
partition='soacustom')
```

Cloning a partition

Another efficient way to create a new metadata partition is to clone an existing partition from a source repository to a different repository. Cloning a partition is advantageous as it preserves the metadata version history including all customizations made to the deployed composites.

Note that cloning a partition is permitted only if the source and the target repository are both database-based repositories with backend databases of the same type and version.

The **MDSDomainRuntime** MBean contains, among other operations, the operation to clone a partition. The `cloneMetadataPartition` operation can be invoked by passing a list of input parameters that specifies the `fromRepository`, `fromPartition`, `toRepository`, and `toPartition`. The arguments required for the function are self-explanatory and should be replaced with actual values specific to your environment. Have a look at the steps outlining the details to clone a partition dynamically at runtime:

1. Log in to Oracle Enterprise Manager Fusion Middleware Control.

2. Expand **Farm_[Domain_Name] | WebLogic Domain**, right-click on your SOA domain and click on **System MBean Browser**.

3. Navigate to the **MDSDomainRuntime** MBean located under **Application Defined MBeans | oracle.mds.lcm | Domain : [Domain_Name] | MDSDomainRuntime** and click on the **Operations** tab.

4. Click on the **cloneMetadataPartiton** operation.

5. In the parameter list enter suitable values to clone an existing partition from an existing source repository to a target one.

6. Ensure that the partition name is unique for a particular repository. If the **toPartition** property is left blank, the name of the source partition is used for the target partition.

7. Click on **Invoke** to clone a partition, as shown in the following screenshot:

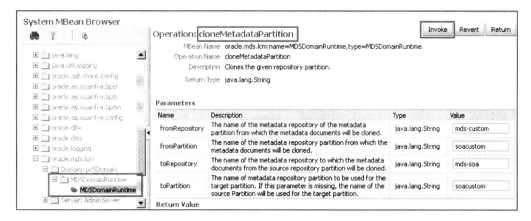

8. Optionally, you can verify that the partition has been created by clicking the repository in the navigation pane. The partition is listed in the **Partitions** table on the **Metadata Repository** home page.

It is often difficult to navigate through the MDS Runtime MBeans available from Oracle Enterprise Manager Fusion Middleware Control particularly if the same configurations need to be duplicated across multiple environments. To maintain consistency, an easy and reusable option is to invoke the WLST command line and enter the metadata partition cloning command provided to clone the soacustom partition in the mds-custom repository to the mds-soa repository as follows:.

```
cloneMetadataPartition(fromRepository='mds-custom',
fromPartition='soacustom', toRepository= 'mds-soa', toPartition=
'soacustom')
```

Deploying a MAR using WLST

Most of the time Oracle SOA Suite 11*g* developers would create an MDS archive during development which would contain bundled composites, shared assets, or reusable resources, and it would be left to the administrator to deploy it to the infrastructure. The easiest and recommended way to deploy an MDS bundle is to use the WLST command line utility. Deploying an MDS archive is a two-step process and involves adding the MDS repository configuration information in a MAR (Metadata Archive) file and then deploying it to a given partition. The following steps would outline how to deploy an archive to a specified partition:

1. Open the WLST command line by executing the wlst.sh script from the $ORACLE_HOME/common/bin directory of your middleware installation.

2. Invoke the getMDSArchiveConfig() command to obtain a handle to the MDSArchiveConfig object for a given MDS bundle and assign it to a variable. The getMDSArchiveConfig() commands take a parameter, fromLocation, pointing to the location of the archive on the file system.

3. The object of MDSArchiveConfig can be used to set the MDS information such as repository name, partition, repository type, and JNDI of repository database connection by invoking the setAppMetadataRepository() operation.

4. Invoke the save() operation on the MDSArchiveConfig object to save changes to the archive. If the toLocation argument is specified in the operation, changes are applied to the target archive file and the original file remains unchanged. Otherwise, the changes are saved in the original file itself.

5. Use the connect() command to connect to the instance of the server to which the metadata archive is to be deployed.

6. Finally invoke the deploy() command to deploy the application. The path argument has to specify the directory location of the MAR and the appName argument should determine the name of the deployed archive on the server.

The preceding steps may be executed as follows:

```
wls:/offline>archive = getMDSArchiveConfig(fromLocation='u02/metadata/
archives/testArchive.ear')
wls:/offline>archive.setAppMetadataRepository(repository='mds-custom',
partition='soacustom', type='DB', jndi='jdbc/mds/custom')
wls:/offline>archive.save()
wls:offline>connect()
wls:soaDomain/serverConfig>deploy(appName='MDS', path='u02/metadata/
archives/testArchive.ear')
```

Exporting and importing composites from/to a partition

Moving composite(s) from one environment to another is an activity that will constantly engage your work as the platform administrator. As an example, you may want to move composites from a development system to a test system and then to a production system. The most effective and convenient approach is that of transferring the entire metadata repository and/or the partition. Transferring the metadata gives you an option to not only move composite applications targeted to it but also customizations that are made and tested at runtime. In order to transfer metadata from one partition to another, you will need to first export it from a partition on the source environment and then import it into a partition on the target environment. Depending on your preference, you can either use a graphical interface via Oracle Enterprise Manager Fusion Middleware Control or a scripting approach via WLST to move composites from one environment to another by transferring the metadata repository. It is our recommendation to use scripting as much as possible as it is efficient, saves time, and only requires a small customization. The following list of steps provides a way to export all composites from a partition displayed in the **MDS Configuration** dashboard:

1. Log in to Oracle Enterprise Manager Fusion Middleware Control.

2. You can either export an individual composite or the entire MDS depending upon your requirement. To export the entire partition right-click on the **Farm_[Domain_Name] | soa-infra | Administration | MDS Configuration**.

3. The **MDS Configuration** dashboard page shows the properties such as the repository name, type, and partition being used by the infrastructure to be exported.

4. Enter the file system location to save the archived MDS file and click on the **Export** button to be prompted on where and what to name the export file.

5. If the **Exclude base documents** option is checked, only the customizations made to the composite are exported and not the base documents.

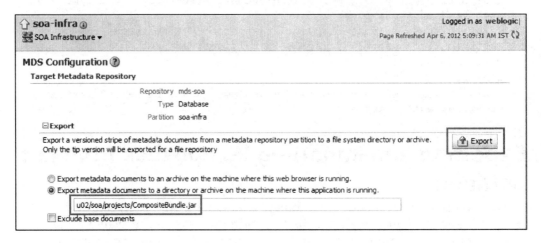

6. Once the MDS archive is exported to the server filesystem you may ftp/copy it to the target filesystem (if it is on a different machine altogether).

7. Navigate to the MDS Configuration page on the target server and under the **Import** panel, either enter the location manually, where the archive is to be copied or use the **Browse** button to go to the directory.

8. Click on the **Import** button to import all archived composites and their customizations on the partition of the target server.

It is important that the export directory specified exists either on the machine where the SOA server is running or where the browser is running, depending upon the export option selected. The browser does not prompt you to browse for a file's path. If the location does not exist in the filesystem, a directory is created. An exception to this is that when the name ends with .jar or .zip, an archive is created. If a directory name is specified then the metadata archive is written to a subdirectory of the directory specified, with the name of the partition that was exported as the name of the subdirectory.

In order to similarly export items from within an MDS and import them in another server using the WLST command line, perform the following steps:

1. Execute the wlst.sh file for administering an MDS repository on the source server instance from the $ORACLE_HOME/common/bin directory:

```
cd $ORACLE_HOME/common/bin
./wlst.sh
```

2. Connect to the server instance from the offline prompt and enter the
   `exportMetadata()` command to extract all composites and metadata
   deployed to a partition in a temporary folder:

```
wls:/offline>connect('<username>', '<password>',
'<host>:<adminport>')
wls:/DomainName/serverConfig>exportMetadata(application='soa-
infra', server='<server_name>', toLocation='<export_folder>',
docs='/**')
wls:/DomainName/serverConfig>exit()
```

If you are unsure about the composite name then you can find it from
the composite dashboard from the Oracle Enterprise Manager Fusion
Middleware Control console. The server name has to be the server to which
the MDS repository is targeted to. The /** wildcard filter indicates that
all documents from the root folder are to be extracted out. However, you
can even specify a path filter to traverse the MDS path internally to export
any desired file or folder. The following WLST command illustrates how to
export all the .xml files from the /soa/configuration/default directory
under the MDS root:

```
exportMetadata(application='soa-infra', server='soa_server1',
toLocation='export_folder',docs='/soa/configuration/default/*.
xml')
```

3. Next, copy the export folder containing the extracted archive to the machine
   where the target server is running.

4. Open a new WLST command line prompt from the Middleware installation
   on the destination machine.

5. Execute the `importMetadata()` command to import the exported metadata
   archive to the target server.

```
wls:/DomainName/serverConfig>importMetadata(application='soa-
infra', server='<server_name>', fromLocation='import_folder',
docs='/**')
```

The value of the `fromLocation` parameter must be on the
same system that is running WLST or on a mapped network
drive or directory mount. Direct network references such as
\\sharedFolder\repositories\ cannot be used though.

Purging metadata version history

As the metadata repository is usually backed by a database, it would be necessary to purge unnecessary and archaic customizations made to composites that are no longer applicable. Purging is only required for database-based MDS repositories as file-based repositories do not maintain composite version histories. Purging metadata version history from a partition deletes all unlabeled documents from it, leaving only the tip version (the latest version), even if it is unlabeled. Purging metadata version history on a regular basis is a necessary maintenance activity to prevent the database from running out of space or when its performance starts to degrade. Purging an MDS repository is performance intensive and hence should either be attempted in a maintenance window or when the system is not busy. To use Oracle Enterprise Manager Fusion Middleware Control to purge the metadata version history, perform the following:

1. Log in to Oracle Enterprise Manager Fusion Middleware Control.

2. You can purge the version history of unlabeled documents from the partition that are older than a selected time period. Navigate to **Farm_[Domain_ Name]** | **soa-infra** | **Administration** | **MDS Configuration**.

3. The **MDS Configuration** dashboard page is displayed.

4. In the **Purge all unlabeled past versions that are older than field**, enter a number and select the unit of time.

5. Click on **OK**.

6. A progress box is displayed. When the operation completes, a completion box is displayed.

7. Click on **Close**.

It is also possible to purge metadata version history using the `purgeMetadata()` command in WLST. You specify the documents to be purged by using the `olderThan` parameter and specifying the time in number of seconds. The following example purges all documents older than `100` seconds:

```
purgeMetadata(application='soa-infra', server='soa_server1',
olderThan=100)
```

Purging metadata version history older than four weeks is not unusual and should be performed on a regular basis as part of your standard MDS maintenance activities. As a minimum, consider purging under the following circumstances:

- When the database is running out of space
- When overall performance is becoming slower

However, note that purging may be performance intensive, so schedule it during a time of low activity.

Managing the Dehydration Store

Until now you have been learning about common administration tasks involving the MDS repository. The MDS maintains a small database footprint as it is simply used to store application metadata, common reusable artifacts, and runtime configuration changes. Another important schema that would require more frequent monitoring and close administration is the [PREFIX]_SOAINFRA, which is used to store instance and transactional data of all the composites being executed in the infrastructure. This database schema is also referred to as the **Dehydration Store**. Oracle SOA Suite 11*g* leverages the Dehydration Store database to maintain long-running processes and their current state information while they are executing over a period of time. Storing the process in a database preserves the process and prevents any loss of state or reliability in case of a system shut down or when a network problem occurs.

Configurations affecting the SOA Suite 11*g* Dehydration Store

It is important to understand how the nature of a deployed composite affects what is saved in the Dehydration Store. Business processes in general can be categorized either as transient processes (short lived, request-response style synchronous processes) or durable processes (long running asynchronous processes). Transient processes do not incur any intermediate dehydration during their execution. Furthermore, the instances of a transient process do not leave a trace in the system in the event of unhandled faults or system downtime. Also, instances of transient processes cannot be saved in-flight whether they complete normally or abnormally. On the other hand, durable processes can have one or more activities during execution that cause instances to dehydrate in the database. For example, in a BPEL component, a few activities that cause this intermittent dehydration are Receive, Pick, Wait, Reply, and Checkpoint.

Instance data being saved to the Dehydration Store database depends upon several factors such as the design of the process, the nature of its synchronicity, audit and logging levels, persistence policies, whether the instance is being optimized to execute in the runtime memory of the engine, and others. Practically there are several combinations through which the amount of data being saved to the database can be controlled. It is vital to know about some typical configurations that can be set either at the individual process level or at a domain wide level and what their impact is on the Dehydration Store.

These configuration properties can be applied at the domain level, enabling you to set a global configuration for all composites deployed to the domain. You can also override these configuration properties at the individual component level. If a setting at the domain level conflicts with the same setting at the component level, the component level setting takes priority. The following table shows the various properties that control data persistence in the Dehydration Store and their respective descriptions.

Property	Configuration Level	Description
completionPersistLevel	Domain and Component (BPEL only)	This property controls the type and amount of instance data being saved after its completion. When process instances complete, Oracle SOA Suite 11*g* engine by default saves the final state (for example, the variable values) of the instance. If these values are not required to be saved after completion, this property can be set to save only instance metadata (completion state, start and end dates, and so on). This property is used only when the inMemoryOptimization performance property is set to true and can have the following values:

all (default): The engine saves the complete instance, including the final variable values, work item data, and audit data.

instanceHeader: Only the instance metadata is saved. |

Property	Configuration Level	Description
completionPersistPolicy	Domain and Component (BPEL only)	This property controls if and when to persist instances. If an instance is not saved, its flow trail does not appear in the Enterprise Manager Console. This property is only used when inMemoryOptimization is set to true. This parameter strongly impacts the amount of data stored in the database and can also impact the throughput. It can be set to either of the values: • on (default): Completed instances are saved normally. • deferred: Completed instances are saved with a different thread and in another transaction. If the server fails, some instances may not be saved. • faulted: Only faulted instances are saved. • off: No instances (and their data) are saved.
inMemoryOptimization	Component (BPEL only)	Works hand in hand with completionPersistLevel and completionPersistPolicy. This property can be set for transient processes. If inMemoryOptimization is set to true, the completionPersistLevel is set to all and the completionPersistPolicy is set to faulted. The process will run in memory without saving anything to the dehydration database unless the instance faults out, in which case all instance data is saved.

Property	Configuration Level	Description
deliveryPersistPolicy	Component (BPEL only)	This property enables and disables database persistence of messages entering Oracle SOA Suite 11*g* engine. By default, incoming requests are saved in intermediate delivery service database tables, later acquired by worker threads and delivered to the targeted processes. In the case where performance is preferred over reliability, persisting the incoming messages in the database can be skipped. This property persists delivery messages and is applicable to durable processes.
largeDocumentThreshold	Domain	This property sets the large XML document persistence threshold. This is the maximum size (in kilobytes) of a variable before it is stored in a separate location from the rest of the instance scope data. This property is applicable to both durable and transient processes. Large XML documents impact the performance of the entire Oracle SOA Suite 11*g* engine if they are constantly read in and written out whenever processing on an instance must be performed.
auditDetailThreshold	Domain	This property sets the maximum size (in kilobytes) of an audit trail details string before it is stored separately from the audit trail. If the size of a detail is larger than the value specified for this property, it is placed in the AUDIT_DETAILS table. Otherwise, it is placed in the AUDIT_TRAIL table.
auditLevel	Domain and Component	This property sets the audit trail logging level. This process is applicable to both durable and transient processes.

For all asynchronous processes, inMemoryOptimization should be set to False. If left as True you will need to set completionPersistPolicy to Off in order to avoid any dangling and orphaned references in the database tables.

Component level properties can be set at design time. Refer to *Chapter 4, Tuning Oracle SOA Suite 11g for Optimum Performance* for examples on how to set these in the composite.xml of the SOA project.

Database objects of the SOA Dehydration Store

The next important area to understand is the structure of the underlying Dehydration Store database. It is somewhat difficult to comprehend the data model and objects maintained by Oracle SOA Suite 11g Dehydration Store as the tables maintained in them have no foreign key constraints to police referential integrity and are intentionally designed as such for performance reasons. Without these constraints, the relationship between master and detail tables needs to be protected to avoid dangling references in the detail tables. Hence, utmost care needs to be taken when engaging with any kind of manual interactions with the database. It is with experience that an administrator will gain insight on the different tables and ways to perform common administration tasks like purging, partitioning, and reclaiming disk space. Improper purging or ignorantly using a wrong mix of configuration parameters will eventually lead to orphaned instances that will make managing the database difficult. A good starting point is to use the out-of-the-box packages that are provided by Oracle to take care of the purging and partitioning activities. It is essential to have an overall understanding of key tables that make up a majority of the Dehydration Store.

A few of them are described in the following table ,along with the nature of the instance related data they store.

Table	Description
ATTACHMENT	Attachments of a process instance are persisted as variables in this table.
ATTACHMENT_REF	An attachment can be referenced by multiple process instances. The references to an attachment are saved in the ATTACHMENT_REF table.
AUDIT_DETAILS	Activities inside a process such as an assign activity log variables as audit details by default in this table. This behavior is controlled through the auditLevel configuration property in place. The auditDetailThreshold configuration property is used by this table. If the size of a detail is larger than the value specified for this property, it is placed in this table. Otherwise, it is placed in the AUDIT_TRAIL table.
AUDIT_TRAIL	This table stores the audit trail for instances. The audit trail viewed in Oracle SOA Suite 11*g* Enterprise Manager console is created from an XML document. As an instance is processed, each activity writes events to the audit trail as XML. The table contains a column named LOG which is a Large Object RAW Column. Each step in a process gets logged into the LOG Column in XML zipped form.
CUBE_INSTANCE	Process instance metadata such as the instance creation date, current state, title, and process identifier are stored in this table. For each process instance an entry gets created in this table. The table also contains the relationship between parent and child instances in fields: cikey, parent_id, and root_id.
CUBE_SCOPE	This table stores the scope data for an instance (that is, all variables declared in the process flow and some internal objects that help route logic throughout the flow).
DLV_MESSAGE	The DLV_MESSAGE table stores callback messages when they are received by running instances. It only stores the metadata for a message such as the current state, process identifier, and receive date.
DLV_SUBSCRIPTION	This table stores delivery subscriptions for an instance. Whenever an instance expects a message from a partner (for example, the receive or onMessage activity) a subscription is written out for that specific receive activity.
DOCUMENT_CI_REF	This table stores cube instance references to data stored in the XML_DOCUMENT table.

Table	Description
INSTANCE_PAYLOAD	All asynchronous invocation messages are stored in this table before being dispatched to the engine. It stores incoming invocation messages (messages that result in the creation of an instance). This table only stores the metadata for a message that invokes a composite instance.
WORK_ITEM	This table stores information related to activities created by an instance. All process activities in a flow will have a column in the WORK_ITEM table created for it. This WORK_ITEM column contains metadata for the activity such as current state, label, expiration date (used by wait activities), etc. When the engine needs to be restarted and instances recovered, pending flows are resumed by inspecting their unfinished work items.
XML_DOCUMENT	This table stores all large objects in the system (for example, instance_payload documents, dlv_message documents, and so on). It stores the data as **binary large objects** (BLOBs). Separating the document storage from the metadata enables the metadata to change frequently without being impacted by the size of documents.

Measuring database growth

It will be necessary to measure the size of the Dehydration Store database at regular intervals to be able to see if there is enough free space available in it. Database free space and growth can be measured in a variety of ways, the easiest being executing a set of queries to get the free size of the tablespace for a given schema. Apart from regular measurements, if you are planning to execute purging, these free space measurements should be taken before and after purging, to ensure there is a visible difference indicating the effectiveness of the purge. Execute the free space measurement script that is provided here to calculate the percentage and free space in MB in the [PREFIX]_SOAINFRA schema:

```
-- Measuring free space in SOA_INFRA tablespace
SELECT * FROM (SELECT C.TABLESPACE_NAME, ROUND(A.BYTES/1048576,2) MB_
ALLOCATED,ROUND(B.BYTES/1048576,2)                               MB_
FREE,ROUND((A.BYTES-B.BYTES)/1048576,2) MB_USED, ROUND(B.BYTES/A.BYTES
* 100,2) TOT_PCT_FREE, ROUND((A.BYTES-B.BYTES)/A.BYTES,2) * 100  TOT_
PCT_USED FROM (SELECT TABLESPACE_NAME, SUM(A.BYTES) BYTES FROM SYS.
DBA_DATA_FILES A GROUP BY TABLESPACE_NAME) A, (SELECT A.TABLESPACE_
NAME, NVL(SUM(B.BYTES),0) BYTES FROM SYS.DBA_DATA_FILES A, SYS.DBA_
FREE_SPACE B WHERE A.TABLESPACE_NAME = B.TABLESPACE_NAME
```

```
(+) AND A.FILE_ID = B.FILE_ID (+) GROUP BY A.TABLESPACE_NAME) B, SYS.
DBA_TABLESPACES C WHERE A.TABLESPACE_NAME = B.TABLESPACE_NAME(+) AND
A.TABLESPACE_NAME = C.TABLESPACE_NAME) WHERE TOT_PCT_USED >=0 AND
TABLESPACE_NAME='DEV_SOAINFRA' ORDER BY TABLESPACE_NAME;
```

The output of the previous free space SQL command will look similar to the following screenshot:

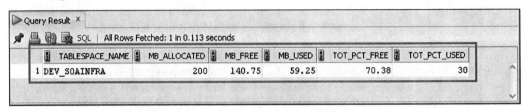

Another important measurement that is to be taken is to record the column count of key tables that store instance related data before and after applying the purging. As these tables in the Dehydration Store have no foreign keys, there is always a case where purging leaves dangling or orphaned instances in some of the tables. Executing the following script provided here, measures the column count in the various Dehydration Store tables. If executed before and after initializing purging, you can determine whether the purging scripts have effectively deleted instance data completely.

```
--Get All Counts of SOA related instance tables
SELECT
(SELECT COUNT(*) FROM CUBE_INSTANCE) AS CUBE_INST,
(SELECT COUNT(*) FROM COMPOSITE_INSTANCE) AS COMP_INST,
(SELECT COUNT(*) FROM COMPONENT_INSTANCE) AS COMPNT_INST,
(SELECT COUNT(*) FROM COMPOSITE_INSTANCE_FAULT) AS COMPST_INST_FLT,
(SELECT COUNT(*) FROM REFERENCE_INSTANCE) AS REF_INST,
(SELECT COUNT(*) FROM CUBE_SCOPE) AS CUBE_SCP,
(SELECT COUNT(*) FROM COMPOSITE_SENSOR_VALUE) AS COMP_SEN_VAL,
(SELECT COUNT(*) FROM XML_DOCUMENT) AS XML_DOC,
(SELECT COUNT(*) FROM XML_DOCUMENT_REF) AS XML_DOC_REF,
(SELECT COUNT(*) FROM AUDIT_TRAIL) AS AUDIT_TRAIL,
(SELECT COUNT(*) FROM AUDIT_COUNTER) AS AUDIT_CNTR,
(SELECT COUNT(*) FROM AUDIT_DETAILS) AS AUDIT_DET,
(SELECT COUNT(*) FROM INSTANCE_PAYLOAD) AS INST_PYLD,
(SELECT COUNT(*) FROM HEADERS_PROPERTIES) AS HDRS_PROPS,
(SELECT COUNT(*) FROM WFTASK) AS WFTASK,
(SELECT COUNT(*) FROM WI_FAULT) AS WI_FLT,
(SELECT COUNT(*) FROM DLV_MESSAGE) AS DLV_MSSG,
(SELECT COUNT(*) FROM DLV_SUBSCRIPTION) AS DLV_SUBC,
(SELECT COUNT(*) FROM DOCUMENT_DLV_MSG_REF) AS DOC_DLV_MSG_REF,
```

```
(SELECT COUNT(*) FROM DOCUMENT_CI_REF) AS DOC_CI_REF,
(SELECT COUNT(*) FROM WORK_ITEM) AS WRK_ITEM
FROM DUAL;
```

These queries are not intended to replace the DBA's traditional monitoring tools, but rather to provide guidance to potential areas of table growth.

Available maintenance strategies

To manage the database growth as a result of a high volume of instance processing and transactions, there must be a strategy in place that can delete historical data that are no longer required in order to reclaim the disk space back. It is also impossible to have a generic strategy that can be applied to all types of infrastructure as there is no one-size-fits-all solution to this, but this chapter will provide an insight into all the available mechanisms, depending upon the database profile, process requirements, and other factors. Once there is enough understanding of these various factors, a combination of these strategies can be applied to have the most relevant and optimal permutations in place. We recommend that regardless of which purging strategy is chosen, it needs to be followed up with proper testing against a production-like dataset. It is also advisable to engage a skilled DBA to review the Dehydration Store data management mechanism. In any case the purging strategy cannot be left as an afterthought and needs to become a part of the performance exercise, a thorough testing is recommended to complete this cycle. If an ineffective purging strategy is implemented, the Oracle SOA Suite 11*g* tables may grow to very large sizes, thereby affecting the overall system performance and leading to an urgent need to reclaim space. The larger the size of tables, the harder it becomes to delete rows and reclaim space and hence it is important to schedule a maintenance strategy to frequently purge data from them.

Chapter 2, Management of SOA Composite Applications, showed a graph indicating the database usage based on the number of instances and their message sizes. The graph is indicative of a small process with a few dehydration points; however it gives a benchmark of how much a database may grow so that you can provision a database suiting the need of business processes running on the infrastructure. Depending upon the size and nature of your database you may be required to schedule more frequent maintenance. In any case, you can follow the recommendations given that cover three different kinds of database footprints that you may have and ways to maintain them.

Purging prerequisites

Running the following maintenance scripts on the database requires certain privileges to be granted as it involves scheduling, creating jobs, deletion, and partitioning. An out-of-the-box purge package is already available with your Oracle SOA Suite 11*g* installation. Before you choose to purge component tables, it is essential to specify a directory to log the output of the executed maintenance scripts to assist in troubleshooting, should a problem arise. The following steps set up all the necessary prerequisites to effectively begin purging your Dehydration Store:

1. Connect to the database as SYSDBA to grant privileges to the SOAINFRA schema user to execute the purging scripts:

    ```
    SQL> GRANT EXECUTE ON DBMS_LOCK TO [PREFIX]_SOAINFRA;
    SQL> GRANT CREATE ANY JOB TO [PREFIX]_SOAINFRA;
    ```

2. On the command prompt, create an environment variable named SQLPATH and point it to the directory containing the scripts used to create the purge packages:

    ```
    export SQLPATH="$MW_HOME/Oracle_SOA1/rcu/integration/soainfra/sql/
    soa_purge"
    ```

3. Reconnect to the database but this time as the SOAINFRA user.

4. Verify that the relevant SOA purge packages are available for the user. Otherwise manually create them by executing the soa_purge_scripts.sql script:

    ```
    SQL>@soa_purge_scripts.sql
    ```

5. To set up a logging and diagnostics directory where logs are written, reconnect to the database as SYSDBA again, specify the directory location, and grant read/write permission to the [PREFIX]_SOAINFRA user. You can also optionally execute the script to turn debugging on by executing the debug_on.sql script from the common directory. <DIAG_LOCATION> should be replaced with a directory of your choice:

    ```
    SQL> CREATE OR REPLACE DIRECTORY SOA_PURGE_DIR AS '<DIAG_
    LOCATION>/purge_logs';
    SQL> GRANT READ, WRITE ON DIRECTORY SOA_PURGE_DIR TO [PREFIX]_
    SOAINFRA;
    SQL>@common/debug_on.sql;
    ```

6. By default, the command line does not read what a query program has written with dbms_output. You have to enable the serveroutput by setting it to on, to change the default behavior. Additionally, if the output needs to be captured, a spool file needs to be configured in the logging directory:

    ```
    SQL> SET SERVEROUTPUT ON;
    SQL> SPOOL '<DIAG_LOCATION>/purge_logs/spool.log'
    ```

7. After the scripts are run, you can choose to set it to `off`, when no longer needed:

```
SQL> SPOOL OFF
```

Selective purging from Enterprise Manager

If there are only a few composites deployed to the service infrastructure that in turn have only a limited number of instances being processed, the database footprint is not expected to grow by much. In these cases you can rely on the use of available out-of-the-box purging scripts and run either the multithreaded looped or single-threaded looped purge procedure to take care of database space management. Alternatively, Oracle Fusion Middleware Enterprise Manager Control can also be used for selective or bulk deletion of instances. For a small footprint of backend database a partitioning methodology can be completely avoided.

Filtering out completed, closed, and terminated composite instances from Oracle Enterprise Manager Fusion Middleware Control is the easiest way to purge instances from the Dehydration Store that are no longer running. It also provides the ability to delete instances for a particular composite or from the entire infrastructure and the steps involved to achieve this are already covered in *Chapter 2, Management of SOA Composite Applications*.

Single-threaded or looped purging

Although deleting instances using the **Delete with Options** button from Oracle Enterprise Manager Fusion Middleware Control may seem to be simple, it is not recommended for deleting a large number of instances. This operation tends to be time consuming and may result in a timeout on the console and it is also harder to tell whether it is completed or not. Instead, it is best to use the standard looped purging scripts available in the `[PREFIX]_SOAINFRA` package to delete instances that are no longer required. The instance purging scripts are effective and can be executed to delete process instances that are in the following states:

- Completed Successfully
- Faulted
- Terminated
- Stale
- Closed and Non Recoverable

Instances that are live, running, and pending recovery, either at the service engine level or at the composite application level are left untouched by the looped purging script. To purge these instances, it is first required to move them to states that are supported by the purging scripts. Another important fact to note is that purging deletes only closed composite instances that are beyond their retention period. The retention_period is applied only on process instances executing on the BPEL engine where users would want to retain the composite instances based on the modify_date in the cube_instance table. The script also has advanced filters to set a commit batch size and maximum run time to control execution time and prevent them from running indefinitely. A sample purging script provided here, demonstrates the use of a looped purging that iterates through the tables in the Dehydration Store to delete instances falling in the date ranges specified by the max_creation_date and min_creation_date timestamps:

```
ALTER SESSION SET CURRENT_SCHEMA=[PREFIX]_SOAINFRA;
DECLARE
    MAX_CREATION_DATE TIMESTAMP;
    MIN_CREATION_DATE TIMESTAMP;
    BATCH_SIZE INTEGER;
    MAX_RUNTIME INTEGER;
    RETENTION_PERIOD TIMESTAMP;
BEGIN
    MIN_CREATION_DATE := TO_TIMESTAMP('2005-11-01','YYYY-MM-DD');
    MAX_CREATION_DATE := TO_TIMESTAMP('2012-11-09','YYYY-MM-DD');
    MAX_RUNTIME := 120;
    BATCH_SIZE := 20000;
    SOA.DELETE_INSTANCES(
    MIN_CREATION_DATE => MIN_CREATION_DATE,
    MAX_CREATION_DATE => MAX_CREATION_DATE,
    BATCH_SIZE => BATCH_SIZE,
    MAX_RUNTIME => MAX_RUNTIME,
    PURGE_PARTITIONED_COMPONENT => TRUE);
END;
```

The following table explains the different filters that can be set in the looped purging script:

Table	Description
MAX_RUNTIME	This option defines when scripts should break and exit the loop (regardless of completion status). The default value is 60 and is specified in minutes.
MAX_CREATION_DATE	MAX_CREATION_DATE specifies the top level date filter within which all composite instances should be handled for purging.
MIN_CREATION_DATE	All composite instances that have their creation date more than the MIN_CREATION_DATE are taken up for purging.

Table	Description
BATCH_SIZE	BATCH_SIZE determines the size of batch used to loop the purge. The default value is 20000.
RETENTION_PERIOD	This property is used only by the BPEL service engine to check for and delete records in the CUBE_INSTANCE table. To purge records successfully the value for this property must be greater than or equal to MAX_CREATION_DATE. If a value for this property is not specified RETENTION_PERIOD defaults to the value of MAX_CREATION_DATE.
PURGE_PARTITIONED_ COMPONENT	This Boolean flag is used to let the purge scripts delete partitioned data as well. The default value is false.

The purging filters for the looped purge scripts depend on the version of Oracle SOA Suite 11*g* installation. The scripts shown in this book are valid for 11.1.1.4 (PS3) and 11.1.1.5 (PS4). Beginning with 11.1.1.6 (PS5), composite_name, composite_revision, and soa_partition_ name can also be included in the purging filters to delete instances specific to a particular composite.

Multithreaded or Parallel Purging

The looped purge script is good enough to purge historical data of instances from the Dehydration Store for small database profiles or SOA Suite 11*g* environments that do not have significant inflow of instances for composites deployed to them. There is however, a performance implication of using these scripts if purging is to happen during business hours as database cycles are taken away from the production system as a result. To overcome this limitation, purging can either be scheduled to run at regular intervals at the end of business hours, or use the multithreaded script to spawn multiple jobs and shorten the time required to purge. The parallel threaded purge is functionally the same as the single-threaded purge with one performance advantage: it distributes the workload across multiple jobs to fully utilize host resources and optimizes the amount of data that can be deleted in a period. The parallel purge script uses a dbms_scheduler package to spawn multiple purge jobs, with each job working on a subset of data. This procedure is designed to purge large Dehydration Stores housed on high-end database nodes with multiple CPUs and a good I/O subsystem. It is recommended that this procedure is executed during non-peak times as it acquires a lot of resources and may contend with normal online operations. Determining the optimal number of jobs to spawn will require constant on-site testing and tuning.

As a rule of thumb, the number of jobs should not exceed the number of CPUs on the node by more than one. For example, on a database box with 4 CPUs, the degree of parallelism can be set to a value of 1 to 4 to match the number of CPUs. The following script depicts the use of parallel purging:

```
DECLARE
  MAX_CREATION_DATE TIMESTAMP;
  MIN_CREATION_DATE TIMESTAMP;
  RETENTION_PERIOD TIMESTAMP;
BEGIN
  MIN_CREATION_DATE := TO_TIMESTAMP('2010-01-01','YYYY-MM-DD');
  MAX_CREATION_DATE := TO_TIMESTAMP('2011-08-06','YYYY-MM-DD');
  RETENTION_PERIOD := TO_TIMESTAMP('2011-08-06','YYYY-MM-DD');
  SOA.DELETE_INSTANCES_IN_PARALLEL(
    MIN_CREATION_DATE => MIN_CREATION_DATE,
    MAX_CREATION_DATE => MAX_CREATION_DATE,
    BATCH_SIZE => 10000,
    MAX_RUNTIME => 60,
    RETENTION_PERIOD => RETENTION_PERIOD,
    DOP => 3,
    MAX_COUNT => 1000000,
    PURGE_PARTITIONED_COMPONENT => FALSE);
END;
```

Most of the filters allowed in the parallel purging script are the same as in the looped purging except a few, which are described in following table.

Table	Description
DOP	This defines the number of parallel jobs to schedule. The default value is 4.
MAX_COUNT	This defines the number of rows processed (not the number of rows deleted). A big temp table is created and then jobs are scheduled to purge based on the data. This is the maximum purge row count to use. The default value is 1000000.

The performance of the parallel purge relies on factors such as CPU resources and the speed of disk I/O. Deleting very large tables is challenging as parsing large amounts of data can impact the elapsed time of the entire purge script. It is also recommended that you drop indexes before expected large purges to speed up the process and then recreate them afterwards.

Reclaiming disk and segment space

After purging old and unused data in the Dehydration Store, as an administrator you will sometimes be surprised that the freed space is not visible on disk. Reclaiming disk and segment spaces is not included in the purging script as this is a database maintenance task that needs to be performed depending on the type and nature of backend database in use. Seen at a very high level, space occupied by data in an Oracle database is spread over tablespaces, which themselves are spread over data files. Data files have a given size determined during tablespace creation. One approach is to allocate a small size to the data files initially and configure them to autoextend when additional space is required. However, these data files do not shrink automatically if data contained in them is deleted. After executing the purge scripts a certain amount of space will be freed up from the [PREFIX]_SOAINFRA tablespace. However, the freed space is not visible on disk, because the size of the data files belonging to that tablespace is not decreased. You can execute the script discussed earlier to measure the free size in the tablespaces to get a rough indication of the amount of free space made available within the database by the purge operations. You can reclaim disk space from the database using some common techniques as follows:

- Deallocate unused space
- Enable database row movement
- Rebuild indexes and coalesces
- Shrink and compact segment space

Each of the preceding activities can be applied by using the following commands in their respective order:

```
ALTER TABLE <TABLE_NAME> DEALLOCATE UNUSED;
ALTER TABLE <TABLE_NAME> ENABLE ROW MOVEMENT;
ALTER TABLE <TABLE_NAME> SHRINK SPACE COMPACT;
ALTER TABLE <TABLE_NAME> SHRINK SPACE;
ALTER TABLE <TABLE_NAME> DISABLE ROW MOVEMENT;
```

The code bundle of this chapter contains a ReadMe.txt file containing details to execute scripts to reclaim disk space from the database tablespaces after running the purging operation. We recommend engaging your Oracle DBA in any database related administration activities.

Database partitioning

Database partitioning (not to be confused with metadata repository partitions) is a feature specific to the Oracle database that allows a table, index, or index-organized table to be divided into smaller pieces. For example, partitions can allow you to segregate data based on a date range, where data of one date range can reside in one partition while that of another will reside elsewhere. From an application perspective, there is absolutely no difference, as it will view all partitioned and non-partitioned tables identically. But from a database administration perspective, each of the partitions can be administered as a whole or individually. This provides the administrator with the ability to maintain different storage characteristics for each partition, take different partitions offline without affecting others, and improve DML efficiency.

 Taking advantage of database partitions will improve both console and transactional performance particularly if you maintain a lot of historical audit data.

From an Oracle SOA Suite 11*g* perspective, you might want to consider partitioning your database if you decide to maintain a lot of historical audit data. Partitioning is not enabled by default, so this is an activity that must be performed manually in conjunction with an experienced DBA any time after the product has been installed.

 Converting your non-partitioned Oracle SOA Suite 11*g* product tables to partitioned tables is a nontrivial effort, and it is strongly recommended to involve an experienced DBA.

The following points should be noted when considering the move to partitioned tables:

- Certain product tables in the Dehydration Store must be partitioned together.

- Converting your partitioned tables back to non-partitioned ones requires first executing the `soa_exec_verify.sql` script to determine when to drop a partition and its equipartitioned dependent table. Refer to the Oracle Fusion Middleware Administrator's Guide for Oracle SOA Suite 11*g* and Oracle Business Process Management Suite 11*g* Release 1 at `http://docs.oracle.com/cd/E23943_01/admin.1111/e10226/soaadmin_partition.htm#CJHFJDII` for more information.

- Database partitioning is only supported for Oracle SOA Suite 11*g* Release 1 (11.1.1.4 or higher).

- There is no one-size-fits-all strategy to configuring and tuning your partitions.

The steps described in this section are specific to implementing database partitioning on the Oracle SOA Suite 11*g* product tables. The approach first involves identifying which product component(s) to partition. Afterwards, for each component, you must identify which tables will be affected and what range partition keys are to be used. The appropriate tablespaces are then created based on your environment and performance needs. Finally, the actual activity of partitioning the tables is performed.

Identifying components to partition

Each of the following Oracle SOA Suite 11*g* components has its own database schemas. From the following list, begin by choosing one or more components to partition:

- SOA Infrastructure
- Oracle BPEL Process Manager
- Oracle Mediator
- Human workflow
- Oracle BPM Suite

Identifying tables to partition

For the component(s) selected, refer to the following table. Say that you choose to partition the tables in the SOA Infrastructure. In this case, there will be a total of nine tables that must be partitioned based on the range partition key listed for each table.

Component	Table	Range Partition Key
SOA Infrastructure	COMPOSITE_INSTANCE	PARTITION_DATE
	REFERENCE_INSTANCE	CPST_PARTITION_DATE
	COMPOSITE_INSTANCE_FAULT	CPST_PARTITION_DATE
	COMPOSITE_SENSOR_VALUE	CPST_PARTITION_DATE
	COMPONENT_INSTANCE	CPST_PARTITION_DATE
	REJECTED_MESSAGE	CREATED_TIME
	REJECTED_MSG_NATIVE_PAYLOAD	RM_PARTITION_DATE
	INSTANCE_PAYLOAD	CREATED_TIME
	COMPOSITE_INSTANCE_ASSOC	CREATED_TIME

Component	Table	Range Partition Key
Oracle BPEL Process Manager	CUBE_INSTANCE	CPST_INST_CREATED_TIME
	CI_INDEXES	CI_PARTITION_DATE
	CUBE_SCOPE	CI_PARTITION_DATE
	DOCUMENT_CI_REF	CI_PARTITION_DATE
	AUDIT_TRAIL	CI_PARTITION_DATE
	AUDIT_DETAILS	CI_PARTITION_DATE
	DLV_SUBSCRIPTION	CI_PARTITION_DATE
	WORK_ITEM	CI_PARTITION_DATE
	AUDIT_COUNTER	CI_PARTITION_DATE
	WI_FAULT	CI_PARTITION_DATE
	DLV_MESSAGE	RECEIVE_DATE
	HEADERS_PROPERTIES	DLV_PARTITION_DATE
	DOCUMENT_DLV_MSG_REF	DLV_PARTITION_DATE
	XML_DOCUMENT	DOC_PARTITION_DATE
Oracle Mediator	MEDIATOR_INSTANCE	COMPOSITE_CREATION_DATE
	MEDIATOR_CASE_INSTANCE	MI_PARTITION_DATE
	MEDIATOR_CASE_DETAIL	MI_PARTITION_DATE
	MEDIATOR_AUDIT_DOCUMENT	MI_PARTITION_DATE
	MEDIATOR_DEFERRED_MESSAGE	CREATION_TIME
	MEDIATOR_PAYLOAD	CREATION_TIME

Component	Table	Range Partition Key
Human Workflow	WFTASK	COMPOSITECREATEDTIME
	WFTASK_TL	COMPOSITECREATEDTIME
	WFTASKHISTORY	COMPOSITECREATEDTIME
	WFTASKHISTORY_TL	COMPOSITECREATEDTIME
	WFCOMMENTS	COMPOSITECREATEDTIME
	WFMESSAGEATTRIBUTE	COMPOSITECREATEDTIME
	WFATTACHMENT	COMPOSITECREATEDTIME
	WFASSIGNEE	COMPOSITECREATEDTIME
	WFREVIEWER	COMPOSITECREATEDTIME
	WFCOLLECTIONTARGET	COMPOSITECREATEDTIME
	WFROUTINGSLIP	COMPOSITECREATEDTIME
	WFNOTIFICATION	COMPOSITECREATEDTIME
	WFTASKTIMER	COMPOSITECREATEDTIME
	WFTASKERROR	COMPOSITECREATEDTIME
	WFHEADERPROPS	COMPOSITECREATEDTIME
	WFEVIDENCE	COMPOSITECREATEDTIME
	WFTASKASSIGNMENTSTATISTIC	COMPOSITECREATEDTIME
	WFTASKAGGREGATION	COMPOSITECREATEDTIME
Oracle BPM Suite	BPM_AUDIT_QUERY	CI_PARTITION_DATE
	BPM_MEASUREMENT_ACTIONS	CI_PARTITION_DATE
	BPM_MEASUREMENT_ACTION_EXCEPS	CI_PARTITION_DATE
	BPM_CUBE_AUDITINSTANCE	CI_PARTITION_DATE
	BPM_CUBE_TASKPERFORMANCE	CI_PARTITION_DATE
	BPM_CUBE_PROCESSPERFORMANCE	CI_PARTITION_DATE

Creating tablespaces and table partitions

At this point, you will have to decide how you want to partition your tables, specifically what date range to divide the data, as well as identify which tablespace each of the partitions will reside in. The DBA may also decide to specify different storage parameters for each tablespace. In this section, we cover generic examples that should be customized by the DBA.

Before proceeding, make sure you shut down your Oracle SOA Suite 11*g* infrastructure (but not the database!). In this example, we separate the data by year, having each range in its own separate tablespace. To do this, we will create two separate tablespaces; soa_ts_2011 and soa_ts_2012, residing on two separate physical disks:

```
CREATE TABLESPACE soa_ts_2011
DATAFILE '/u01/app/oracle/oradata/orcl/soa_ts_2011.dbf'
SIZE 5G
REUSE
AUTOEXTEND ON
NEXT 128M
BLOCKSIZE 8192
EXTENT MANAGEMENT LOCAL AUTOALLOCATE
SEGMENT SPACE MANAGEMENT AUTO;

CREATE TABLESPACE soa_ts_2012
DATAFILE '/u02/app/oracle/oradata/orcl/soa_ts_2012.dbf'
SIZE 5G
REUSE
AUTOEXTEND ON
NEXT 128M
BLOCKSIZE 8192
EXTENT MANAGEMENT LOCAL AUTOALLOCATE
SEGMENT SPACE MANAGEMENT AUTO;
```

We have already identified that the SOA Infrastructure requires partitioning of all of the following nine tables: COMPOSITE_INSTANCE, REFERENCE_INSTANCE, COMPOSITE_ INSTANCE_FAULT, COMPOSITE_SENSOR_VALUE, COMPONENT_INSTANCE, REJECTED_ MESSAGE, REJECTED_MSG_NATIVE_PAYLOAD, INSTANCE_PAYLOAD, and COMPOSITE_ INSTANCE_ASSOC, as they are part of the same component.

Let's start with the INSTANCE_PAYLOAD table. Create a completely new table that is partitioned by the year range on the CREATED_TIME column:

```
CREATE TABLE instance_payload_temp PARTITION BY RANGE (created_time) (
   PARTITION P01_2011 VALUES LESS THAN ('01-JAN-12 12.00.00.000000 AM')
TABLESPACE soa_ts_2011,
   PARTITION P01_2012 VALUES LESS THAN ('01-JAN-13 12.00.00.000000 AM')
TABLESPACE soa_ts_2012
)
NOLOGGING
AS
SELECT * FROM instance_payload;
```

As shown in the preceding command, the entire data is selected from the base table `INSTANCE_PAYLOAD` and copied into our newly created, partitioned table called `INSTANCE_PAYLOAD_TEMP`.

Now rename the existing product table, maintaining it temporarily for backup purposes:

```
RENAME instance_payload TO instance_payload_delete;
```

Then rename the temp table to replace the original table:

```
RENAME instance_payload_temp TO instance_payload;
```

Finally, drop the original table if all goes well and it is no longer needed:

```
DROP TABLE instance_payload_temp;
```

Now repeat these same instructions for all tables within the component.

The preceding set of steps are used to provide a working example of how to partition the Oracle SOA Suite 11*g* tables. It is recommended to capture basic metrics before and after you partition the tables to observe the performance impact and involve an Oracle DBA to fine tune the tablespace characteristics as needed. Though database partitioning of the Oracle SOA Suite 11*g* product tables is an activity that is rarely performed, it does support certain use cases and may be appropriate for your particular installations.

Reducing audit levels

Another way to maintain database growth is to reduce the audit level for composites by controlling the instance data being written to the Dehydration Store. We recommend that all production environments should have the audit level set to `Production`. This setting should be applied as a standard default for all domains in production. Depending upon the business requirement each component can override the default with its own audit level as needed. Changing audit level from `Development` to `Production` results in significantly less to and fro interaction with the database and greatly enhances performance. You can further improve performance by turning `Off` auditing although this may not be ideal. Configuration and management of audit levels is covered in detail in *Chapter 2, Management of SOA Composite Applications*.

Summary

The MDS, or Metadata Services, is a repository used by Oracle SOA Suite 11*g* to store metadata of composites and their customizations that are deployed to the service infrastructure. The Dehydration Store, on the other hand, maintains instance related information. As an Oracle SOA Suite 11*g* administrator, you will likely be required to manage both of these database-based repositories.

This chapter covered numerous administrative activities as they pertain to the MDS and Dehydration Store, namely:

- Introducing file-based and database-based MDS repositories, as well as how to register database-based MDS repositories with an Oracle SOA Suite 11*g* environment.

- Creating and cloning metadata repository partitions.

- Deploying MARs as well as importing and exporting metadata to and from MDS partitions to promote or replicate code and shared artifacts across environments.

- Understanding the underlying database objects that comprise the Dehydration Store.

- Understanding configurations that impact the Dehydration Store and ways to measure database growth through SQL queries.

- Purging through the use of Oracle Enterprise Manager Fusion Middleware Control as well as single-threaded and multithreaded purge scripts and reclaiming freed space.

- Implementing database partitioning on the Oracle SOA Suite 11*g* product tables for improved data management and performance.

In the next chapter, we wrap up with the last major tasks surrounding Oracle SOA Suite 11*g* administration; backup and recovery.

9
Backup and Recovery

As an administrator, you will have already recognized the importance of establishing well defined backup and recovery procedures. It is easy to write in length on this topic alone, discussing various backup, restore, failover, migration, and disaster recovery strategies. Fortunately, we will focus on the most important areas in this chapter to simplify the process for you as best we can. As long as you understand a few core concepts regarding the overall backup and recovery strategy for Oracle SOA Suite 11*g*, you can implement it in any number of ways.

Establishing a backup and restore strategy is important because it provides you with the ability to restore your environment in the event of a critical infrastructure or hardware failure. For instance, if you experience a hard drive failure, the disks may have to be replaced and the software restored from backup. It also provides you with the ability to restore your environment to a previously working snapshot in the event of a faulty patch, faulty code deployment, or faulty configuration. In some cases, these faulty updates are not undoable and thus a restore may be needed.

In this chapter, we will cover the following key areas:

- Understanding what needs to be backed up
- Recommended backup strategy
- Implementing the backup process
- Recovery strategies
- Cloning Oracle SOA Suite 11*g*

There are really two types of backups you can perform—offline backups and online backups. **Offline backups** are taken when the entire environment is down. This is the preferred approach, as all tiers are backed up at the same point, ensuring that a full restore will be an exact point in time snapshot. Unfortunately, it is usually difficult to find the downtime needed for a full offline backup, and **online backups** may have to be utilized in certain cases. You may now be wondering what kind of data is important and needs to be backed up.

The types of data that are typically backed up are:

- Static files (for example, domain configuration files, software binaries, and patches)
- Runtime artifacts (for example, application deployments, instance data and metadata, and transaction logs)

So when should you backup your environments? As long as the static files don't change, technically a single valid backup is all that is required. Configuration changes or the application of patches tend to change the contents of these static files, hence prompting the need to create another backup. Runtime artifacts or dynamic data, such as continually updated instance data in the database, may need to be backed up regularly. There are cases where both online and offline backups may be valid for these types of data, and we will discuss them in more detail later on in this chapter.

In the unfortunate event that a recovery is needed, performing a complete restore can guarantee full restoration of your environment. However, this is time consuming and the appropriate downtime may not be sufficient to do so. Thus, once you understand the different types of files that need to be backed up, you will know what needs to be restored.

Understanding what needs to be backed up

Before describing how to back up your environment, it is important to understand what needs to be backed up first. We differentiate between static files, files which do not change frequently such as the software installation binaries, and dynamic data, otherwise referred to as runtime artifacts, which could include frequently updated data such as instance information and deployment metadata.

Static files

Static files and directories are those that do not change frequently. These files should be regularly backed up, particularly when configuration changes, patching, or installations have been performed since the last backup. In most cases, static files can be backed up both online and offline.

Oracle system files

System files include the `oraInst.loc` and `beahomelist` files. These files point to the location of the Oracle Inventory and the Middleware Home respectively. Thus, future patching or installations of other Oracle products can easily recognize where your software is installed, check for their existing versions, and update these inventories accordingly, if needed.

The `beahomelist` file is typically located in the user's home directory and varies according to the operating system. The BEA Home List contains the location of your Oracle WebLogic Server installation.

The `oraInst.loc` configuration file contains the location of your Oracle Inventory. The Oracle Inventory contains metadata of all installed Oracle products on your server. It is updated when new Oracle products are installed on your server or the existing software is upgraded. An example of the contents of `oraInst.loc` is:

```
inventory_loc=/u01/app/oracle/oraInventory
inst_group=oinstall
```

The locations of each of these files, by operating system, are shown in the following table:

File	Description	Operating system	Sample location
BEA Home List	This file points to the Oracle WebLogic Server installation directory and is typically created in the user's home directory.	Linux	`/home/oracle/bea/beahomelist`
		Windows	`C:\bea\beahomelist`
		Solaris	`/home/oracle/beahomelist`
Oracle Installation Location	This is a registry key in Microsoft Windows.	Linux	`/etc/oraInst.loc`
		Windows	`HKEY_LOCAL_MACHINE\SOFTWARE\Oracle`
		Solaris	`/var/opt/oracle/oraInst.loc`
Oracle Inventory	Location is determined by `oraInst.loc`.	Linux	`/home/oracle/oraInventory`
		Windows	`C:\Program Files\Oracle\Inventory`
		Solaris	`/home/oracle/oraInventory`

These files should be backed up after initial installation or after any patch update or upgrade. A standard file system backup is sufficient.

JDK

Your installation may rely on Sun JDK, JRockit JDK, or both. The JDK can be installed in Middleware Home or elsewhere. The location of your JDK can be shared between the servers in your cluster, or may be installed standalone on each server.

Regardless of its location, your JDK should be backed up after new installations and/or a patch update or upgrade.

Here are examples of the locations of both Sun and JRockit JDKs installed outside your Middleware Home:

```
/u01/app/oracle/jdk1.6.0_26
/u01/app/oracle/jrockit1.6.0_29
```

And here are examples of both Sun and JRockit JDKs installed inside your Middleware Home:

```
/u01/app/oracle/middleware/jdk1.6.0_26
/u01/app/oracle/middleware/jrockit1.6.0_29
```

Middleware Home

The Middleware Home contains numerous files, components, and shared components. This includes, as a minimum, the binaries and configuration files for Oracle WebLogic Server, the Oracle SOA Suite Home, and Oracle Common components. The location of the Middleware Home in your system can be found in the `beahomelist` file.

For example, your Middleware Home may reside in `/u01/app/oracle/middleware`. The following table lists all the static files that should be backed up as part of the Middleware Home backup after initial installation or after any patch update or upgrade. A standard filesystem backup is sufficient.

Product	Description	Sample Location
Coherence (optional)	Coherence is installed on some environments, particularly Oracle SOA Suite 11g clusters.	`$MW_HOME/coherence_3.6`
JDK (optional)	This refers to the Sun or JRockit JDK, if they have been installed under the Middleware Home.	`$MW_HOME/jrockit1.6.0_29`

Product	Description	Sample Location
Logs	These are installation and WLST logs. These are not transactional logs.	`$MW_HOME/logs`
Modules	These are modules (that is, JAR files) that are shared across all products in this Middleware Home.	`$MW_HOME/modules`
Oracle Common	This includes common Oracle files and binaries that are shared across all products in this Middleware Home. This can include OPatch, installation scripts and the WLST script.	`$MW_HOME/oracle_common`
Oracle SOA Suite 11*g* Home	This is the root folder of Oracle SOA Suite 11*g* installation.	`$MW_HOME/Oracle_SOA1`
Utilities	These include utilities such as cloning and uninstall libraries and scripts.	`$MW_HOME/utils`
Oracle WebLogic Server 11*g* Home	This is the root folder of Oracle WebLogic Server 11*g* installation.	`$MW_HOME/wlserver_10.3`

Windows registry keys

For Microsoft Windows based installations, the following registry keys would need to be backed up:

```
HKEY_LOCAL_MACHINE\Software\Oracle
HKEY_LOCAL_MACHINE\System\CurrentControlSet\services
```

These keys point to the current locations of the Oracle installed software as well as registered Windows services. These registry keys should be backed up after initial installation or after any patch update or upgrade.

Runtime artifacts

Oracle documentation refers to data that is dynamically updated and required for runtime operations as **runtime artifacts**. In essence, it is the data and/or configuration that are regularly accessed and/or updated during runtime. We will describe each of these areas in later sections of this chapter.

Database

A database is configured during installation to contain the SOA infrastructure and MDS and messaging data. Although Oracle SOA Suite 11*g* is certified on a range of databases such as Microsoft SQL Server, MySQL, and IBM DB2, discussions in this book assume an Oracle database, which is more common. The Oracle database can be backed up via a tool such as Oracle **Recovery Manager** (**RMAN**).

The database maintains data related to in-flight instances, deployed composites, and configuration, among other things. For example, if you deploy a composite today and perform a database restore to the day before, that deployed composite will not be available. Also note that some configurations, such as that of the Oracle BPEL Process Manager Engine, are stored in the database so that they are available to all the managed servers.

The schemas that need to be backed up are listed in the following table. It is recommended to have nightly backups of the database.

Schema	Description
<ENV>_MDS	Metadata Services
<ENV>_SOAINFRA	SOA Infrastructure
<ENV>_ORABAM	**Business Activity Monitoring (BAM)**
<ENV>_ORASDPM	User Messaging Service

JMS File Stores

Persistent stores host information such as JMS destinations. Though persistent stores can either be file-based or JDBC-enabled (that is, saved in the database), most Oracle SOA Suite 11*g* high availability installations utilize file-based stores for performance reasons. File-based stores essentially provide persistence capabilities to Oracle WebLogic Server subsystems and services through the use of a built-in, high performance storage solution.

Because these file-based persistent stores save JMS messages, durable subscriber information, and temporary messages sent to unavailable destinations by using the Store-and-Forward features, it is not possible to take consistent backups of them. Restoring these persistent stores may result in data inconsistency, even if they were backed up offline. These persistent stores often (and should) reside on redundant fault-tolerant storage that is accessible to all nodes of the Oracle SOA Suite 11*g* cluster. Alternatively, you may have already used JDBC-enabled stores for your JMS destinations so that they are maintained in and backed up with the database.

 Backing up and restoring the JMS file-based persistent stores may result in data inconsistency. Instead, ensure the availability of the file store to all servers in your cluster.

The following table shows an example of the location of persistent stores required by Oracle SOA Suite 11*g* clusters. These stores are shared and accessible to all nodes of the clusters (in this example a two node cluster).

JMS file store name	Sample location	Shared
UMSJMSFileStore_auto_1	/share/soa_domain/soacluster/jms/ UMSJMSFileStore_auto_1	Yes
UMSJMSFileStore_auto_2	/share/soa_domain/soacluster/jms/ UMSJMSFileStore_auto_2	Yes
WseeFileStore_auto_1	/share/soa_domain/soacluster/jms/ WseeFileStore_auto_1	Yes
WseeFileStore_auto_2	/share/soa_domain/soacluster/jms/ WseeFileStore_auto_2	Yes
FileStore_auto_1	/share/soa_domain/soacluster/jms/ FileStore_auto_1	Yes
FileStore_auto_2	/share/soa_domain/soacluster/jms/ FileStore_auto_2	Yes
BPMJMSFileStore_auto_1	/share/soa_domain/soacluster/jms/ BPMJMSFileStore_auto_1	Yes
BPMJMSFileStore_auto_2	/share/soa_domain/soacluster/jms/ BPMJMSFileStore_auto_2	Yes
SOAJMSFileStore_auto_1	/soa_domain/soacluster/jms/ SOAJMSFileStore_auto_1	Yes
SOAJMSFileStore_auto_2	/soa_domain/soacluster/jms/ SOAJMSFileStore_auto_2	Yes

By virtue of the file stores being shared, they are accessible to all nodes in the cluster. The recommendation here is to implement one of the following backup strategies for JMS file-based persistent stores:

- Move the JMS modules to a JDBC-enabled persistent store. Database backups will ensure the consistency of the data in the event of a database restore, but restoring to older backups of the database may result in data inconsistency.

- Ensure that the file-based persistent stores reside in fully redundant shared storage accessible to all nodes of the cluster, and guarantee its availability. Backing up these stores is possible, but there are implications regarding message loss and message duplication should you choose to restore them.

The only scenario perhaps where file stores can be backed up is in non-production environments where data consistency is not critical such as development or test environments. In this case, it is still recommended to take an offline backup (that is, where all mid-tier nodes are shut down while the backup is being performed). Restoring from this backup essentially performs a point-in-time recovery where the file stores may contain older JMS messages that have already been consumed and processed. It may also result in lost messages. For example, messages may have been enqueued but not consumed before the backup. The only advantage to backing up your JMS file store is that it allows the administrator to always take a single, working, and consistent backup of the environment, but with the risk of data duplication and/or inconsistency as a result of restoring older file stores.

Transaction logs

Transaction logs store information about committed transactions, coordinated by the Oracle WebLogic Server, that may not have been completed. The transaction logs provide Oracle WebLogic Server with a mechanism to recover from system crashes or network failures.

It is recommended to configure the default persistent store of the transaction logs to a directory on highly available and shared storage. This is typically a requirement for multinode installations of Oracle SOA Suite 11*g* anyway. To identify where this directory is, log in to the Oracle WebLogic Server Administration Console, navigate to **Environment | Servers | soa_server1 | Configuration | Services**, and observe the value of **Directory**.

Unfortunately, transaction logs can only be stored in the default store and must be file-based. Thus, the backup behavior is similar to that of JMS file-based persistent stores. Oracle WebLogic 12*c*, however, allows transaction logs to be stored in a JDBC store, but Oracle SOA Suite is not yet released for that version.

Since transaction logs are based on file-based persistent stores, do not delete or restore them. It may result in data inconsistency.

The recommendation, therefore, is to ensure that the transaction logs reside in fully redundant shared storage accessible to all nodes of the cluster, and guarantee its availability. Backing up the transaction logs is suggested, but there are implications regarding message loss and message duplication should you choose to restore them.

SOA domain

Typically, every Oracle SOA Suite 11*g* installation includes at least one domain extended with SOA extensions (for example, `soa_domain`), which hosts your administration and managed servers. Though many of the files in your Domain Home are static in nature, several of them change periodically (for example, log files). By default, the domain home is located under Middleware Home (for example, `$MW_HOME/user_projects/domains/soa_domain`), but it may reside elsewhere depending on what was specified during the domain creation. A typical SOA domain will fall within the 1 GB to 2 GB size range and will contain a multitude of file types that include:

- Startup scripts
- Libraries
- Domain configuration files
- Logs
- Deployed and extracted Java applications

The configuration files most relevant to your domain installation are listed in the following table. Backing up your domain is usually recommended if one or more of these files are updated.

Component	Configuration File Location
Oracle WebLogic Server SOA Domain	`$DOMAIN_HOME/config/config.xml`
Oracle WebLogic Server JMS	`$DOMAIN_HOME/config/jms/*`
Oracle WebLogic Server Startup Scripts	`$DOMAIN_HOME/bin/*`
Oracle BAM	`$DOMAIN_HOME/config/fmwconfig/servers/ AdminServer/adml/server-oracle_bamweb-11.0.xml`

Component	Configuration File Location

Oracle BAM	`$DOMAIN_HOME/config/fmwconfig/servers/`
	`AdminServer/adml/server-oracle_bamserver-`
	`11.0.xml`

Oracle BAM	`$DOMAIN_HOME/config/fmwconfig/servers/bam-` `server-name/adml/server-oracle_bamweb-11.0.xml`

Oracle BAM	`$DOMAIN_HOME/config/fmwconfig/servers/bam-`
	`server-name/adml/server-oracle_bamserver-`
	`11.0.xml`

Oracle B2B	`$DOMAIN_HOME/config/soa-infra/configuration/` `b2b-config.xml`
Oracle Business Rules	`$DOMAIN_HOME/config/soa-infra/configuration/` `businessrules-config.xml`
Oracle Business Process Management (BPM)	`$DOMAIN_HOME/config/fmwconfig/logging/oracle.` `bpm-logging.xml`
Oracle BPM	`$DOMAIN_HOME/config/jms/bpmjmsmodule-jms.xml`
Oracle Web Services Manager (OWSM)	`$DOMAIN_HOME/config/fmwconfig/policy-accessor-` `config.xml`
Oracle Platform Security Services (OPSS)	`$DOMAIN_HOME/config/fmwconfig/jps-config.xml`
Oracle WebLogic Server Node Manager	`$MW_HOME/wlserver_10.3/common/bin/nodemanager.` `properties`
Oracle WebLogic Server	`$MW_HOME/wlserver_10.3/common/bin/wlsifconfig.` `sh`
Oracle WebLogic Server	`$MW_HOME/wlserver_10.3/common/bin/setPatchEnv.` `sh`
Oracle WebLogic Server	`$MW_HOME/wlserver_10.3/common/bin/commEnv.sh`

In most cases, you do not need to back up managed server directories separately because the `AdminServer` contains information about all of the managed servers in its domain.

Managed servers do not require the `AdminServer` to be up during normal operation. However, as an administrator, your view of the health and performance of the managed server may be restricted. Furthermore, it prevents you from making any changes to the domain's configuration if the `AdminServer` is down.

A managed server maintains a local copy of the domain configuration. If you attempt to start a managed server while the AdminServer is down, the managed server uses a local copy of the domain configuration and continues to periodically attempt to reconnect with the AdminServer. The managed server, thus, is running in what is called the **Managed Server Independence (MSI)** mode. When it connects successfully, the configuration state is synchronized.

It is, therefore, recommended to take a full backup of your Domain Home periodically while your infrastructure, and especially the AdminServer, are offline. Technically, backing up the Domain Home on the machine running the AdminServer is sufficient, though it might make your life easier to back up the domain on the other servers in your cluster as well.

Recommended backup strategy

Generally speaking, your environment should be backed up on a regularly scheduled basis. This is typically a standard operation, and we will discuss it in more detail towards the end of this section. In addition, occasional one-off backups may be needed. By considering the proposed backup strategy outlined here, you should be protected for the majority of cases and will be able to perform effective recovery, if needed.

The following table is a summary of the actions described in this section, as well as when and what type of backup to perform:

Action		Backup schedule	Backup type
New installation	After installation	One-off	Offline
Upgrading	Before and/or after upgrading	One-off	Offline
Applying patches	Before and/or after patching	One-off	Offline
Configuration changes	Before and/or after changes	One-off	Offline
Architectural changes	Before and/or after changes	One-off	Offline
Code deployment	Only if needed	Never	Offline

After a new installation

Installing Oracle SOA Suite 11*g* involves installing and creating a database, running the **Repository Creation Utility (RCU)** to create all required database schemes, installing Oracle WebLogic Server 11*g*, Sun JDK, or JRockit JDK (or both), and Oracle SOA Suite 11*g*, followed by the creation of the SOA domain. In high availability installations of two or more nodes, further configuration and setup is required.

It is, therefore, recommended to perform a full offline backup of your environment after confirming the successful installation of your infrastructure. This includes backing up:

- Oracle system files
- JDK
- Middleware Home
- SOA domain
- Database (using a tool such as RMAN)

Before upgrading

If you are planning on upgrading from Oracle SOA Suite 11*g* PS4 to PS5, this involves upgrading the Oracle WebLogic Server from 10.3.5 to 10.3.6 and Oracle SOA Suite from 11.1.1.5 to 11.1.1.6. Prior to patching, it is a good idea to perform a backup of the environment, so that you can roll back in the event of an unforeseen upgrade problem.

In this case, it is recommended to perform a full offline backup of the entire infrastructure, which includes:

- Oracle system files
- JDK
- Middleware Home
- JMS file stores
- Transaction logs
- SOA domain
- Database (using a tool such as RMAN)

Before applying patches

The overwhelming majority of Oracle patches are downloaded from Oracle Support and come in the form of an OPatch. Many, but not all of these patches provide some form of rollback mechanism. If the patch application is unsuccessful, it will not be installed. If the patch application is successful, but does not resolve your particular problem, it can be rolled back (in other words, uninstalled).

These patches can be OPSS patches, JDK patches, OWSM patches, Oracle WebLogic Server patches, Oracle SOA Suite patches, Oracle BPM patches, BAM patches, or any type of patch related to one of the many underlying subcomponents. Even though most (but not all) patches can be rolled back, there are rare cases where patches can corrupt or produce undesirable results in your system. It is both our and Oracle's recommendation to backup your environment prior to applying a patch. However, with a little bit of understanding of the patch, it may not be necessary to perform a full backup, and only a partial backup may be needed.

If the patch is a JDK patch, simply perform an offline backup of JDK (this being the common JDK directory or the one specific to your installation).

If the patch is an Oracle SOA Suite 11*g* patch, simply perform an offline backup of the following:

- Middleware Home
- SOA domain
- Database (using a tool such as RMAN)

If the patch is an Oracle WebLogic Server 11*g* patch, simply perform an offline backup of Middleware Home (and specifically, only the `$MW_HOME/wlserver_10.3` directory may need to be backed up).

If the patch is an Oracle BAM, OWSM, BPEL Process Manager, or any of the other subcomponents, simply perform an offline backup of the following:

- Middleware Home
- SOA domain
- Database

When in doubt, perform a full offline backup of the entire infrastructure, which includes backing up the following:

- Oracle system files
- JDK
- Middleware Home

- JMS file stores
- Transaction logs
- SOA domain
- Database

Before configuration changes

There are many types of configuration changes that can be performed, and there is an even more endless list of possible backup scenarios for each of the configuration changes. Some settings are stored in configuration files (for example, `config.xml`) and startup scripts (like `setSOADomainEnv.sh`), while other settings such as BPEL Service Engine configuration settings are stored in the database. When in doubt, perform a full offline backup prior to making any configuration change.

In most cases, configuration changes can be rolled back by simply undoing the configuration change itself, though there are scenarios where damaging repercussions have occurred. For example, modifying the number of maximum connections in your connection pool typically involves zero risk. On the other hand, in certain scenarios where a second SOA server has never yet been started and conflicting JVM configurations are found across the servers, irrecoverable startup issues may occur on that second SOA server.

We, therefore, recommend performing a backup, as a minimum, of the following prior to making any configuration changes:

- SOA domain
- Database

Configuration changes that are committed to the database can usually be rolled back by undoing them or restoring the database itself. Configuration changes to any of the software installs (for example, files under the `$MW_HOME/Oracle_SOA1`, `$JAVA_HOME`, and `$MW_HOME/wlserver_10.3`) are usually undoable by simply restoring the configuration change to its original settings.

Before architectural changes

Examples of architectural changes include extending your domain to install additional products or converting your single node installation to a cluster. Even though performing these activities should not be a problem, the administrator often has to deal with unforeseen setbacks. Some architectural changes are simple, while others are more involved. Performing a full offline backup of the entire infrastructure is recommended in these cases.

The database, JMS file stores, and transactions logs may not necessarily be backed up, as the impact on transactional data due to these changes is extremely low.

After upgrade, patch, configuration, or architectural changes

After finishing an upgrade, applying one or more patches, or performing major configuration or architectural changes, you probably want to perform a full offline backup of your environment in order to maintain a snapshot of a working installation that you can recover to in the future, if need be.

For that reason, performing a full offline backup of the entire infrastructure in the event of any of these actions is recommended. The components to be backed up are:

- Oracle system files
- JDK
- Middleware Home
- JMS file stores
- Transaction logs
- SOA domain
- Database

Before or after a code deployment

It is often unnecessary to perform backups before or after a code deployment, unless major architectural changes or high risk activities are involved. You should have a change control strategy for code deployments defined, wherein if a deployment fails or a code deployment is successful but needs to be rolled back, you have the ability to redeploy the previous version of the code. Code could include Java applications, SOA composites, DVMs, or even schemas and WSDLs.

All SOA composites and artifacts are stored in the MDS. In the event that no formal change control strategy is in place, reverting to a previous snapshot of the database will restore your SOA composites to their original version at the time of the database backup. Therefore, if you require it, you may perform a full database backup before or after SOA code is deployed to protect yourself.

Ongoing backups

As part of your operation, maintenance, and support activities, you will want to regularly schedule backups of your environment. Some backups may be nightly while others may be weekly. If little to no changes take place on your midtiers, nightly delta filesystem backups of the Middleware Home, JDK, and SOA domain may suffice (after a full offline backup is performed at least once). In this case, the only ongoing changes that really do occur are growth of log files.

As for the JMS file store and transaction logs, as mentioned earlier, these are not backed up. In the event of an irrecoverable failure to them, the best option will be to recreate them.

As a good practice, your databases should be backed up consistently. Daily and weekly full backups of databases are not uncommon, and the database administrator will need to be engaged in this activity.

> Files within your SOA domain rarely change unless there is a code deployment or configuration change. If neither of these two activities are performed, delta file system backups are often sufficient.

As for ongoing backups, certain components such as the Oracle system files, JDK, and Middleware Home do not require frequent backing up unless changes occur to them. Regardless, implementing some type of ongoing and regular backup is typically recommended. This table provides a guideline for your backup schedule, but should be customized based on your needs and operational standards:

Component	Backup schedule	Backup type	Comments
Oracle system files	Monthly	Online	
JDK	Monthly	Online	
Middleware Home	Monthly	Online	
JMS file store	Never	-	Recreate if recovery needed. Data loss or inconsistency may occur.
Transaction logs	Never	-	Recreate if recovery needed.
SOA domain	Weekly	Online	Online backups are acceptable as long as no changes to the domain have been made.
Database	Daily	Online	

Implementing the backup process

Now that we have described the types of files to be backed up, the frequency of backup needed, and the locations of what needs to be backed up, you may use alternate third-party tools or commands to perform your filesystem backups. The backup commands and instructions in this section are meant to serve as a workable guideline to cover all areas requiring backup and are general in nature. They assume a Linux-based operating system with gtar installed, but they may be substituted with alternate file manipulation commands as needed. We recommend dedicating a backup mount point with ample storage and timestamping each backup file with the date and time in the file name. Many backup solutions that can be leveraged to automate and simplify the administration of the entire backup process are available in the market.

Oracle system files

The Oracle system files are comprised of the server specific files under the `/etc` system directory as well as the Oracle Inventory. The `oraInst.loc` file location varies depending on the flavor of Unix being used:

1. Set your environment, if not already set. This may vary depending on your installation:

   ```
   export BACKUP_DIR=/backup
   export TIME=`date "+%Y%m%d_%k%M"`
   ```

2. Execute the following command to backup the Oracle system files under `/etc`:

   ```
   gtar -czvf $BACKUP_DIR/etcora.${TIME}.tgz /etc/oraInst.loc /etc/oratab
   ```

3. The following command extracts the Oracle Inventory location and places it in the `INVENTORY_HOME` environment variable:

   ```
   export INVENTORY_HOME=`cat /etc/oraInst.loc | grep inventory_loc | cut -f2 -d=`
   ```

4. Execute the following command to backup the Oracle Inventory:

   ```
   gtar -czvf $BACKUP_DIR/oraInventory.${TIME}.tgz $INVENTORY_HOME
   ```

JDK

Backup the JDK as per the following instructions and modify the environment variables depending on whether you are running JDK, JRockit, or both:

1. Set your environment, if not already set. This may vary depending on your installation:

   ```
   export BACKUP_DIR=/backup

   export JDK_HOME=/u01/app/oracle/middleware/jdk1.6.0_26

   export JROCKIT_HOME=/u01/app/oracle/middleware/jrockit1.6.0_29

   export TIME=`date "+%Y%m%d_%k%M"`
   ```

2. Execute the following commands to backup both Sun JDK and JRockit JDK:

   ```
   gtar -czvf $BACKUP_DIR/jdk.${TIME}.tgz $JDK_HOME

   gtar -czvf $BACKUP_DIR/jrockit.${TIME}.tgz $JROCKIT_HOME
   ```

Middleware Home

The Middleware Home consists of several installed components such as Oracle SOA Suite, Coherence (if installed), Oracle WebLogic Server, and shared libraries and utilities:

1. Set your environment, if not already set. This may vary depending on your installation:

   ```
   export BACKUP_DIR=/backup

   export MW_HOME=/u01/app/oracle/middleware

   export TIME=`date "+%Y%m%d_%k%M"`
   ```

2. Execute the following commands to back up the files:

   ```
   gtar -czvf $BACKUP_DIR/mwhome.${TIME}.tgz $MW_HOME/coherence_3.6
   $MW_HOME/logs $MW_HOME/modules $MW_HOME/oracle_common $MW_HOME/
   Oracle_SOA1 $MW_HOME/utils $MW_HOME/wlserver_10.3
   ```

Domain Home

Although the Domain Home is often created under the $MW_HOME/user_projects/ domains directory, that is not necessarily a requirement. It is only necessary to backup the domain on which the AdminServer is running, but you may also opt to backup the domain on all other nodes of the cluster for ease of restoration in the future:

1. Set your environment, if not already set. This may vary depending on your installation:

   ```
   export BACKUP_DIR=/backup
   ```

   ```
   export DOMAIN_HOME=/u01/app/oracle/middleware/user_projects/
   domains/soa_domain
   ```

   ```
   export TIME=`date "+%Y%m%d_%k%M"`
   ```

2. Execute the following commands to back up the files:

   ```
   gtar -czvf $BACKUP_DIR/domain.${TIME}.tgz $DOMAIN_HOME
   ```

Windows registry keys

For Windows-based installation, certain registry keys need to be backed up.

Via the Window Registry Editor, navigate to the following registry keys and export them:

```
HKEY_LOCAL_MACHINE\Software\oracle
HKEY_LOCAL_MACHINE\System\CurrentControlSet\Services
```

Database

Contact your DBA and use a backup utility such as RMAN to perform nightly hot backups.

Another crude way to take a backup of your database is to use the Oracle Data Pump utility commands such as `expdp` that can be used to export the database schema and the `impdp` command that is used for importing the dump file to the database. Because these are the low level database methods, this approach is more suitable when performing an initial data migration to a fresh installation or cloning an environment that does not yet contain any business data.

Recovery strategies

The purpose of recovering your environment is to restore it due to a software failure (such as a faulty patch or misconfiguration), hardware failure (such as an internal hard disk failure), or due to a need to perform a point-in-time recovery (to undo configuration or architectural changes that have proven defective or problematic).

Multiple factors should be considered before recovering an environment. It depends on which component failed and what point in time you want to recover to. Additional factors such as ensuring consistency among components is equally important. Full restores of the entire mid-tier and database to the same point in time are perhaps the simplest and least risky of all approaches, but are time consuming in nature. Furthermore, when a simple faulty configuration change needs to be rolled back, do you really need to restore the entire environment or just restore that particular component?

The installation of an Oracle SOA Suite 11*g* environment relies on interdependent components that contain configuration information, applications (both Java and composite), and data that must be kept in synchronization. As a consequence, both backing up and restoring an Oracle SOA Suite 11*g* installation requires more thought than merely unzipping the backup files.

By now, you have a good understanding of how Oracle SOA Suite 11*g* functions, what files and components it requires and relies on, and what area to perhaps recover in the event of a failure. You also understand the implications of restoring different components separately.

All components, with the exception of the database, are backed up by using standard file system commands or tools. To recover your Oracle SOA Suite 11*g* environment, simply restore the file or files of the component that needs to be restored. For example, any combination of the following may need to be restored depending on the type of failure:

- **Domain**: In the event of a severe configuration failure of the domain in which it is unable to start.
- **Middleware Home**: For example, to restore the entire infrastructure to a previous release after a patch has been applied.
- **Oracle Home**: For example, restoring Oracle SOA Suite 11*g* to a previous version after it has been upgraded.
- **JDK**: For example, if desiring to revert to a previous version of your JDK.
- **Oracle system files**: In the event of a bad software installation where you wish to restore the Oracle Inventory to its original state.

In almost all cases, your Oracle SOA Suite 11*g* environment must be offline to recover. Though possible, it is dangerous to try to recover Oracle SOA Suite, Oracle WebLogic Server, JDK, or any other component while the infrastructure is running.

There are implications to recovering JMS data to a previous point in time. As discussed earlier, we generally do not recommend backing up (or restoring) the JMS file store. It can result in duplicate or lost messages. In many cases, it is probably better to recreate the persistent stores in the event that they are accidentally deleted or are in need of recovery.

Since the transaction log is accessible to all nodes of your cluster, in the event of a server failure, the other machines should be able to process the transactions. Even in the unlikely event of a full environment crash, the Transaction Recovery Service gracefully handles transaction recovery once the servers are brought up.

Cloning Oracle SOA Suite 11*g*

Another very important utility to back up your environment and create an exact replica of it at a later stage, or at a different location altogether, is **cloning**. As the word suggests, cloning not only copies an existing environment to a different location, but also preserves its state, enabling you to create a new Middleware Home with all post-installation patches. Cloning is also a highly effective way to have the same snapshot and configurations across different distributed environments.

Cloning an existing Oracle SOA Suite 11*g* infrastructure is a multistep process that needs to be executed in a sequential manner as shown in the following screenshot:

1. The Middleware binary movement involves activities needed to create a backup archive of your Middleware Home. Then, if required, paste it elsewhere.

2. The Middleware configuration movement involves steps to back up, extract, edit, and paste domain configuration. Broadly, the activities can be divided into the following two steps:

    ◦ Backing up and moving the Middleware Home installation
    ◦ Cloning the WebLogic Server domain

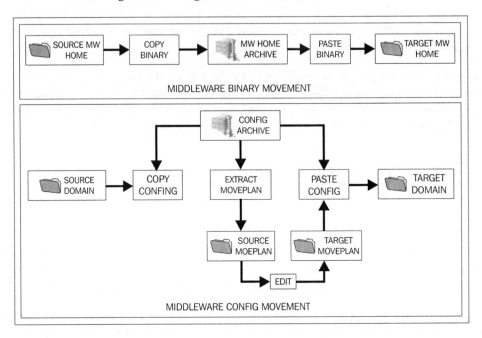

Backing up and moving a Middleware installation

The Middleware Home can be backed up and moved using the `copyBinary` and `pasteBinary` scripts available in `$MW_HOME/oracle_common/bin` directory.

Archiving the Middleware installation

You can execute the `copyBinary` script to create an archive of a Middleware Home containing the Oracle WebLogic Server home, and one or more Oracle homes, such as SOA, BAM, OSB, and so on.

The `copyBinary.sh` script can be executed in a terminal by passing a few arguments in the following syntax:

```
copyBinary -javaHome $JAVA_HOME -archiveLoc <ARCHIVE_LOC>
-sourceMWHomeLoc $MW_HOME
```

Replace the <ARCHIVE_LOC> argument with the actual name and location of the directory to save the archive, for example, /backup/soa/cloning/archive/mw_backup.jar.

Copying archive to remote location

If you intend to extract and copy the compressed Middleware Home archive to a remote location, ensure that the $MW_HOME/oracle_common/bin/pasteBinary.sh and $MW_HOME/oracle_common/jlib/cloningclient.jar files are copied to the target system, and an execute permission is granted on them.

It is important to note that the pasteBinary.sh script and cloningclient.jar file have to be copied to the same directory on the target system as they were in the source system.

Extracting the archive

The pasteBinary.sh script is used to extract the files from the archive at a target host by using the following syntax:

```
copyBinary -javaHome $JAVA_HOME -archiveLoc <ARCHIVE_LOC>
-targetMWHomeLoc $MW_HOME
```

Backing up and moving a domain

Backing up a live server domain enables you to obtain a snapshot of all the custom modifications, deployments, and configurations made to it and then apply the snapshot to a different environment.

Archiving the SOA domain

The first thing that is needed to create a backup of your SOA domain is archiving it by using the copyConfig.sh script located in the $MW_HOME/oracle_common/bin directory. Before running the script, ensure that the administration server and all managed servers in the source Middleware Home are in running state. The script can be used with the following syntax by replacing the highlighted variables with actual values corresponding to your environment:

```
copyConfig -javaHome $JAVA_HOME -archiveLoc <ARCHIVE_LOC>
-sourceDomainLoc <SRC_DOMAIN_LOC> -sourceMWHomeLoc $MW_HOME
-domainHostName <HOST_NAME> -domainPortNum  <ADMIN_PORT>
-domainAdminUserName <USER_NAME> -domainAdminPassword <PWD>
```

Extracting move plans

A **move plan** is a migration property file containing configurable information that can be extracted from the domain backup archive, edited, and then applied to the target system. For example, you can edit the move plan (`moveplan.xml`) to change the server instance start modes, listening addresses, as well as other resource configurations, such as data sources, JMS, adapters, and so on.

To extract the migration properties from the archive, run the `extractMovePlan.sh` script as per the following syntax:

```
extractMovePlan -javaHome $JAVA_HOME -archiveLoc <ARCHIVE_LOC>
-movePlanDir <PLAN_DIR>
```

> The directory specified for the `PLAN_DIR` property in the `extractMovePlan.sh` argument list must not exist in the filesystem. However, its parent location must exist in the filesystem and you must have write permission on it.

Editing move plan files

Move plans are extracted and placed in the following directory structure:

- `<PLAN_DIR>/moveplan.xml`: The main move plan configuration file
- `<PLAN_DIR>/adapters`: The directory that contains plan files for the resource adapters configured for the domain
- `<PLAN_DIR>/composites`: The directory that contains subplans for SOA composites
- `<PLAN_DIR>/deployment_plans`: The directory that contain subplans for the `soa-infra` application

The `moveplan.xml` captures the key information in the `config.xml` file for a particular server domain. You can modify the domain configurations, such as server startup mode, data sources, authentication providers, and other available properties, and then apply the changes to the new domain on the target host. For example, to change the database connection URLs of the data sources used by the server components, edit the line in the `moveplan.xml` file as highlighted:

```
<configProperty>
  <name>Url</name>
  <value>jdbc:oracle:thin:@dBHost:1521:SERVICE_NAME</value>
  <itemMetadata>
```

```
        <dataType>STRING</dataType>
        <scope>READ_WRITE</scope>
    </itemMetadata>
</configProperty>
```

You can also modify the configuration of resource adapters such as database adapters, JMS adapters, BAM adapters, and so on by editing the corresponding adapter plan file in the `<PLAN_DIR>/adapters` directory.

Extracting the archive in a target system

Finally, to complete the domain movement to the target host, extract the files from the archive by using the `pasteConfig.sh` script. While extracting the domain, you would need to specify the directory where the edited move plans are located:

```
pasteConfig -javaHome $JAVA_HOME -archiveLoc <ARCHIVE_LOC>
-targetDomainLoc <DOMAIN_LOC> -targetMWHomeLoc $MW_HOME -movePlanLoc
<PLAN_DIR> -domainAdminPassword <PWD>
```

> The move plans are applied only when the $MW_HOME directory is the same on both the source and target host. If you choose to back up your Middleware installation to a different directory on the target host, you need to manually edit the `config-root` property in all the plans under the `<PLAN_DIR>/adapters` and the `<PLAN_DIR>/deployment_plans` directories.

Summary

Backing up and restoring an environment should be relatively simple. After all, software is merely a bunch of files scattered on various filesystems. However, the two challenges that Oracle SOA Suite 11*g* administrators face when the need to restore arises are:

- To identify what exactly needs to be recovered
- To establish at what state or point in time you should recover to

In this chapter, we described all the various components that need to be backed up in an Oracle SOA Suite 11*g* environment and then followed up with detailing how to actually perform the backup. Specifically, we covered the following:

- The various static files in an Oracle SOA Suite 11*g* installation such as Oracle system files, the JDK, and the Middleware Home

- Runtime artifacts that include the database and SOA domain

- The implications of backing up and restoring JMS file stores and transaction logs

- A backup strategy, focusing on what needs to be backed up after installations, upgrades, patches, and configuration changes, as well as a recommended regular backup schedule

- The backup commands for Linux-based installations

- Key recovery strategy considerations

- The mechanism to back up and restore a Middleware installation and domain from one environment to another via cloning

At this point, you should be fully capable of backing up your environment with a thorough enough understanding of when to restore individual components as needed.

Advance administration topics such as silent installations, patching, and upgrading the SOA infrastructure, upgrading from Oracle SOA Suite 10*g*, and setting up a highly available clustered installation for Oracle SOA Suite 11*g*, are available as a downloadable chapter from Packt's website.

Index

Symbols

[PREFIX]_MDS schema 284
-Xms (minimum heap size) 106
-Xmx (maximum heap size) 106
-XX:+HeapDumpOnOutOfMemoryError 107
-XXtlasize:min=16k,preferred=128k,wasteLimit=8k 107

A

Abandon Timeout Seconds parameter 111
ADCServerName 205
ADCServerPort 205
Add Fields button 69
Add URI button 189
adf-config.xml file 244
AdminServer
  setting up 149
  shutting down 150
Advanced Queue (AQ) 238
ant
  artifacts, importing to MDS 50, 51
  composite, deploying via ant 49
  composites, deploying 48
  composites, packaging 48
  composites, packaging via ant 48
  composites, starting 48
  composites, stopping 48
  composites, undeploying 48
  composite, undeploying via ant 49
  environment path, setting 45
  environment, setting 45
  MDS artifacts, exporting 49, 50
  On Linux/Unix 45, 46

  on Windows 46, 47
  setting up, for composite management 45
ant-worklist-t2p.xml 195
application parameter 270
appName argument 290
AQ_TM_PROCESSES parameter 141
archive
  extracting 339
  in target system, extracting 341
artifacts
  importing, to MDS 50, 51
ATTACHEMNT_REF table 300
ATTACHMENT table 300
AUDIT_DETAILS table 300
auditDetailThreshold property 298
Audit Framework 166
Audit Level property 169, 177
audit level, settings
  precedence order 60, 61
AuditStorePolicy parameter 127
AUDIT_TRAIL table 300
Audit Trail Threshold parameter 126
Audit Trail Threshold property 169
authorization policies 259, 260

B

B2B 16
B2B Server Properties 29
backup
  offline backup 317
  online backup 317
  runtime artifacts 318
  static files 318
  strategy (recommended) 327

JVM, settings
  -Xgcprio:throughput 107
  -Xms and -Xmx 106
  -XX:+HeapDumpOnOutOfMemoryError
    107
  -XXtlasize:min=16k,preferred=128k,wasteL
    imit=8k 107

K

Keep XA Connection Until Transaction
  Complete parameter 116
key administration areas
  navigating to 152-156
keystores
  about 257
  configuring 261-263

L

Large Document Threshold parameter 126
Large Document Threshold property 169
last update time, instances 76, 77
Linux operating system
  tuning 144
listCred() command 263
log file entries
  identifying 84-86
  logger levels, modifying 88-90
  relevant 86-88
  viewing 84-86
logger levels
  modifying 88-90
logging assertion
  adding, to policy 278, 279
log level
  adjusting 122
log rotation
  enabling 151, 152
logs
  checking 230
looped purging 305-307

M

Managed Server Independence (MSI) 327
managed servers
  monitoring 94

Management Policies 251
map.file property 197
MAR
  deploying, WLST used 290
MaxCapacity attribute 114
MAX_COUNT table 308
MAX_CREATION_DATE table 306
Maximum Capacity parameter 114
Maximum Duration of XA Calls parameter
    111
maximum heap size (-Xmx) 106
MaxRaiseSize property 137
MAX_RUNTIME table 306
MaxTransactionSize property 138
MDS 283
MDS artifacts
  exporting, with Ant 49, 50
MDS assets 284
MDSDomainRuntime MBean 289
MDS repository, database-based
  registering 285-287
MEDIATOR_INSTANCE table 76
Mediator Properties 29
Mediator Service Engine
  administering 176-178
  properties 129
  tuning 128
memory
  checking 229
Message Driven Beans (MDB) 107
Message Transmission Optimization
    Mechanism (MTOM) 251
metadata 210
Metadata Archive (MAR) 283
metadata repository partitions
  about 287
  cloning 288-290
  MAR deploying, WLST used 290
  new metadata partition, creating 288
Metadata Store (MDS) 33
metadata version history
  purging 294, 295
metrics level property 177
Middleware Home
  about 320, 321
  backing up 334

Thank you for buying
Oracle SOA Suite 11g Administrator's Handbook

About Packt Publishing

Packt, pronounced 'packed', published its first book "Mastering phpMyAdmin for Effective MySQL Management" in April 2004 and subsequently continued to specialize in publishing highly focused books on specific technologies and solutions.

Our books and publications share the experiences of your fellow IT professionals in adapting and customizing today's systems, applications, and frameworks. Our solution based books give you the knowledge and power to customize the software and technologies you're using to get the job done. Packt books are more specific and less general than the IT books you have seen in the past. Our unique business model allows us to bring you more focused information, giving you more of what you need to know, and less of what you don't.

Packt is a modern, yet unique publishing company, which focuses on producing quality, cutting-edge books for communities of developers, administrators, and newbies alike. For more information, please visit our website: www.packtpub.com.

About Packt Enterprise

In 2010, Packt launched two new brands, Packt Enterprise and Packt Open Source, in order to continue its focus on specialization. This book is part of the Packt Enterprise brand, home to books published on enterprise software – software created by major vendors, including (but not limited to) IBM, Microsoft and Oracle, often for use in other corporations. Its titles will offer information relevant to a range of users of this software, including administrators, developers, architects, and end users.

Writing for Packt

We welcome all inquiries from people who are interested in authoring. Book proposals should be sent to author@packtpub.com. If your book idea is still at an early stage and you would like to discuss it first before writing a formal book proposal, contact us; one of our commissioning editors will get in touch with you.

We're not just looking for published authors; if you have strong technical skills but no writing experience, our experienced editors can help you develop a writing career, or simply get some additional reward for your expertise.

Getting Started With Oracle SOA Suite 11g R1 – A Hands-On Tutorial

ISBN: 978-1-84719-978-2   Paperback: 482 pages

Fast track your SOA adoption— Build a Service-Oriented composite Application in just hours!

1. Offers an accelerated learning path for the much anticipated Oracle SOA Suite 11g release

2. Beginning with a discussion of the evolution of SOA, this book sets the stage for your SOA learning experience

3. Includes a comprehensive overview of the Oracle SOA Suite 11g Product Architecture

Oracle SOA Suite Developer's Guide

ISBN: 978-1-84719-355-1   Paperback: 652 pages

Design and build Service-Oriented Architecture Solutions with the Oracle SOA Suite 10gR3

1. A hands-on guide to using and applying the Oracle SOA Suite in the delivery of real-world SOA applications

2. Detailed coverage of the Oracle Service Bus, BPEL Process Manager, Web Service Manager, Rules, Human Workflow, and Business Activity Monitoring

3. Master the best way to combine / use each of these different components in the implementation of a SOA solution

WS-BPEL 2.0 for SOA Composite Applications with Oracle SOA Suite 11g

ISBN: 978-1-84719-794-8   Paperback: 616 pages

Define, model, implement, and monitor real-world BPEL business processes with SOA-powered BPM

1. Develop BPEL and SOA composite solutions with Oracle SOA Suite 11g

2. Efficiently automate business processes with WS-BPEL 2.0 and develop SOA composite applications

3. Get familiar with basic and advanced BPEL 2.0

Oracle SOA Suite 11g R1 Developer's Guide

ISBN: 9781849680189   Paperback: 720 pages

Develop Service-Oriented Architecture Solutions with the Oracle SOA Suite

1. A hands-on, best-practice guide to using and applying the Oracle SOA Suite in the delivery of real-world SOA applications

2. Detailed coverage of the Oracle Service Bus, BPEL PM, Rules, Human Workflow, Event Delivery Network, and Business Activity Monitoring

3. Master the best way to use and combine each of these different components in the implementation of a SOA solution

Please check **www.PacktPub.com** for information on our titles

Lightning Source UK Ltd.
Milton Keynes UK
UKOW021043100912

198769UK00003B/17/P